PHARMACOLOGY OF EATING DISORDERS

THEORETICAL AND CLINICAL DEVELOPMENTS

Pharmacology of Eating Disorders

Theoretical and Clinical Developments

EDITORS

Michele O. Carruba,
M.D., Ph.D.
*Department of Pharmacology,
Chemotherapy, and Medical Toxicology
University of Milan
Milan, Italy*

John E. Blundell,
B.Sc., Ph.D., F.B.Ps.S.
*BioPsychology Group
Psychology Department
University of Leeds
Leeds, England*

Raven Press ■ New York

Raven Press, 1140 Avenue of the Americas, New York, New York 10036

Made in the United States of America

Library of Congress Cataloging-in-Publication Data
Main entry under title:

Pharmacology of eating disorders.

Based in part on contributions delivered to a symposium at the 14th Congress of the Collegium Internationale Neuro-Psychopharmacologicum (C.I.N.P.) held in Florence, June 19–23, 1984.
Includes bibliographies and index.
1. Appetite depressants—Physiological effect—Congresses. 2. Appetite disorders—Chemotherapy—Congresses. 3. Appetite disorders—Psychological aspects—Congresses. I. Carruba, Michele O. II. Blundell, J. E. (John E.), 1942– III. Collegium Internationale Neuro-Psychopharmacologicum. Congress (14th : 1984 : Florence, Italy)

[DNLM: 1. Appetite Depressants—pharmacodynamics—congresses. 2. Appetite Disorders—drug therapy—congresses. 3. Feeding Behavior—drug effects—congresses. 4. Obesity—drug therapy—congresses.
QV 129 P5365]
RM332.3.P47 1986 613.2'5 85-32329
ISBN 0-88167-201-7

Preface

The present time is particularly appropriate for the appearance of a volume concerning eating disorders; this type of pathology is one of the most prominent abnormalities of the decade. Indeed obesity has been a major problem for decades past and is now an urgent sociomedical issue in modern industrialized countries. Van Itallie (2) has reported that more than 36 million people in America can be regarded as being statistically overweight, whilst Garrow (1) has estimated that between one third and one quarter of the adult population of the United Kingdom may be defined as mildly obese (body mass index between 25 and 30). Moreover, the cultural ethos is extremely antagonistic toward obesity and obese people are frequently regarded by the media as being either unhealthy, unfit, aesthetically displeasing, or all of these. This strong cultural disapproval, together with the absence of a treatment available on the scale required, has led individuals (mainly women) to resort to drastic measures to attain or preserve an acceptable body weight. These measures include uncontrolled bouts of starvation and bingeing, vomiting, and the excessive use of purges and laxatives. There is evidence that disordered patterns of eating affect a sizeable fraction (2 to 10% of young adult women).

To this class of eating disorders should be added aberrant patterns of eating that arise as symptoms of affective disorders as well as those unwanted changes in appetite and consumption that may occur as a result of medication with antidepressant and neuroleptic agents. These disorders combined with the existing problems of anorexia nervosa and severe overweight constitute a major challenge for scientists and clinicians to initially understand and then to treat.

Within this arena the pharmacological approach can provide a useful strategy for research and, in certain cases, for therapy. However, it should be recognized that adopting this orientation need not imply that all eating disorders depend on neurochemical or physiological causes which may be manipulated by a drug. Nor, in the case of obesity, should it be assumed that this disorder is primarily or exclusively a function of maladjusted eating. A productive framework emphasizes the *interrelationships* among eating behaviors, body weight regulation and neurochemical mechanisms. Adjustments in one of these elements will provoke changes in the others. In addition, this system of inter-dependent components is influenced by environmental conditions—physical, nutritional, and psychosocial—and by psychological feelings and sensations.

The chapters in this volume, written by researchers who collectively have made a massive contribution to this field of study, consider various relationships in the biopsychological system of which eating and body weight form a part. The contributors have been invited for their specific expertise in animal or human research (psychopharmacological, physiological, nutritional, or psychiatric) and for their capacity to embrace both theoretical developments and clinical applications. This book is intended to extend and strengthen the theoretical framework underlying disorders of eating and weight regulation to the point of important clinical implications. The use of drugs as experimental tools or as potential therapeutic devices represents a theme that appears in every chapter. The editors are indebted to the authors for generating a volume that provides both a synthesis of the current level of knowledge and a pointer to future developments. This book should be stimulating and helpful to researchers and clinicians.

John E. Blundell
Michele O. Carruba

REFERENCES

1. Garrow, J. (1982): *Nutr. Bull.* 7:49–53.
2. Van Itallie, T. B. (1983): Proceedings of IV Int. Cong. Obesity, New York.

Acknowledgments

This volume is based, in part, on contributions delivered to a symposium on the Psychopharmacology of Eating Disorders at the 14th Congress of the Collegium Internationale Neuro-Psychopharmacologicum (C.I.N.P.) held in Florence (June 19–23, 1984). The symposium convenors and editors wish to thank the Institute de Recherches Internationales Servier of Neuilly sur Seine Cedex (Paris, France) for supporting the symposium by means of an educational grant, and we are indebted to Dr. Christine Nathan, Dr. Beatrice Guardiola-Lemaitre, Dr. Yves Rolland, and Dr. Bernadette Biasi for help in the publication of this book.

Contents

Contributors

John E. Blundell
BioPsychology Group
Psychology Department
University of Leeds
Leeds, LS2 9JT, England

Michele O. Carruba
Department of Pharmacology, Chemotherapy and Medical Toxicology
University of Milan
via Vanvitelli, 32
20129 Milano, Italy

Stuart A. Checkley
Institute of Psychiatry and Maudsley Hospital
Denmark Hill
London, SE5 8AF, England

Emanuela Coen
Department of Pharmacology, Chemotherapy and Medical Toxicology
University of Milan
via Vanvitelli, 32
20129 Milano, Italy

Patrick Even
Laboratoire de Neurobiologie des Régulations C.N.R.S.
Collège de France
11 place Marcelin Berthelot
75231 Paris Cédex 05, France

Elizabeth Goodall
Academic Unit of Human Psychopharmacology
Medical Colleges of St. Bartholomew's and London Hospitals
Ritson Road
London, EC1, England

Andrew J. Hill
BioPsychology Group
Psychology Department
University of Leeds
Leeds, LS2 9JT, England

Sarah F. Leibowitz
The Rockefeller University
1230 York Avenue
New York, NY 10021

Allen S. Levine
Neuroendocrine Research Unit
Minneapolis V A Medical Center
Departments of Medicine and Food Science and Nutrition
University of Minnesota
Minneapolis - St. Paul, MN 55417

Paolo Mantegazza
Department of Pharmacology, Chemotherapy and Medical Toxicology
University of Milan
via Vanvitelli, 32
20129 Milano, Italy

Maurizio Memo
Institute of Pharmacology and Experimental Therapeutics
School of Medicine, University of Brescia
via Valsabbina, 19
25124 Brescia, Italy

Cristina Missale
Institute of Pharmacology and Experimental Therapeutics
School of Medicine, University of Brescia
via Valsabbina, 19
25124 Brescia, Italy

John E. Morley
Education and Clinical Center
V A Medical Center
Sepulveda, CA

Stylianos Nicolaidis
Laboratoire de Neurobiologie des Régulations C.N.R.S.
Collège de France
11 place Marcelin Berthelot
75231 Paris Cédex 05, France

Marina Pizzi
Institute of Pharmacology and Experimental Therapeutics
School of Medicine, University of Brescia
via Valsabbina, 19
25124 Brescia, Italy

Paul H. Robinson
Institute of Psychiatry and Maudsley Hospital
Denmark Hill
London, SE5 8AF, England

Gerald F. M. Russell
Institute of Psychiatry and Maudsley Hospital
Denmark Hill
London, SE5 8AF, England

Gail Shor-Posner
The Rockefeller University
1230 York Avenue
New York, NY 10021

Trevor Silverstone
Academic Unit of Human Psychopharmacology
Medical Colleges of St. Bartholomew's and London Hospitals
Ritson Road
London, EC1, England

Pier Franco Spano
Institute of Pharmacology and Experimental Therapeutics
School of Medicine, University of Brescia
via Valsabbina, 19
25124 Brescia, Italy

Albert J. Stunkard
Department of Psychiatry
University of Pennsylvania
Philadelphia, PA 19014

Mark L. Willenbring
Departments of Psychiatry
Minneapolis V A Medical Center
University of Minnesota
Minneapolis - St. Paul, MN 55417

Judith J. Wurtman
Department of Nutrition and Food Science
Massachusetts Institute of Technology
Cambridge, MA 02139

PHARMACOLOGY OF EATING DISORDERS

THEORETICAL AND CLINICAL DEVELOPMENTS

Pharmacology of Eating Disorders: Theoretical and Clinical Developments, edited by M. O. Carruba and J. E. Blundell. Raven Press, New York © 1986.

Mechanism of Action of Anorectic Drugs: An Overview

Michele O. Carruba, Emanuela Coen, *Marina Pizzi, *Maurizio Memo, *Cristina Missale, *Pier Franco Spano, and Paolo Mantegazza

*Department of Pharmacology, Chemotherapy, and Medical Toxicology, School of Medicine, University of Milan, 20129 Milano; and *Institute of Pharmacology and Experimental Therapeutics, School of Medicine, University of Brescia, 25100 Brescia, Italy*

It has become increasingly clear that in the treatment of obesity a unique therapeutic solution does not exist. Nevertheless, results can be achieved combining various treatments. Therefore, the pharmacological approach should be considered not as a means that alone can cure obesity but rather as an important element of a wider therapeutic strategy (23). In general the two basic therapeutic tactics remain the reduction of energy intake and the increase in energy expenditure.

Unfortunately, attempts to increase metabolic utilization by pharmacological means have generally been unsatisfactory because of undesirable side effects and/or frank toxicities. Therefore, the most common pharmacological treatment for weight reduction is the administration of anorectic drugs that reduce food consumption by either inhibiting hunger or by enhancing satiety.

The first reports of pharmacologically-induced reduction of food intake were those of Ehrich and Krumbhaar in 1937 (47) on rats, followed by a report of Nathanson (82) on humans. The pharmacological agent in these studies was amphetamine, and this drug can be considered to be the founder of the family of anorectics.

Since amphetamine has been found to cause a series of side effects, including central stimulation, mood enhancement and cardiovascular changes, which hinder wide therapeutic use of the drug, a series of compounds have been developed with the aim of reducing these undesirable stimulatory side effects while maintaining the anorectic potency of the prototype drug. The vast majority of these compounds have been derived from amphetamine and possess chemical structures that resemble those of the sympathomimetic amines, with various substitutions on the common β-phenylethylamine nucleus (Fig. 1). Among the various changes in the ring, side chain or amino structure of amphetamine used to reduce central stimulation without changing anorectic potency, the

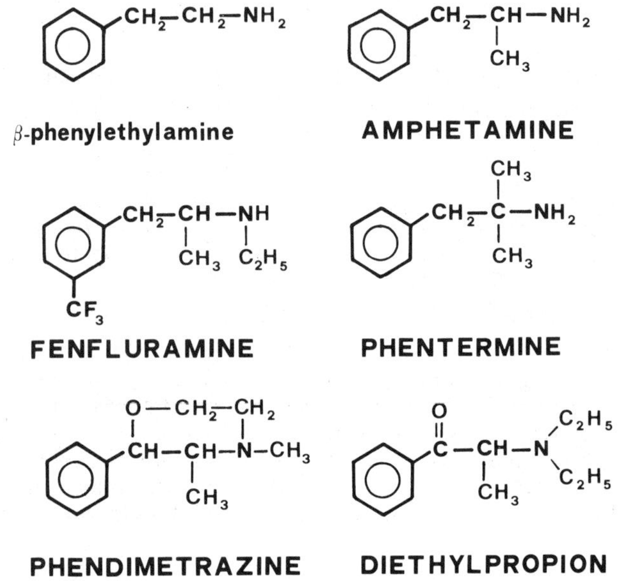

β-phenylethylamine

AMPHETAMINE

FENFLURAMINE

PHENTERMINE

PHENDIMETRAZINE

DIETHYLPROPION

FIG. 1. Chemical structures of some of the more widely used anorectic drugs.

most successful was the introduction of the halogen group CF_3 into the ring plus a C_2H_5 group on the amine. The resulting compound, fenfluramine, differs markedly from amphetamine not only because it possesses central depressant rather than stimulant properties but also because its overall pharmacological profile is completely different.

Initial inquiry into the mechanism of action of anorectic drugs showed that their ability to reduce food intake depends on their ability to cross the blood-brain barrier and enter the central nervous system (CNS). A change in the amphetamine molecule, such as introduction of an OH group into the ring, which lessens the lipid solubility necessary for the molecule to enter the brain, causes the disappearance of the anorectic and central stimulant activities while leaving unaltered the peripheral sympathomimetic potency (41).

Therefore, although some anorectic drugs have been reported to also affect peripheral mechanims controlling carbohydrate and lipid metabolism (see Nicolaidis et al., this volume), they seem to reduce food intake mainly by acting within the CNS.

ANATOMICAL AND PHYSIOLOGICAL SUBSTRATES

A large and fairly consistent body of evidence has been collected showing that food intake is controlled in mammals by a delicate balance between several brain neuronal circuits involving different monoamines, aminoacids and peptides as neurotransmitters.

The first attempts to clarify the participation of brain neuronal structures in the regulation of eating behaviour involved experimental manipulations of the ventromedial nucleus (VMH) and the lateral area (LHA) of the hypothalamus. These early experiments lead to the proposal of the dual-center theory for the regulation of food intake (17, 106). The VMH was considered a "satiety center" since a lesion in the VMH leads to overeating (18), while stimulation of the VMH inhibits eating (97). In the LHA, the opposite occurs and this area was consequently considered to be an "eating center" (2, 78). More recent experiments by Grossman (61) and especially by Leibowitz (69) indicate that microinjection of noradrenaline (NA) or adrenaline (A) into the paraventricular nucleus of the hypothalamus (PVH) produces a vigorous feeding response in a satiated rat. Tests with selective stimulants of and adrenergic receptors have demonstrated that an eating response can be elicited by an receptor stimulant such as metaraminol but not by the receptor stimulant isoproterenol. Studies with and receptor antagonists have confirmed that noradrenergic or adrenergic systems terminating in the region of the PVH do have a stimulatory effect on feeding.

Leibowitz (69) and Margules (75) found that hypothalamic injections of the three catecholamines (CA): A, NA, dopamine (DA) and of isoproterenol, could produce a marked suppression of feeding in hungry rats. This phenomenon occurs more reliably after injection into the perifornical (PF) area of the lateral hypothalamus. Furthermore, it appears to involve receptors that are -adrenergic and dopaminergic in type. These studies provide clear evidence in support of the idea that there are two opposing CA systems with effects on feeding behaviour: one that stimulates feeding through α-adrenergic receptors in the PVH and one that suppresses feeding through β-adrenergic and dopaminergic receptors located in the PF area of the lateral hypothalamus.

A second line of research in which chemical and electrolytic lesions have been used to study the involvement of brain CAs in feeding, has yielded some results which are in apparent disagreement with those already described. It has been shown that intracerebroventricular (ICV) or intracerebral injections of the neurotoxic agent 6-hydroxydopamine (6-OHDA) which selectively destroys CA neurons (63) produce a state of aphagia (110). It is believed that the primary system involved in this phenomenon is the nigrostriatal DA pathway (107). Although these findings suggest that DA has a role in facilitating feeding, there is some question concerning the specificity of this phenomenon to feeding per se (60, 107). It has been clearly shown, in fact, that this DA system is involved in mediating arousal, motivation and motor functions that are required for normal performance not only of ingestive behaviour but also of all voluntary behaviour (107).

It has been shown that food intake can also be modified by manipulation of the central 5-hydroxytryptamine (5-HT) system. Indeed, ICV injection of p-chlorophenylalanine (PCPA) which reversibly depletes brain 5-HT (67), results in transient hyperphagia (15). ICV injection of 5,7-dihydroxytryptamine (5,7-DHT) which selectively destroys serotoninergic terminals (64), results in a more persistent hyperphagia and even obesity (92). Conversely, the central injection of 5-HT results in a decrease in the amount of food eaten by deprived rats (56). The most sensitive area for 5-HT-induced suppression of feeding is the PVH (70).

Recently, in our laboratories using a micro-punch method to dissect out the PF and the PVH from rat brains, it has been possible to study the adenylate cyclase activity [measured by a sensitive Radio Immuno Assay technique (37)] as a biochemical index of the DA, NA and 5-HT receptor function in those areas.

The results obtained indicated that DA strongly reduces adenylate cyclase activity in homogenates from rat PF region. This effect was dose-dependent with a half maximal inhibitory concentration of 1 μM. The reduction of adenylate cyclase activity induced by maximal effective concentration of DA was reversed by 10 μM haloperidol or 10 μM l-sulpiride but not by the pharmacological inactive isomer d-sulpiride (Table 1 and 2). Like DA, a selective D_2 agonist bromocriptine (tested at 10 μM) was able to inhibit adenylate cyclase activity and its effect was antagonized by haloperidol (Table 1). These data indicate that PF region contains DA receptors which are negatively coupled with adenylate cyclase activity. The pharmacological characterization suggests the involvement of the D_2 receptor subtype. This hypothesis was further confirmed by the fact that SKF 82526, which is a selective D_1 agonist, was completely inactive in modifying the enzyme function (Table 2).

In addition to DA receptors, the PF region appears to contain β-adrenergic receptors. Adenylate cyclase activity was indeed sensitive to stimulation by isoproterenol (data not shown).

TABLE 1. Effect of three different dopaminergic agonists on adenylate cyclase activity in rat hypothalamic perifornical area.

	Cyclic AMP (pmol/mg prot/min)	
	In the absence of (1) sulpiride	In the presence of (1) sulpiride
Basal	93	-
Dopamine 100 μM	2*	80
Bromocriptine 10 μM	33*	87
SKF 82526 100 μM	92	-

* $p \leq 0.01$ vs the correspondent basal values by Student's t test. Numbers are from a representative experiment and are the means of triplicate determinations which varied less than 10 %. (1) sulpiride, 10 μM.

TABLE 2. Effect of haloperidol, 1-sulpiride and d-sulpiride on dopamine inhibited adenylate cyclase activity in rat hypothalamic perifornical area.

	cAMP (pmol/mg prot/min)
Basal	120
DA 100 μM	10*
DA 100 μM + haloperidol 10 μM	116
DA 100 μM + 1-sulpiride 10 μM	102
DA 100 μM + d-sulpiride 10 μM	18*

* $p \leq 0.01$ vs basal values by Student's t test. Numbers are from a representative experiment and are the means of triplicate determinations which varied less than 10 %.

When the experiments were performed using homogenates from rat PVH, DA, SKF 82526, and bromocriptine, were not able to affect adenylate cyclase activity. Moreover, the addition of 100 μM 5-HT to the incubation buffer did not significantly modify the enzyme basal activity (Table 3).

According to these data, the putative serotoninergic receptors in the PVH, which have been previously proposed by Leibowitz (70), if present, appear to be of the 5-HT_2 type that is uncoupled to adenylate cyclase (therefore undetectable with our method).

TABLE 3. Effect of different agonists on adenylate cyclase activity in rat hypothalamic paraventricular nucleus.

	cAMP (pmol/mg prot/min)
Basal	101
DA 100 μM	107
SKF 82526 100 μM	100
Bromocriptine 10 μM	102
5-HT 100 μM	91

Numbers are from a representative experiment and are the means of triplicate determinations which varied less than 10 %.

In conclusion, our data indicate that dopaminergic and β-adrenergic receptors are present in PF region but not in PVH. According to the classification of DA receptors (D_1 and D_2) (76), which are linked to adenylate cyclase in a stimulatory and inhibitory way respectively, we can deduce that the PF DA receptors belong to the D_2 subtype.

All these observations plus others implicate brain CA and 5-HT in the physiological regulation of food intake so that these neurotransmitters could potentially mediate the anorectic effect induced by drugs. Other hypothalamic mechanisms involving glucoreceptors (83), opiate receptors (57), GABA (57, 66) and some endogenous peptides (55) have also been reported to affect food intake and have all been suggested to play a role in determining the organism's tendency to eat (9, 79). However, until now, no evidence exists that non aminergic mechanisms play a crucial role in mediating anorectic drug action.

NEUROCHEMICAL MECHANISMS UNDERLYING ANORECTIC DRUG ACTION

After it was established that anorectics act within the brain, the major research efforts have been aimed at determining specific changes in the function of particular monoamine systems which are correlated with specific anorectic effects. The results obtained clearly indicate that drugs suppressing food intake do not all function by a single defined neurochemical mechanism of action. Indeed, biochemical evidence indicates that while amphetamine activates central noradrenergic and dopaminergic systems (59), fenfluramine increases central serotoninergic function (40). Pharmacological evidence suggests that increased synthesis and release of CA, and especially DA, from nerve terminals is responsible for amphetamine-induced anorexia. The evidence includes the observation that the anorectic effect of amphetamine can be antagonized by both DA receptor blocking agents, such as pimozide, and also by α-methyl-p-tyrosine (α-MpT) (Table 4), an inhibitor of CA synthesis (104) and by a treatment with 6-OHDA plus desmethylimipramine, which selectively destroys DA nerve terminals (58, 62).

The involvement of noradrenergic mechanisms in amphetamine induced anorexia appears to be complex. That central noradrenergic neurons play a role in the anorectic activity of amphetamine is suggested by the fact that selective lesions of noradrenergic fibers passing through the ventral noradrenergic bundle completely prevent amphetamine reducing food intake (1, 12, 93) without affecting the drug's action on motor behaviour (88). On the other hand, systemic administration of α- and β-adrenergic blockers do not counteract amphetamine anorexia (22, 52) and amphetamine retains its ability to reduce food intake even after selective blockade of NA synthesis by dopamine- β-hydroxylase inhibitors (49), thus arguing against a NA involvement. Moreover, Groppetti et al. (59) reported that low doses of d-amphetamine (up to 1 mg/kg), active in reducing food intake, do not modify telediencephalic or hypothalamic NA turnover rate while enhancing the turnover rate of DA. In addition, the reduction of food intake caused by local application of amphetamine to the PF hypothalamus is prevented by dopamine and β-adrenergic blockers (72). Amphetamine, however, being an indirect acting sympathomimetic agent, also possesses α-adrenergic properties that can affect feeding in the opposite direction by acting on a different noradrenergic system. Indeed, increased feeding has been observed on injecting amphetamine in the medial part of the hypothalamus, particularly the PVH, an effect selectively antagonized by α-adrenergic blockers (68). Amphetamine also elicits feeding when given systemically to animals with lateral hypothalamic lesions (112). The bulk of data suggests that DA is the CA primarily involved in the anorectic effect of amphetamine, although NA may play a supporting role. Several of structural analogues of amphetamine, such as phentermine, phendimetrazine and diethylpropion, seem to share with amphetamine a similar mechanism of action in reducing food intake (38, 45). On the other hand the mechanism by which another amphetamine analogue, fenfluramine, induces anorexia has been identified as an inhibition of 5-HT reuptake mechanisms together with an increased release of 5-HT from nerve terminals (27, 86), since its anorectic effect can be antagonized by pretreatment with 5-HT receptor blockers such as metergoline, or with chlorimipramine, a drug which prevents fenfluramine entry into 5-HT neurons and thus counteracts its releasing properties (Table 4). Fenfluramine-induced anorexia can also be antagonized by PCPA, by 5, 7-DHT and by electrolytic lesions of the Raphe Nuclea (51), all treatments which impair 5-HT function. All these data refer to the racemic compound. Recently the dextro isomer of fenfluramine has been introduced in the clinical practice. This compound has also been shown to act

TABLE 4. Comparison among different anorectics: efficacy in reducing food intake (ID_{50}), relative antagonisms and CNS stimulant porperties.

	ID_{50} (1)	ANTAGONISM BY							Locom.	Stereot.
	μ mol/kg	PIM	α MpT	DOMP	MET	CIIM	PROP	PHEN	activ.	behav. (2)
d-Amphetamine	5.43 (5.15- 5.91)	YES	YES	NO	NO	NO	NO	NO	++	+
Mazindol	3.79 (3.12- 4.81)	YES	YES	NO	NO	NO	NO	NO	+	-
Diethylpropion	19.00 (15.55-22.80)	YES	YES	NO	NO	NO	NO	NO	+	-
Apomorphine	1.02 (0.77- 1.21)	YES	NO	NO	NO	NO	NO	NO	++	+
Lisuride	0.12 (0.11- 0.14)	YES	NO	NO	NO	NO	NO	NO	-	-
Lergotrile	2.12 (1.85- 2.40)	YES	NO	NO	NO	NO	NO	NO	-	-
Bromocriptine	4.49 (4.25- 4.83)	YES	NO	NO	NO	NO	NO	NO	+	-
Piribedil	36.75 (35.10-38.36)	YES	NO	NO	NO	NO	NO	NO	-	-
d,1-Fenfluramine	7.43 (6.91- 8.03)	NO	NO	NO	YES	YES	NO	NO	-	-
d-Fenfluramine	5.49 (4.67- 6.21)	NO	NO	NO	YES	YES	NO	NO	-	-
p-Cl-Amphetamine	7.51 (6.83- 8.27)	NO	NO	NO	YES	YES	NO	NO	-	-
Quipazine	7.23 (6.01- 8.45)	NO	NO	NO	YES	NO	NO	NO	-	-
m-CPP	6.49 (5.80- 7.32)	NO	NO	NO	YES	NO	NO	NO	-	-
Salbutamol	13.87 (10.05-17.95)	NO	NO	NO	NO	NO	YES	NO	-	-

m-CPP = m-chlorophenylpiperazine; PIM = pimozide; HAL = haloperidol; α MpT = α -methyl-p-tyrosine; DOMP = domperidone; MET = metergoline; ClIM = chlorimipramine; PROP = propranolol; PHEN = phentolamine.
(1): Experiments performed in rats trained to eat 4h a day. Values refer to the effect at 1h after food presentation.
(2): - no change; + slightly increased; ++ increased.

throughout a 5-TH mechanism (11) and resulted more active in reducing food intake than the racemic form both in animal (table 4) and human studies (11, 100). Furthermore, it also appears that dextrofenfluramine displays less side effects than the parent compound, particularly with regard to sedation. Indeed, the sedative effect of racemic fenfluramine has been shown to be mainly linked to the effect of the l-isomer in reducing brain DA function, as judged by the increase of brain homovanillic acid levels (42) and by the ability of l-fenfluramine to antagonize, at low doses, the stimulant effects of amphetamine and apomorphine (6).

We have also studied the mechanism of action of mazindol, an anorectic drug that possesses a chemical structure completely different from those of amphetamine and fenfluramine (Fig. 2). The results of these studies lead us to the conclusion that mazindol, although not chemically related to the β -phenylethylamine group, has a pharmacological profile very similar to that of amphetamine. It causes anorexia, increases in motor activity and body temperature, it induces stereotyped behaviour and, when injected into rats with unilateral nigrostriatal lesions, it provokes turning towards the lesion-bearing side (116). Like amphetamine, mazindol appears to reduce food intake through a mechanism involving brain DA, since its anorectic effect is antagonized by α -MpT, and pimozide (Table 4). Mazindol and amphetamine inhibit uptake of DA by caudate synaptosomal preparations and provoke its release (25). Furthermore, both drugs enhance the turnover rate of DA (21).

In contrast to amphetamine (59), mazindol decreases the incorporation rate of ^{3}H-tyrosine into brain NA and does not alter tissue levels of CA (21). As the reduction of the NA turnover rate induced by mazindol may be a consequence of overstimulation at the receptor site, possibly caused by inhibition of the re-uptake mechanisms (48) that reduce synthesis through a feedback mechanism, the difference between the effects of mazindol and amphetamine on the brain noradrenergic system may be unimportant functionally because both drugs induce stimulation of NA function in the end even though by different mechanisms (35).

FIG. 2. Chemical structure of mazindol (5-hydroxy-5-p-chlorophenyl-2,3-dihydro-5H-imidazo-2,1-a-isoindole)

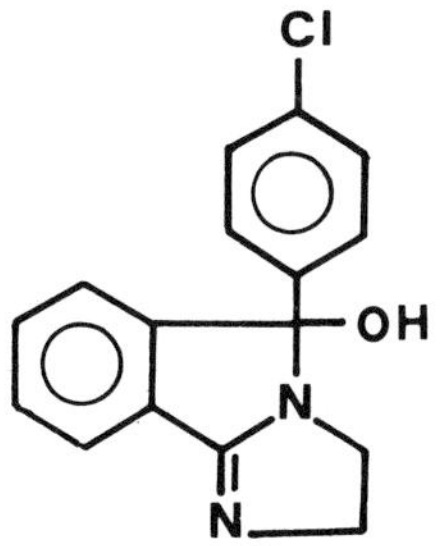

Cl

OH

N

N

Apart from anorexia, mazindol shares no behavioural effect with fenfluramine; unlike fenfluramine, the anorectic action of mazindol is not antagonized by chlorimipramine or by metergoline (Table 4). Like fenfluramine, mazindol inhibits in vitro the high-affinity uptake of 5-HT by guinea pig blood platelets (86) and rat forebrain synaptosomes (27), but whereas fenfluramine is also able to release the amine, mazindol does not share this action (21). Proof of mazindol's ability to inhibit 5-HT re-uptake by presynaptic neurons has been obtained *in vivo* too (26). Probably owing to its ineffectiveness in releasing 5-HT, in contrast to fenfluramine (40, 46) mazindol fails either to decrease brain 5-HT concentration or to change the 5-HT turnover rate (21), ruling out a serotoninergic involvement in its anorectic effect (35).

Thus, it appears that in animals, despite the great number of neuronal systems that play roles in controlling food intake, the effects of the more widely used anorectic drugs are mediated essentially by activation of dopaminergic or serotoninergic mechanisms.

It is worthwhile also noting that there is a dichotomy between these two eating-suppressive systems. Indeed, on the basis of some differences observed between fenfluramine and amphetamine in modifying particular aspects of feeding such as onset of feeding, meal size, rate of eating, it has been suggested that serotoninergic mechanisms are primarily involved in satiety, while dopaminergic neurons act mainly on appetite (7).

OTHER DRUGS WITH ANORECTIC PROPERTIES

More recently attention has been focused on seeing whether drugs that stimulate the dopaminergic or the serotoninergic system by different mechanisms from those of amphetamine and fenfluramine are also anorectic.

Along this line, it has been reported that quipazine and m-chlorophenylpiperazine are able to induce anorexia by direct activation of 5-HT receptor sites in the brain (94, 95). The observation that chlorimipramine, at a dose that is able to counteract fenfluramine anorexia, did not overcome the anorexia induced by quipazine or m-chlorophenylpiperazine (Table 4) would indicate that these two drugs can act even when their entry into presynaptic 5-HT neurons is prevented, confirming that direct 5-HT receptor activation is the primary mechanism responsible for the anorectic effect.

Direct activation of DA receptor sites also seems to bring about reduction of food intake, since amorphine (4), lisuride, lergotrile, bromocriptine (32) and piribedil (29) can induce striking dose-related anorexia in the rat. That this effect, as opposed to those of amphetamine and mazindol, is actually due to activation of DA receptors and does not depend on newly synthesized brain CA is shown by the ability of pimozide and haloperidol, but not of α-MpT, to antagonize apomorphine-, lisuride-, lergotrile-, bromocriptine- and piribedil-induced anorexia (Table 4).

The likelihood that the site of action for these compounds is in the CNS is strongly suggested by the evidence that they can cause anorexia even when injected ICV (Carruba, unpublished observations) and that two DA-receptor blockers which do not cross (domperidone) or only minimally cross (sulpiride) (89) the blood-brain barrier did not oppose the anorexia induced by these DA agonists (29, 32). Therefore, since all these compounds are potent agonists of D_2 dopamine receptors (103, 111), the most likely site of action of these drugs could be those D_2 dopamine receptors previously reported to be present in the PF area of the hypothalamus.

DA-mimetic drugs are known to cause nausea and vomiting by stimulation of DA receptors located in the chemoreceptor trigger zone of the area postrema (39). Since this area lies outside the blood-brain barrier, it is easily accessible to the DA receptor blocker domperidone, which does not cross the blood-brain barrier, and thus counteracts the emetic and nauseating effects of DA agonists, without modifying their central actions (89). Therefore, the inability of domperidone to antagonize the anorectic action of the DA-mimetics can also be taken as evidence that their effects on food intake do not result from a non-specific nauseating action of the drugs.

It also seems worth noting that, under our experimental conditions, some of the direct acting DA-mimetics lisuride, lergotrile and piribedil, reduced food intake at doses lower than those required to increase spontaneous motor activity or to induce stereotyped behaviour, unlike amphetamine which induces anorexia in rats at doses which increase locomotor activity and cause stereotyped movements (22).

There are several possible ways of explaining this dissociation between the anorectic and motor stimulant effects of some of these DA agonists. We can speculate that the DA receptors involved in suppression of feeding, located in the hypothalamus, are more sensitive to the action of these compounds than those involved in increasing motor activity, which are located in the extrapyramidal or limbic system.

Morevoer, the observation that the hypothermia induced by these drugs, an effect most probably mediated by hypothalamic DA receptors, occurs within the same range of doses as the anorectic effect (33) also supports this view. It seems unlikely that the differential effects of lisuride may result from easier access of the drug to hypothalamic regions than to extrapyramidal or limbic ones. Indeed, a dose of 25 μg/kg of lisuride, for instance, which is active in lowering food consumption and body temperature, is associated with hypomotility and sedation (32), probably reflecting activation of dopaminergic autoreceptors in the extrapyramidal or limbic system (20, 65).

Thus, in contrast to the situation with traditional anorectics such as amphetamine and mazindol, acting indirectly through enhancing DA release, by giving drugs that directly activate DA receptor sites in the brain, it is possible to obtain marked anorexia divorced from concomitant central stimulation.

Salbutamol, an agonist of β_2-adrenergic receptors (16, 43), known to induce anorexia when injected into the PF hypothalamic area of the rat (71), has been shown recently to cause a dose-dependent reduction in food intake of starved rats even after systemic administration (14). The effect was prevented by the β-adrenolytic drug propranolol, given either systemically or ICV (14), but not by antagonists of α-adrenergic, dopaminergic or serotoninergic receptors (Table 4), indicating that the anorectic effect of salbutamol is mediated by stimulation of central β-adrenergic sites. The fact that salbutamol reduces food intake with no apparent motor stimulation and that activation of peripheral β-adrenoceptors can potentially increase thermogenesis suggest new interesting possibilities in the pharmacological treatment of obesity.

Another interesting observation is that (-)-hydroxycitrate and (-)-threo-chlorocitric acid can decrease food intake and body weight not only when given to normal rats and dogs, but also in a number of experimentally induced obese states, such as the VMH-lesioned rat and the gold-thioglucose-induced obese mouse (108). The most interesting aspect of these findings is the fact that (-)-hydroxycitrate and (-)-threo-chlorocitric acid do not cross the blood-brain barrier and therefore their anorectic effects must be mediated in the periphery. It remains an open question whether the inhibition of gastric emptying and/or the antilipogenic activity of these compounds might be responsible for the suppression of appetite.

Although similarities between effects of anorectic drugs in animals and in humans are at times striking, conclusions drawn from animal studies cannot always be applied to clinical situations. Nevertheless, these results are encouraging and provide a rationale for clinical trials. In this regard it is noteworthy that among the side-effects of some direct DA agonists in patients with neuroendocrine disturbances, loss of appetite and body weight have been reported (10 and personal communications).

EFFECTS OF ANORECTIC DRUGS ON EXPERIMENTALLY-INDUCED HYPERPHAGIAS

Rats trained to eat their daily meal within 4 h a day are the most common experimental model for testing the efficacy of anorectic drugs (8). Under these experimental conditions, several agents with direct or indirect stimulatory effects on dopaminergic or serotoninergic systems all reduce food consumption (22), with variable degrees of potency (Table 4). This non-hyperphagic model, although widely used to evaluate anorectic properties of drugs, may not be really representative of the clinical situation, in which these drugs are used to control the overeating of obese people who often have concomitant dysfunctions of glucose metabolism and/or utilization (8, 9).

Hypoglycemic doses of insulin or administration of 2-deoxy-d-glucose (2-DG), a glucose analogue that induces intracellular glucopenia (19), for instance, causes hyperphagia in rats as a result of cerebral glucoprivation (101). Since 2-DG causes not only hyperphagia, but also hyperglycemia and a state of relative insulin deficiency or resistance (50), similar to that observed in diabetes mellitus, rats given this compound may be considered experimental models for obese diabetic people (109). On the other hand, the insulin-induced increase in food intake seems more representative of the hyperphagia present in obese subjects with hyperinsulinemia (5, 113).

Therefore, study of the effects of anorectic drugs on these and other experimentally induced hyperphagias should provide information not only about the neuronal organization of the brain systems that control feeding, but also about possible therapeutic strategies against obesity.

In order to compare the effects of anorectics that act upon either dopaminergic or serotoninergic mechanisms on insulin- and 2-DG-induced hyperphagias, the drugs were given rats at doses equal to their ID_{50}s (dose inhibiting food intake by 50%, evaluated previously in rats trained to eat 4 h per day). Subsequently, the rats were given a second injection of either insulin (6 U/kg) or 2-DG (750 mg/kg) or saline and the food eaten by the animals during the following 5 h was measured. These doses of insulin and 2-DG were given because they cause constant and substantial increases in food consumption (101, 102). Fig. 3 shows that dextrofenfluramine, p-chloroamphetamine, fluoxetine and quipazine, which cause anorexia by enhancing, through different mechanisms, brain serotoninergic neurotransmission (22), can antagonize both insulin- and 2-DG-induced hyperphagia, whereas d-amphetamine, diethylpropion, lisuride, mazindol and bromocriptine, which induce anorexia by enhacing brain dopaminergic neurotransmission (31), were only effective in antagonizing the hyperphagia induced by 2-DG and not that induced by insulin (24, 34). It seems unlikely that these different effects of serotoninergic and dopaminergic anorectics on insulin-induced hyperphagia could be due to different effects of these drugs on insulin-induced hypoglycemia. Indeed, neither d-amphetamine and lisuride nor dextrofenfluramine and quipazine modified the hypoglycemic response to insulin (34).

These results showing differential effects of serotoninergic and dopaminergic anorectic drugs on glucoprivation-induced eating, support the previously proposed notion that different neuronal circuits are involved in the hyperphagic responses to insulin and 2-DG glucoprivation (61). Evidence for this is also provided by the observation that 2-DG needs functional α-adrenoceptors in order to bring about increased food intake, while insulin does not. Indeed, under our experimental conditions, the hyperphagic response to 2-DG could be antagonized by pre-treatment with the α-adrenergic receptor blocker phentolamine (81), but insulin-induced hyperphagia was not modified by this pre-treatment (Fig. 3).

The opiate antagonist, naloxone, has been shown by several authors to decrease the eating response induced by 2-DG (74, 80, 99, 115), whereas there is disagreement concerning the effect of naloxone on insulin-induced hyperphagia in rats. Indeed both no effect and a reduction of insulin-induced eating have been reported (74, 80, 84, 91, 115). Under our experimental conditions, naloxone had the same selective effect as dopaminergic agents and phentolamine on 2-DG-induced eating but not on insulin hyperphagia (data not shown). It therefore seems likely that a complex interaction between glucose metabolism, opiate receptors and both the serotoninergic and the catecholaminergic systems are activated by 2-DG administration. Insulin-induced eating appears to involve mainly the serotoninergic system. Since insulin and meal-related insulin secretion can increase 5-HT synthesis in the brain (114), this could serve as a satiety signal for cessation of insulin-induced overeating, even without exogenous administration of a 5-HT agonist. Therefore, one would expect that administration of a 5-HT receptor antagonist, such as metergoline, could somehow enhance or prolong the hyperphagic effect of insulin. This, however, did not occur under our experimental conditions. Activation of brain serotoninergic mechanisms did antagonize the overeating induced by insulin but impairment of 5-HT function did not seem to facilitate it.

On the whole, from these data it appears that different neuronal or humoral circuits underly insulin- and 2-DG-induced eating and that serotoninergic and dopaminergic anorectic drugs modulate the eating responses of rats to cerebral glucoprivation induced by insulin or by 2-DG in different ways. In turn, this suggests that glucose dysmetabolims in obesity may be a determining factor in the choice of therapeutic strategy.

Other animal models of hyperphagias include tail pinch-induced eating and muscimol injection into the nucleus raphe dorsalis (NDR). The first of these will not be considered here (see Morley et al., this volume). For muscimol injection into the NDR it has been reported to elicit eating together with a concomitant reduction in the hypothalamic and striatal turnover of 5-HT (87). Although this result

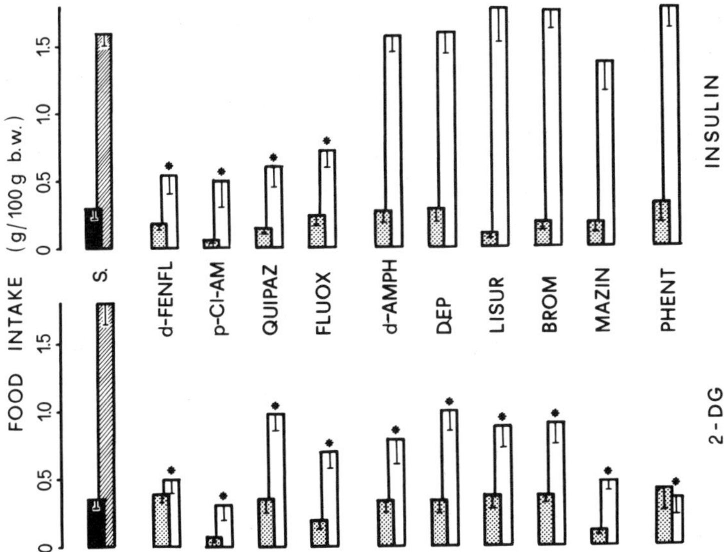

FIG. 3. Effects of different drugs on 2-DG-and insulin-induced increase in food intake.
Rats were given ip a) saline plus saline (black bars) or b) saline plus 750 mg/kg 2-DG or 6 U/kg insulin (dashed bars) or c) the drug to be tested plus saline (shaded bars) or d) the drug to be tested plus 2-DG or insulin (doses as before) (open bars).
The following drugs were tested at doses corresponding to the ID_{50}s (see Table 4): dextrofenfluramine (d-FENFL); p-chloroamphetamine (p-Cl-AM); quipazine (QUIPAZ); fluoxetine (FLUOX); d-amphetamine (d-AMPH); diethylpropion (DEP); lisuride (LISUR); 2-Br- α -ergocriptine (BROM); mazindol (MAZIN). Phentolamine (PHENT) was given at 1 mg/kg (this dose does not change food intake in rats trained to eat 4 h per day). Bars represent mean values $\pm$ SEM of food eaten within 5 h expressed as g/100 g body weight. Twelve animals per group were used. $^*p \leq 0.01$ vs saline plus 2-DG or insulin-treated rats, by Dunnett's test.

was interpreted as evidence that the injection of muscimol into the NDR causes eating by depressing brain 5-HT function, further experiments did not confirm this view. Indeed, eating induced by muscimol injection in the NDR was not significantly modified in rats which had received 5,7-DHT in the same area 11 days before, indicating that the integrity of 5-HT neurons in the NDR is not necessary for muscimol to induce eating (13). The eating response to muscimol injection into the NDR appeared to be mediated by both α-adrenergic and dopaminergic mechanisms since it was markedly reduced by doses of phenoxybenzamine and penfluridol reported to block central α-adrenergic and dopaminergic receptors respectively (13). Interestingly, d-amphetamine, at doses which markedly reduce food intake by starved rats, was unable to modify muscimol induced eating whereas dextrofenfluramine did antagonize the muscimol effect (13). Therefore, eating elicited by muscimol injected in the NDR appears to represent a CA-mediated model of hyperphagia selectively inhibited by agents which increase 5-HT transmission.

A series of interesting similarities and differences can be noted between eating induced by insulin, 2-DG, muscimol injection in the NDR or tail pinch. As is the case with 2-DG-induced eating α-adrenergic mechanisms seem to contribute to both muscimol- and tail pinch-induced eating (13, 90) whereas insulin hyperphagia is independent of such mechanisms (34). On the other hand, insulin-induced eating resembles eating caused by tail pinch and by muscimol injection in the NDR in that all are insensitive to the anorectic effect of d-amphetamine (3, 13, 34). Indeed, d-amphetamine was able to counteract only the overeating caused by 2-DG (34). Interestingly, all the experimentally-induced hyperphagias examined were sensitive to dextrofenfluramine (3, 13, 34) indicating that serotoninergic mechanisms do play some fundamental role in controlling overeating.

TOLERANCE AND CROSS TOLERANCE STUDIES

It is well known that the initial anorectic effect of amphetamine and other appetite suppressants is diminished after repeated administration. This apparent tolerance, which develops both in laboratory animals and in man, limits the therapeutic effectiveness of long-term anorectic drug treatment of obesity (53). The acute behavioural effects of drugs might undergo drastic modification after repeated administration because of metabolic adaptation or because of modified receptor number or sensitivity (96, 98), or because of behavioural adaptation (44). The exact mechanism through which the anorectic effect of drugs undergoes tolerance has not yet been fully clarified. It has been hypothesized that tolerance to the anorectic effect of amphetamine could be interpreted as a learning process (44), or it could be simply due to a loss of body weight (73) or to increased deprivation of food (36, 54, 85). This uncertainty, as pointed out by Blundell and McArthur (9), rests upon methodological problems that hinder the interpretation of tolerance studies on anorectic agents.

In an attempt to better understand the mechanisms responsible

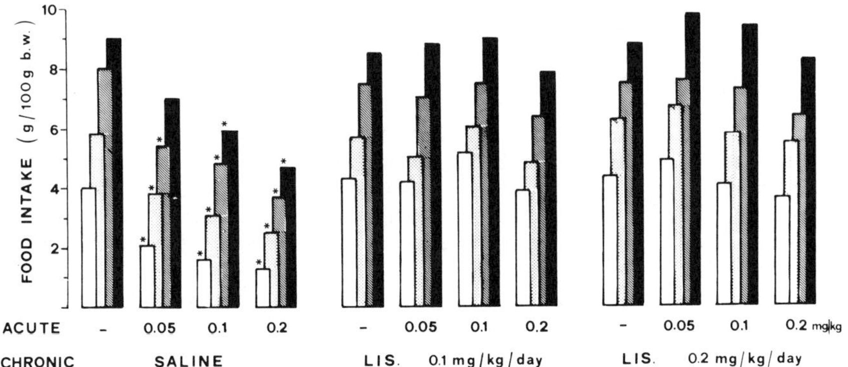

FIG. 4. Effects of different doses of lisuride on food intake of rats trained to eat 4 h a day and chronically pretreated with either saline or lisuride, 0.1 or 0.2 mg/kg, ip, daily for 24 days.
Bars represent food eaten (g per 100 g body weight) 1 (open bars), 2 (dotted bars), 3 (dashed bars) and 4 h (black bars) after food presentation.
The mean standard errors were 9.23 ± 0.54% of the reported values (min 3 and max 18.3%).
Acute injections of lisuride were given 24 h after the last injection of the chronic treatment and 15 min before food presentation.
Six rats per group. * $p \leq 0.01$ by Dunnett's t-test.

for the changes in the behavioural effects of a drug following repeated administration, we investigated the pattern of modification of the effect of the drug lisuride on food intake and on other behavioural parameters after long-term treatment. It was found that rats given daily injections of lisuride showed a progressive decline in the anorectic potency of the drug. Complete tolerance to the anorectic effect of lisuride was reached 24 days after the beginning of the treatment (Fig. 4). The growth of the rats, treated daily with lisuride, was inhibited during the first 24 days of treatment. However, once complete tolerance to the anorectic effect of the drug developed, the rats began to grow at the same rate as controls, indicating a clear-cut cause-effect relationship between reduced intake of food and reduced gain in body weight (28).

Rats that developed tolerance to the anorectic effect of lisuride also developed tolerance to its hypothermic effect. Interestingly, rats treated chronically with lisuride, at the time when they became tolerant to the anorectic and hypothermic effects of the drug also developed reverse tolerance (sensitization), rather than tolerance, to some other behavioural effects, such as locomotor activity, stereotypy and mounting behaviour (28). Therefore, two behavioural effects of lisuride, anorexia and hypothermia, both probably mediated through activation of hypothalamic DA receptors, are subject to tolerance, while other behavioural effects, locomotor activity and stereotypy, probably mediated by activation of DA receptors located in the extrapyramidal or limbic system, are sensitized. Among other possibilities, this could be because hypothalamic DA receptors have different characteristics from those in extrapyramidal or limbic sites: otherwise, both populations of DA receptors should have reacted in the same way to prolonged stimulation by lisuride. One of these differences might be that there are functionally-defined autoreceptors within the extrapyramidal and limbic regions but not within the hypothalamus. This would imply that repeated administration of lisuride, which has a preferential affinity for DA autoreceptors (32), desensitizes mainly the autoreceptors, thus causing less autoregulation and more postsynaptic stimulation, which leads to sensitization.

The hypothesis of a lack in the hypothalamus of functionally-defined DA autoreceptors would also explain why the anorexic and the hypothermic effects of lisuride occurred after doses smaller than those required to increase spontaneous motor activity or to induce stereotyped and mounting behaviour. Indeed, in the extrapyramidal system, where DA autoreceptors seem to be present, the stimulatory effects of lisuride, due to activation of postsynaptic DA receptors, occurred at doses large enough to overcome the inhibitory effects after activation of the autoreceptors. It is worth emphasizing that, as opposed to the situation with locomotor activity, the effects of lisuride on those behavioural responses mediated by hypothalamic DA receptors (decreased food intake and body temperature) were not biphasic: small doses of the drug did not cause any increase in the intake of food or in body temperature (Carruba, unpublished data).

It is still a matter of debate whether anorectics, such as amphetamine and apomorphine, are truly anorectic or merely obstruct the process of eating by facilitating incompatible behaviour, such as hyperactivity and stereotypy. The observation that after repeated administration of lisuride, an additional dose of the drug caused hyperactivity and stereotypy, because of sensitization, without altering food consumption, because of tolerance, would indicate that increased motor activity, at least up to a certain degree, can coexist with a normal feeding pattern and these behavioural effects are not competitive.

The series of events, which develops following repeated administration of a DA agonist, may well confer an advantage when the drug is used for reasons other than the treatment of obesity, for example in Parkinson's disease where the food intake suppressant effect of the drug is an undesirable side effect. In such circumstances, the side effect (anorexia) would disappear with prolonged treatment while the desired effect would be potentiated. However, when considering a DA agonist drug as a possible candidate in the management of obesity it must not be forgotten that the anorectic effect of the drug will undergo tolerance following repeated administration while the CNS stimulant effects, in this case undesirable, will undergo sensitization.

Another interesting observation is that when rats develop tolerance to the anorectic effect of lisuride, they become cross tolerant to the anorexigenic effect of other DA-mimetics, such as amphetamine, mazindol, etc. and also to anorectics which act throughout the 5-HT system, such as fenfluramine and quipazine (30). The next step was to verify whether the reverse occurs. Accordingly, we made rats tolerant to the anorectic effect of fenfluramine. At this stage neither fenfluramine nor quipazine were able to cause anorexia in those animals. In contrast the anorectic activities of amphetamine, mazindol and lisuride were unchanged (30). These data therefore indicate the existence of cross-tolerance between fenfluramine and quipazine, both serotoninomimetics, but a lack of cross-tolerance between serotoninergic and dopaminergic anorectics.

The existence of cross-tolerance between fenfluramine and quipazine can be taken as evidence that fenfluramine tolerance is not due to the decrease in brain 5-HT store which could have prevented fenfluramine-induced 5-HT release and thus anorexia. It therefore seems more likely to depend on a modification taking place at the level of 5-HT receptor sites otherwise quipazine, whose anorectic action does not depend on presynaptic events, would have remained effective in reducing food intake in fenfluramine tolerant rats. More direct evidence on this issue has been reported by Mennini et al. (77) who found that tolerance to the anorectic effect of dextrofenfluramine was correlated with a significant decrease in the number of 5-HT receptor sites in the brain. In the case of lisuride the mechanism underlying tolerance to its anorectic action seems much more complex since, once activated, it also impedes the capacity of other anorectics, acting through DA or 5-HT systems, to exert their anorectic action.

The clinical implications of these findings would foresee a sequential therapeutic scheme utilizing first a serotoninergic anorectic such as dextrofenfluramine so that, when tolerance develops to this agent, there is still the possibility of successfully continuing the treatment with DA-mimetics. The reverse procedure would not be so effective. In keeping with these results is the observation that the monthly weight losses that occurred in obese patients when the dopaminomimetic phentermine followed the serotoninomimetic fenfluramine were greater than those achieved either during continuous fenfluramine therapy or when fenfluramine followed phentermine (105).

CONCLUDING REMARKS

The studies described in the present review point out the increase complexity in knowledge about the pharmacology of anorectic drugs made in the last few years. Since research on pharmacology of anorectic agents has become more closely linked with basic research on the brain systems involved in appetite control, a number of interesting relationships between drugs, CNS and appetite have become evident. In turn, studies on the pharmacological manipulation of eating have been useful in providing better insight into the physiological mechanisms of feeding control, regulation of body weight (see Stunkard, this volume) and the pathologic events that disturb these mechanisms. Although research in this field has not yet discovered the "ideal" drug for the management of obesity, nevertheless more has been learned about the way in which the present generation of drugs exert their effects and about the different ways in which they intervene in processes controlling eating.

The present family of anorectic drugs do not however conform to a single class and therefore they should be used selectively to counteract specific eating difficulties in obese people with particular feeding problems. Indeed, obesity, like other metabolic disturbances, may well have many different subtypes each with its own appropriate style of management and in which different anorectic drugs have distinct parts to play.

REFERENCES

1. Ahlskog, J.E. (1974): *Brain Res.*, 82: 211-240.

2. Anand, B.K., and Brobeck, J.R. (1951): *Proc. Soc. Exp. Biol. Med.*, 77: 323-324.

3. Antelman, S.M., Caggiula, A.R. Block, C.A., and Edwards, D.J. (1978): *Brain Res.*, 143: 580-585.

4. Barzaghi, F., Groppetti, A., Mantegazza, P., and Müller, E.E. (1973): *J. Pharm. Pharmacol.*, 25: 909-911.

5. Belloff-Chain, A. (1979): In: *Animal Models of Obesity*, edited by M.F.W. Festing, pp. 91-106. MacMillan Press, London.

6. Bendotti, C., Borsini, F., Zanini, M.G., Samanin, R., and Garattini, S. (1980): *Pharmacol. Res. Comm.*, 12: 567-574.

7. Blundell, J.E., and Latham, C.J. (1978): In: *Central Mechanisms of Anorectic Drugs*, edited by S. Garattini and R. Samanin, pp. 83-109. Raven Press, New York.

8. Blundell, J.E., and Latham, C.J. (1982): In: *Drugs and Appetite*, edited by T. Silverstone, pp. 41-80. Academic Press, London.

9. Blundell, J.E., and McArthur, R.A. (1979): *Obesity and its Treatment*, vol. 1. Annual Research Reviews. Churchill Livingstone, Edinburgh.

10. Bommer, J., Ritz, E., Del Pozo, E., and Bommer, G. (1979): *Lancet*, 2: 496-497.

11. Borsini, F., Bendotti, C., Aleotti, A., Samanin, R. and Garattini, S. (1982): *Pharmacol. Res. Comm.*, 14: 671-678.

12. Borsini, F., Bendotti, C., Carli, M., Poggesi, E., and Samanin, R. (1979): *Res. Comm. Chem. Pathol. Pharmacol.*, 26: 3-11.

13. Borsini, F., Bendotti, C., Przewlocka, B., and Samanin, R. (1983): *Eur. J. Pharmacol.*, 94: 109-115.

14. Borsini, F., Bendotti, C., Thurlby, P., and Samanin, R. (1982): *Life Sci.*, 30: 905-911.

15. Breisch, S.T., Zelman, F.P., and Hoebel, B.G. (1976): *Science*, 192: 382-384.

16. Brittain, R.T., Farmer, J.B., Jack, D., Martin, L.E., and Simpson, W.T. (1968): *Nature*, 219: 862-863.

17. Brobeck, J.R. (1946): *Physiol. Rev.*, 26: 541-559.

18. Brobeck, J.R., Tepperman, J., and Long, C.N.H. (1943): *Yale J. Biol. Med.*, 15: 831-853.

19. Brown, J. (1962): *Metabolism*, 11: 1098-1112.

20. Carlsson, A. (1975): In: *Pre- and Postsynaptic Receptors*, Annual ACNP Meeting, Puerto-Rico, edited by E. Usdin and W.E. Bunney Jr., pp. 49-65. Dekker, New York.

21. Carruba, M.O., Groppetti, A., Mantegazza, P., Vincentini, L., and Zambotti, F. (1976): *Br. J. Pharmacol.*, 56: 431-436.

22. Carruba, M.O., and Mantegazza, P. (1981): In: *Obesity: Pathogenesis and Treatment*, edited by G. Enzi, G. Grepaldi, G. Pozza, and A.E. Renold, pp. 261-270. Academic Press, London.

23. Carruba, M.O., and Mantegazza, P., editors (1983): *Obesita, Analisi e Terapia*. Minerva Medica, Torino.

24. Carruba, M.O., Mantegazza, P., Müller, E.E., and Ricciardi, S. (1981): *Br. J. Pharmacol.*, 72: 161 P.

25. Carruba, M.O., Picotti, G.B., Zambotti, F., and Mantegazza, P. (1977): *Naunyn-Schmiedeberg's Arch. Pharmacol.*, 298: 1-5.

26. Carruba, M.O., Picotti, G.B., Zambotti, F., and Mantegazza, P. (1977): *J. Pharm. Pharmacol.*, 29: 242-243.

27. Carruba, M.O., Picotti, G.B., Zambotti, F., and Mantegazza, P. (1977): *Nuanyn-Schmiedeberg's Arch. Pharmacol.*, 300: 227-232.

28. Carruba, M.O., Ricciardi, S., Chiesara, E., Spano, P.F., and Mantegazza, P. (1985): *Neuropharmacology*, 24: 199-206.

29. Carruba, M.O., Ricciardi, S., and Mantegazza, P. (1980): *Life Sci.*, 27: 1131-1140.

30. Carruba, M.O., Ricciardi, S., and Mantegazza, P. (1981): In: *Anorectic Agents: Mechanisms of Action and Tolerance*, edited by S. Garattini and R. Samanin, pp. 101-112. Raven Press, New York.

31. Carruba, M.O., Ricciardi, S., and Mantegazza, P. (1981): In: *Apomorphine and Other Dopaminomimetics*, vol. 1, Basic Pharmacology, edited by G.L. Gessa and G.U. Corsini, pp. 303-310. Raven Press, New York.

32. Carruba, M.O., Ricciardi, S., Müller, E.E., and Mantegazza, P. (1980): *Eur. J. Pharmacol.*, 64: 133-141.

33. Carruba, M.O., Ricciardi, S., Negreanu, J., Calogero, M., and Mantegazza, P. (1980): *Psychopharmacology*, 70: 223-229.

34. Carruba, M.O., Ricciardi, S., Spano, P.F., and Mantegazza, P. (1985): *Life Sci.*, 36: 1739-1749.

35. Carruba, M.O., Zambotti, F., Vincentini, L., Picotti, G.B., and Mantegazza, P. (1978): In: *Central Mechanisms of Anorectic Drugs*, edited by S. Garattini and R. Samanin, pp. 145-164. Raven Press, New York.

36. Cawthorne, M.A. (1981): In: *Anorectic Agents: Mechanisms of Action and Tolerance*, edited by S. Garattini and R. Samanin, pp. 1-77. Raven Press, New York.

37. Clément-Cormier, Y.C., Kebabian, J.W., Petzold, G.L., and Greengard, P. (1974): *Proc. Nat. Acad. Sci.*, 71: 1113-1117.

38. Costa, E., and Garattini, S., editors (1970): *Amphetamines and Related Compounds.* Raven Press, New York.

39. Costa, E., and Gessa, G.L., editors (1977): *Nonstriatal Dopamine Neurons.* Raven Press, New York.

40. Costa, E., Groppetti, A., and Revuelta, A. (1971): *Br. J. Pharmacol.*, 41: 57-64.

41. Cox, R.H. Jr., and Maickel, R.P. (1972): *J. Pharmacol Exp. Ther.*, 181: 1-9.

42. Crunelli, V., Bernasconi, S., and Samanin, R. (1980): *Pharmacol. Res Comm.* 12: 215-223.

43. Cullum, V.A., Farmer, J.B., Jack, D., and Levy, G.P. (1969): *Br. J. Pharmacol.*, 35: 141-151.

44. Demellweek, C., and Goudie, A.J., (1983): *Psychopharmacology*, 79: 58-66.

45. Dobranski, S., and Dogget, N.S. (1979): *Psychopharmacology*, 66: 297-300.

46. Duhault, J., and Verdavainne, C. (1967): *Arch. Int. Pharmacodyn Ther* 170: 276-286.

47. Ehrich, W.E., and Krumbhaar, E.B. (1937): *Ann. Int. Med.* 10: 1874-1888.

48. Engstrom, R.G., Kelly, L.A., and Gogerty, J.H. (1975): *Arch. Int. Pharmacodyn. Ther.* 214: 308-321.

49. Franklin, K.B.J., and Herberg, L.J. (1977): *Neuropharmacology* 16: 45-46.

50. Frohman, L.A., Müller, E.E., and Cocchi, D. (1973): *Horm. Metab. Res.* 5: 21-26.

51. Garattini, S., Borroni, E., Mennini, T., and Samanin, R. (1978): In: *Central Mechanisms of Anorectic Drugs* edited by S. Garattini and R. Samanin, pp. 127-143. Raven Press, New York.

52. Garattini, S., and Samanin, R. (1976): In: *Appetite and Food Intake* edited by T. Silverstone, pp. 83-108. Abakon Verlagsgesellschaft, Berlin.

53. Garattini, S., and Samanin, R., editors (1981): *Anorectic Agents: Mechanisms of Action and Tolerance.* Raven Press, New York.

54. Ghosh, M.N., and Parvathy, S. (1976): *Br. J. Pharmacol.*, 57: 479-486.

55. Gibbs, J., Fauser, D.J., Rowe, E.A., Rolls, B.J., Rolls, E.T., and Maddison, S.P. (1979): *Nature*, 282: 208-210.

56. Goldman, H.W., Lehr, D., and Friedman, E. (1971): *Nature*, 231: 453-455.

57. Grandison, L., and Guidotti, A. (1977): *Neuropharmacology*, 16: 533-536.

58. Groppetti, A., and Mantegazza, P. (1973): In: *First Congress of Hungarian Pharmacological Society*, vol. 1, edited by J. Knoll and K. Magyar, pp. 195-203. Akademiai Kiado, Budapest.

59. Groppetti, A., Zambotti, F., Biazzi, A., and Mantegazza, P. (1973): In: *Frontiers in Catecholamine Research*, edited by E. Usdin, and S.H. Snyder, pp. 917-925. Pergamon Press, Oxford.

60. Grossman, S.P. (1975): *Physiol. Rev.*, 82: 200-224.

61. Grossman, S.P. (1978): In: *Central Mechanisms of Anorectic Drugs*, edited by S. Garattini and R. Samanin, pp. 1-37. Raven Press, New York.

62. Hollister, A.S., Ervin, G.N., Cooper, B.R., and Breese, G.R. (1975): *Neuropharmacology*, 14: 715-723.

63. Iversen, L.L., Uretsky, N.J. (1970): *Brain Res.*, 24: 364-367.

64. Jacoby, J.H., and Lytle, L.D., editors (1978): *Ann. N. Y. Acad. Sci.*, vol. 305.

65. Kehr, W., Carlsson, A., and Lindquist, M. (1975): In: *Dopaminergic Mechanisms*, edited by D. Calne, T.N. Chase, and A. Barbeau, pp. 185-196. Raven Press, New York.

66. Kimura, H., and Kuriyama, K. (1975): *J. Neurochem.*, 24: 903-907.

67. Koe, B.K., and Weissman, A. (1966): *J. Pharmacol. Exp. Ther.*, 154: 499-516.

68. Leibowitz, S.F. (1976): In: *Hunger: Basic Mechanisms and Clinical Implications*, edited by D. Novin, W. Wyrwiwka, and G. Bray, pp. 1-18. Raven Press, New York.

69. Leibowitz, S.F. (1978): In: *Central Mechanisms of Anorectic Drugs*, edited by S. Garattini and R. Samanin, pp. 39-82. Raven Press, New York.

70. Leibowitz, S.F., and Papadakos, P.J. (1978): *Neurosci. Abstr.*, 4: 452.

71. Leibowitz, S.F., and Rossakis, C. (1978): *Neuropharmacology*, 17: 691-702.

72. Leibowitz, S.F., and Rossakis, C. (1978): *Eur. J. Pharmacol.*, 53: 69-81.

73. Levitsky, D.A., Strupp, B.J., and Lupoli, J. (1981): *Pharmacol. Biochem. Behav.*, 14: 661-667.

74. Lowy, M.T., Maickel, R.P., and Yim, G.K.W. (1980): *Life Sci.*, 26: 2113-2118.

75. Margules, D.L. (1970): *J. Comp. Physiol. Psychol.*, 73: 1-21.

76. Memo, M., Carboni, E., Uzumaki, H., Govoni, S., Carruba, M.O., Trabucchi, M., and Spano, P.F. (1984): In: *Principles and Methods in Receptor Binding*, edited by F. Cattabeni and S. Nicosia, pp. 93-111. Plenum Press, New York.

77. Mennini, T., De Blasi, A., Borroni, E., Bendotti, C., Borsini, F., Samanin, R., and Garattini, S. (1981): In: *Anorectic Agents: Mechanisms of Action and Tolerance*, edited by S. Garattini and R. Samanin, pp. 87-100. Raven Press, New York.

78. Mogenson, G.J., and Stevenson, J.A.F. (1967): *Exp. Neurol.*, 17: 119-127.

79. Morley, J.E. (1980): *Life Sci.*, 27: 355-368.

80. Morley, J.E., and Levine, A.S. (1983): *Lancet*, 1: 398-401.

81. Müller, E.E., Cocchi, D., and Mantegazza, P. (1972): *Am. J. Physiol.*, 223: 945-950.

82. Nathanson, M.H. (1937): *Am. J. Med. Ass.*, 108: 528-531.

83. Oomura, Y. (1973): *Adv. Biophysiol.*, 5: 65-142.

84. Ostrowski, N.L., Rowland, N., Foley, T.L., Nelson, J.L., and Reid, L.D. (1981): *Pharmacol. Biochem. Behav.*, 14: 549-555.

85. Panksepp, J., and Booth, D.A. (1973): *Psychopharmacology*, 39: 45-54.

86. Picotti, G.B., Carruba, M.O., Zambotti, F., and Mantegazza, P. (1977): *Eur. J. Pharmacol.*, 42: 217-224.

87. Przewlocka, B., Stala, L., and Scheel-Krüger, J. (1979): *Life Sci.*, 25: 937-946.

88. Quattrone, A., Bendotti, C., Recchia, M., and Samanin, R. (1977): *Comm. Psychopharmacol.*, 1: 525-531.

89. Reyntjens, A.J., Niemegeers, C.J.E., Van Neuten, J.M., Laduron, P., Heykants, J., Schellekens, H.L., Marsboom, R., Jagenau, A., Broeckaert, A., and Janssen, P.A.J. (1978): *Artzneim. Forsch.*, 28: 1194-1198.

90. Robbins, T.W., Everitt, B.J., and Sahakian, B.J. (1981): In: *The Body Weight Regulatory System: Normal and Disturbed Mechanisms*, edited by I.A. Cioffi, W.P.T. James, and T.B. Van Itallie, pp. 289-297. Raven Press, New York.

91. Rowland, N., and Bartness, T.J. (1982): *Pharmacol. Biochem. Behav.*, 16: 1001-1003.

92. Saller, C.F., and Stricker, E.M. (1976): *Science*, 192: 385-387.

93. Samanin, R., Bendotti, C., Bernasconi, S., Borroni, E., and Garattini, S. (1977): *Eur. J. Pharmacol.*, 43: 117-124.

94. Samanin, R., Bendotti, C., Miranda, F., and Garattini, S. (1977): *J. Pharm. Pharmacol.*, 29: 53-54.

95. Samanin, R., Mennini, T., Ferraris, A., Bendotti, C., Borsini, F., and Garattini S. (1979): *Naunyn Schmiedeberg's Arch. Pharmacol.*, 308: 159-163.

96. Schwartz, J.C. Costentin, J., Martres, M.P., Protais, P., and Baudry, M. (1978): *Neuropharmacology*, 17: 666-685.

97. Sclafani, A., and Maul, G. (1974): *Physiol. Behav.* 12: 157-162.

98. Seeman, P. (1980): *Pharmacol. Rev.*, 32: 229-313.

99. Sewel, R.D.E., and Jawaharlal, K. (1980): *J. Pharm. Pharmacol.*, 32: 148-149.

100. Silverstone, J.T. (1985): Communication at the *First International Meeting on Body Weight Control*, Montreux, Switzerland.

101. Smith, G.P., Epstein, A.N. (1969): *Am. J. Physiol.*, 217: 1083-1087.

102. Smith, G.P., Gibbs, J., Trohmayer, A.J., and Stokes, P.E. (1972): *Am. J. Phsysiol.*, 222: 77-81.

103. Spano, P.F., Govoni, S., Uzumaki, H. Bosion, A., Memo, M., Lucchi, L., Carruba, M.O., and Trabucchi, M. (1983): In: *Aging Brain and Ergot Alkaloids: Studies on the Mechanism of Action*, edited by A. Agnoli, G. Crepaldi, P.F. Spano, and M. Trabucchi, pp. 165-177. Raven Press, New York.

104. Spector, S., Sjoerdsma, A., and Udenfriend, S. (1965): J. *Pharmacol. Exp. Ther.*, 147: 86-95.

105. Steel, J.M., Munro, J.F., and Duncan, L.J.P. (1973): *Practitioner*, 211: 232-236.

106. Stellar, E. (1954): *Psychol. Rev.*, 61: 5-23.

107. Stricker, E.M., and Zigmond, M.J. (1976): In: *Progress in Psychobiology*, vol. 6, edited by J.M. Sprague and A.N. Epstein, pp. 121-188. Academic Press, New York.

108. Sullivan, A.C., Guthrie, R.W., and Triscari, J. (1981): In: *Anorectic Agents: Mechanisms of Action and Tolerance*, edited by S. Garattini and R. Samanin, pp. 143-158. Raven Press, New York.

109. Thompson, D.A., and Campbell, R.G. (1977): *Science*, 198: 1065-1068.

110. Ungerstedt, U. (1971): *Acta Physiol. Scand.*, Suppl. 367: 69-93.

111. Uzumaki, H., Govoni, S., Memo, M., Carruba, M.O., Trabucchi, M., and Spano, P.F. (1982): *Brain Res.*, 248: 185-187.

112. Wolgin, D.L., Cytawa, J., and Teitelbaum, P. (1976): In: *Hunger: Basic Mechanisms and Clinical Implications*, edited by D. Novin, W. Wyrwicka, and G. Bray, pp. 33-50. Raven Press, New York.

113. Woods, S.C., and Porte, D. Jr. (1976): In: *Hunger: Basic Mechanisms and Clinical Implications*, edited by D. Novin, W. Wyrwicka, and G. Bray, pp. 273-281. Raven Press, New York.

114. Wurtman, R.J., and Fernstrom, J.D. (1976): *Biochem. Pharmacol.*, 25: 1691-1696.

115. Yim, G.K.W., Lowy, M.T., Davis, J.M., Lamb, D.R., and Malven, P.V. (1982): In: *The Neural Basis of Feeding and Reward*, edited by G.B. Hoebel, and D. Novin, pp. 485-498. Raven Press, New York.

116. Zambotti, F., Carruba, M.O., Barzaghi, F., Vicentini, L., Groppetti, A., and Mantegazza, P. (1976): *Eur. J. Pharmacol.*, 36: 405-412.

Pharmacology of Eating Disorders: Theoretical and Clinical Developments, edited by M. O. Carruba and J. E. Blundell. Raven Press, New York © 1986.

Hypothalamic Monoamine Systems for Control of Food Intake: Analysis of Meal Patterns and Macronutrient Selection

Sarah F. Leibowitz and Gail Shor-Posner

The Rockefeller University, New York, New York 10021

Evidence accumulated over the past two decades indicates the existence of several different monoaminergic systems in the brain that influence feeding behavior (14, 47, 61). Although the importance of these hypothalamic neurochemical systems is widely recognized, the precise nature of the signals to which these systems may respond to influence feeding remains unknown. In order to establish a foundation for understanding the brain's control of normal feeding, in addition to determining the relationship of these systems to the development of abnormal feeding patterns, the precise role of each of these systems, as well as their interaction, will need to be clarified. The primary purpose of this review is to characterize, through behavioral analyses of feeding patterns and macronutrient selection, hypothalmic monoamine mechanisms (noradrenergic, serotonergic, dopaminergic and adrenergic) that are involved in the control of food intake.

Most studies of the neuropharmacology of feeding behavior have been concerned with measurement of total food intake, and, until recently, little attention was focused on either the temporal pattern of feeding behavior or the nutritional composition of diets. In the last few years, the use of sensitive techniques to monitor feeding patterns and evaluate macronutrient selection has proven valuable in revealing differences in neurochemical systems. Through the micro-structural analysis of food intake over time (for determining meal size, meal frequency, rate of eating, intermeal interval), precise changes in consummatory behavior have been documented in freely-feeding animals, and specific actions of neurotransmitters or drugs differentiated (13, 42). Furthermore, in numerous studies employing nutrient choice, it has been demonstrated that peripheral pharmacological manipulations alter macronutrient selection, leading to the hypothesis that specific brain neurotransmitters affected by the drugs may have a function in balancing the proportion of carbohydrate, fat and protein consumed by an animal (1, 13, 53, 62, 139).

The focus in this chapter, on dietary selection as well as the micro-structure of feeding patterns, provides an important dimension in our attempt to identify the specific role of hypothalamic neurotransmitters in coordinating and balancing the ingestion of diets of varied composition. Physiological signals of body energy and nutrient stores are complex in nature, as are the diets that affect them, thus, the ability of animals to respond to these physiological signals and select appropriate foods, in appropriate quantity and sequence, requires the involvement and integration of complex neurotransmitter mechanisms.

NOREPINEPHRINE

Hypothalamic norepinephrine (NE) has been strongly implicated in neural processes underlying feeding behavior (62). When injected in physiological doses, specifically into the medial paraventricular nucleus (PVN) of satiated rats, NE rapidly elicits a robust feeding response (60), through its action on α_2-noradrenergic receptors (41). Furthermore, chronic infusion of NE, or the α-noradrenergic agonist clonidine (CLON) into this nucleus, has been shown to potentiate daily food intake and body weight gain (76, 85). Discrete electrolytic lesions of the PVN also produce hyperphagia and obesity (2, 68) and, in addition, attenuate or abolish the potency of NE and CLON injection (69). In contrast to these hyperphagic effects, destruction of PVN noradrenergic innervation, through 6-hydroxydopamine injection, produces specific disturbances in freely-feeding rats, including a decrease in daily food intake and body weight gain (118). These results suggest that the overeating resulting from PVN electrolytic lesions is not attributable to the destruction of noradrenergic *afferents* to the nucleus. Rather, it appears to reflect damage to a PVN *efferent* projection, through which endogenous NE may act to enhance food intake by inhibiting a specific PVN-controlled satiety function (68, 91, 133).

Norepinephrine within the medial hypothalamus has been shown to have a very specific effect on the temporal pattern of food intake. As indicated by meal pattern analyses, NE potentiates feeding primarily through an increase in meal size, rather than meal frequency (76, 120). Both the rate of feeding, as well as the time spent eating, are increased; the latency of feeding onset, however, is not altered. Administration of CLON into the PVN enhances feeding in a similar manner to NE (Shor-Posner and Leibowitz, unpublished data), suggesting once again a common mechanism of action (91). These results are consistent with the findings of Ritter and Epstein (105), who reported a similar increase in meal size in response to NE infusion at the onset of a spontaneously initiated meal. These data are also in agreement with the demonstration that depletion of brain NE, after peripheral injection of the synthesis inhibitor FLA-63, is associated with an opposite effect on the micro-structure of feeding, namely, a reduction in meal size (112).

In addition to changing the pattern of eating, hypothalamic NE has been found to modulate the animals' apppetite for specific foods. After acute, as well as chronic, injection of NE into the PVN, animals provided with pure macronutrient diets display a preference for carbohydrate, in conjunction with no change or a suppression of protein and fat intake (67, 81). This pattern of diet selection is also observed with PVN and peripheral injection of CLON, as well as with tricyclic antidepressant drugs which are believed to act through the release of endogenous NE (64, 67) and which produce a similar carbohydrate appetite in humans (99, 101). Furthermore, animals with PVN electrolytic damage demonstrate a dramatic rise in daily carbohydrate intake, along with a significant inhibition of protein consumption (117, 119). On the other hand, animals with decreased catecholaminergic innervation to the PVN exhibit a *reduction* in spontaneous carbohydrate ingestion (118). Taken together, these findings support a specific role for the PVN α_2-noradrenergic system in the control of carbohydrate intake.

The possibility that endogenous PVN NE and α_2 receptors are active in appetite regulation is supported by biochemical evidence associating enhanced medial hypothalamic NE release with the onset of natural feeding responses (87, 132). Additional studies have revealed a close relationship between circulating glucose concentration and hypothalamic noradrenergic activity (123), and under conditions of food-deprivation, a significant increase in NE turnover within the medial hypothalamus (50, 124) and a profound down regulation of PVN α_2 receptors (48), have been demonstrated. These studies are of particular interest in light of recent findings demonstrating that animals with PVN damage exhibit a disturbance in compensatory feeding after food deprivation (118, 119). Whereas normal animals compensate by increasing both carbohydrate and fat intake, animals with PVN electrolytic lesions display a disruption in their ability to produce compensatory feeding of carbohydrate in response to both short- and long-term food deprivation (119). Animals with a neurotoxin lesion of catecholaminergic innervation to the PVN show a similar disruption in their compensatory ability and, compared to control rats, display a greater loss of body weight during this period (118).

In view of this link between hypothalamic NE and carbohydrate ingestion, it is important to note that NE must act in close association with two hormones, corticosterone (CORT) and insulin, which are known to have an important impact on carbohydrate metabolism (75, 110, 116). Recent studies have demonstrated that the dorsal vagal system is important for NE-elicited feeding, possibly through its controlling influence over insulin (116). Other evidence indicates that the feeding response elicited by PVN α_2-noradrenergic stimulation is dependent upon an intact PVN-hypophyseal-adrenal axis (75, 110, 111). The full expression of this feeding response is determined by the level of plasma CORT, such that a rise in CORT is associated with an increase in the efficacy of α_2-noradrenergic stimulation. Circulating CORT, in the range of 2-

10 μg%, significantly upregulates α 2 receptors exclusively in the PVN (51) and, in a precise dose-response fashion and with short latency (within minutes), permits NE to function normally in its short-term regulation of meal size in relation to energy (carbohydrate) reserves. Through its connection with the hindbrain and the peripheral autonomic nervous system (129), the PVN is in an ideal position to monitor, integrate and respond to information required for nutrient and energy balance.

SEROTONIN

Whereas α -noradrenergic stimulation of the medial hypothalamus is effective in potentiating eating behavior, hypothalamic serotonin (5-HT) receptor systems appear to exert an inhibitory effect on feeding (14, 62, 115). This suppression of feeding has been demonstrated in all species examined; however, the central site(s) of 5-HT's action have not been clearly defined, and, moreover, there are questions concerning behavioral specificity, particularly with high doses of this monoamine. If 5-HT is truly active in the regulation of normal feeding, then destruction of 5-HT innervation to the forebrain should produce alterations in food intake and body weight. There is evidence to suggest that depletion of brain 5-HT, by neurotoxin injection or micro-knife cuts, may produce hyperphagia and weight gain (26, 35, 44, 114). There is conflicting evidence on this point, however, and it may be that endogenous 5-HT affects aspects of feeding that are not easily revealed by measurements of total food intake (11, 115).

Further insight into the action of 5-HT has been obtained recently from behavioral and pharmacological studies of the hypothalamus, where 5-HT administration is found to reduce food intake (14, 115). In particular, the medial hypothalamus appears to be especially sensitive to direct serotonergic stimulation. The work of Leibowitz (62, 74) has demonstrated a reliable dose-dependent suppression of feeding after PVN injection of 5-HT, with no apparent change in general arousal. Injection of norfenfluramine, into the same site, which is presumed to release endogenous 5-HT, produces similar results. Further analyses of the micro-structure of this feeding effect have revealed specific alterations in meal patterns (43). After PVN 5-HT administration, animals display a significant decrease in the size and duration of meals, as well as reduced rate of eating. However, the latency to meal onset and the frequency of meals taken are not affected. These results are generally consistent with the meal patterns reported in animals receiving peripheral injections of drugs, e.g., fenfluramine (FENF) and 5-hydroxytryptophan, which are presumed to facilitate 5-HT synaptic activity (14, 27, 32, 42). As with PVN injection of 5-HT or norfenfluramine, peripheral administration of FENF is shown in these studies to decrease meal size and feeding rate, without affecting meal initiation or producing a change in the number of meals consumed. These findings, suggesting that centrally and peripherally administered 5-HT agonists share to some extent a common site of action, may have even broader implications for understanding human brain mechanisms of appetite control, which are apparently similarly responsive to FENF in reducing eating rate (21, 109) and possibly, meal size (18).

The pattern of feeding exhibited in PVN 5-HT-injected animals stands in direct contrast to the meal patterns observed in rats receiving PVN injections of NE, as described above. That is, opposite effects have been obtained with 5-HT and NE, in terms of their impact on mechanisms controlling meal size and eating rate. This evidence supports the proposal that these neurochemical systems, perhaps within the medial hypothalamus or PVN, interact in an antagonistic fashion to modulate food intake. The work of Leibowitz and Papadakos (74) provides additional support for this concept. In their study, 5-HT produced a potent inhibitory effect in rats which had been induced to eat by administration of NE into the PVN. Furthermore, agents which are presumed to inhibit feeding through serotonergic action (i.e., FENF, norfenfluramine, fluoxetine, 5-hydroxytryptophan) also suppressed NE-induced, as well as deprivation-induced, feeding when administered into the PVN.

With regard to diet selection, various investigations have implicated a role for 5-HT in control of appetite for specific foods (1, 5, 14, 139). This role appears to involve the control of a protein/carbohydrate ratio, with 5-HT reducing the proportion of carbohydrate in the diet. Evidence for this modulation has been obtained through peripheral administration of drugs which enhance the release of brain 5-HT and which are found to suppress carbohydrate intake while sparing protein consumption. A similar pattern of diet selection can be seen with PVN injection of 5-HT or norfenfluramine (Leibowitz and Tretter, unpublished data), while the opposite occurs when brain 5-HT is reduced (5). As in animal studies, administration of FENF in humans has been shown to inhibit the consumption of carbohydrate, as well as the "craving" for snacks rich in this macronutrient (20, 136, 139). However, it should be noted that some differences in drug-induced diet selection may be observed, depending on whether pure or mixed diets are available and, in particular, whether pure fat is introduced (100).

These findings with 5-HT stimulation reveal, once again, how this monoamine may act antagonistically to NE in the control of feeding behavior. As described earlier, NE administration into the PVN selectively stimulates carbohydrate ingestion, while in some cases causing a significant suppression of protein intake. This is precisely opposite to the effects observed with peripheral injection of 5-HT agonists and PVN injection of 5-HT or norfenfluramine. Thus, as with meal patterns, 5-HT and NE may act antagonistically in their control of macronutrient selection. It is of interest that these neurotransmitters, possibly within the medial hypothalamus, appear to have opposite effects on both carbohydrate and protein ingestion and, thus, may have a role in controlling the ratio between these macronutrients. It could be this ratio, rather than the absolute amounts of protein and carbohydrate, that is a critical factor in maintaining nutrient balance (28, 29).

DOPAMINE

Studies have indicated that dopamine (DA), similar to 5-HT, may in some cases be linked to the inhibition of feeding (47, 61, 62). Systemic administration of DA agonists reduces food intake (140), while DA antagonists, particularly in low doses, may stimulate eating (6, 108, 113, 134). In studies conducted to determine the central site of action, it has been suggested that this CA may act within the hypothalamus, in particular, the lateral perifornical region (PFH), which contains a rich supply of DA terminals and receptors (65, 79, 80, 92). This particular sensitivity of the lateral hypothalamic region to DA appears to be unique, contrasting with other hypothalamic sites where DA produces no behavioral change, and also contrasting with extra-hypothalamic sites, in particular the neostriatum, where DA has a general activating influence on motivated behavior, including feeding (127, 128, 140).

The possibility of a physiological role for lateral hypothalamic DA in the control of food intake is suggested by a variety of studies. Specifically, feeding in hungry animals is reduced by acute DA injection into this site, and daily food intake and body weight regulation is similarly altered by a chronic infusion of DA into the PFH (79, 80, Leibowitz and Roossin, unpublished data). A similar reduction in feeding and body weight gain results from electrolytic lesions of the PFH, in contrast to the enhancement of feeding that is elicited by electrical stimulation of this area (47, 90). Furthermore, anorexic drugs such as amphetamine (AMPH), which are believed to act in part through activation of hypothalamic DA neurons, also suppress feeding when administered specifically into the PFH (23, 43, 59, 78, 90, 92), while DA blockers, e.g., chlorpromazine (CPZ), clozapine and haloperidol, cause the opposite effect, namely, an enhancement of feeding (47, 73). The involvement of PFH DA receptors in these effects is supported by biochemical studies revealing an increase in DA turnover, specifically in this area, subsequent to systemic AMPH and CPZ administration (70, 71).

It should be noted that AMPH, in addition to having an impact on DA neurons, is also believed to act through the release of NE and epinephrine (EPI) in the hypothalamus. A variety of studies has revealed effects with lateral hypothalamic injections of EPI, and to some extent NE, which are similar to those produced by DA (78, 79). This anorexic effect of adrenergic stimulation is mediated by β-adrenergic receptors, which appear to operate in close association with the hypothalamic DA receptors for optimal control of food intake (78).

The nature of the inhibition of the feeding effect caused by brain CA activation has recently been assessed through meal pattern analyses. As revealed in these studies, peripheral injection of AMPH appears to have a particular impact on the process of eating initiation, causing a reduction of food intake (decreased meal size and duration) by delaying the onset of a meal, rather than by altering the point of the meal termination (15, 17). Further examination of AMPH's pattern of effects has shown that the frequency of subsequent meals is not altered and, somewhat paradoxically, that eating rate is increased. Of particular interest is the finding that essentially identical meal patterns are demonstrated in animals receiving lateral hypothalamic administration of AMPH (43). Furthermore, opposite effects are found to occur with DA blockers; for example, CPZ, when administered into the PFH, causes animals to initiate feeding sooner and consequently increase meal size (43), and also, systemic pimozide is effective in antagonizing the impact of AMPH on meal patterns (17). Based on these and related findings, it has been proposed that AMPH, via the release of brain CA, may in part suppress feeding behavior through the *inhibition* of a hunger-stimulating mechanism (15, 16). Support for this suggestion is provided by studies in humans, comparing the effects of anorectic drugs on food intake, meal patterns and subjective experiences (20, 21, 109, 121, 122). These studies have revealed meal pattern changes similar to those obtained in rats. Furthermore, they have actually reported a decrease in subjective hunger ratings after AMPH administration, independent of alterations in general arousal, and also the opposite effect with CPZ treatment.

This impact of dopaminergic agents on meal initiation stands in contrast to the effects of 5-HT and NE, which produce no change in the time of meal onset but alter meal size by affecting the point of meal termination. This evidence suggests the possibility that the CA systems for suppression of food intake may act through inhibition of hunger processes which control meal initiation. The 5-HT systems, in contrast, may control the process of meal termination, through the activation of satiety mechanisms. The above results obtained in rats and humans, with the anorectic monoamine-releasing drugs AMPH and FENF, support this concept and, together with the CA and 5-HT agonists, argue for a specific site of action within the brain. Specifically, it is believed that AMPH, through CA release, acts in the lateral (perifornical) hypothalamus, while the 5-HT-releasing drug FENF suppresses feeding through the medial hypothalamus. It is well known that electrolytic lesions of these medial and lateral hypothalamic areas produce opposite effects on food intake and body weight gain. Whereas damage to the medial hypothalamus causes overeating and obesity, lateral hypothalamic lesions produce anorexia or starvation (47). These effects may, in part, be due to destruction of the efferent component of the endogenous monoaminergic systems, which function in these two areas to mediate signals for satiety and hunger (90, 91, 92, 119, 133). However, while tests with AMPH and FENF yield results generally consistent with this hypothesis, one needs to be particularly cautious in evaluating these effects, since these two anorectic drugs may have multiple actions in various brain sites, especially when systemically injected (11, 12).

Studies with systemic and central administration of DA agents support a role for this CA in appetite regulation for specific nutrients. A low dose of AMPH (0.5 mg/kg), peripherally injected into freely-feeding or only slightly deprived animals provided with either mixed diets (19) or three pure macronutrients (66), produces a dramatic and specific decrease in protein consumption. A similar suppression of protein intake, as compared to smaller and insignificant alterations in carbohydrate or fat ingestion, has been revealed after AMPH injection into the PFH (66) and also after administration of DA and EPI into this brain site (Leibowitz and Shor-Posner, unpublished data). Consistent with these findings, DA blockers have been shown to elicit the opposite effect on diet selection. Leibowitz et al. (66) have demonstrated that systemic administration of either CPZ or clozapine produces overeating, along with a preferential increase in protein consumption and considerably smaller increases in carbohydrate and fat ingestion. This evidence obtained in animals is in agreement with human reports (20) of a strong and significant inhibition of protein intake after AMPH administration, suggesting that similar neurotransmitter mechanisms may be involved in human and animal diet selection. It should be noted, however, that in animals exposed to severe food restriction, the effects of AMPH may be different. Under these conditions, either no selective change in nutrient intake or a suppression in fat ingestion may occur (54, 100, 135). This variation in response to AMPH, in animals maintained on restricted feeding schedules, may reflect an interaction of the drug with the altered baseline feeding scores caused by food restriction.

These results appear to show a specific CA effect on macronutrient selection, rather than an overall attenuation of total food intake. This inhibitory effect of DA (and EPI) on protein consumption may be contrasted to the effect of 5-HT (see above), which appears to spare protein while suppressing carbohydrate consumption. These findings suggest, as shown previously with the mapping studies and in meal pattern analyses, that the hypothalamic catecholaminergic and serotonergic neurotransmitter systems work in opposing directions, respectively influencing hunger and satiety mechanisms for protein appetite regulation.

GENERAL SUMMARY OF NEUROTRANSMITTER EFFECTS ON FOOD INGESTION PATTERNS

It is evident from these studies, that hypothalamic monoamine systems involved in the control of food intake have specific effects on temporal feeding patterns, as well as on appetite for specific nutrients (14, 61, 62). Whereas NE stimulates the consumption of carbohydrate, primarily through an increase in feeding rate, meal size and duration, 5-HT, in contrast, appears to spare protein while suppressing food intake, particularly carbohydrate, through an early termination of feeding. Both of these findings have been interpreted in terms of an action of these monoamines on a satiety mechanism for carbohydrate, rather than a hunger-stimulating process, with NE acting to inhibit satiety and 5-HT potentiating satiety. These neurotransmitter effects appear to occur in the medial hypothalamus, which has long been known to have an active role in satiety and which more recently is believed to act more specifically in control of carbohydrate ingestion. One particular site for neurotransmitter interactions may be the PVN, where NE, in association with CORT is known to be particularly effective in potentiating eating, and where 5-HT has been shown to be active in the inhibition of feeding. This action of the monoamines in the medial hypothalamus contrasts with that of the CAs in the lateral hypothalamus (PFH). At this lateral site, DA and possibly EPI, which may mediate the anorectic properties of AMPH, appear to have an inhibitory action on hunger-stimulating mechanisms that initiate a meal, particularly of protein. Thus, increased CA activation of this hypothalamic area causes a delay in the onset of feeding, resulting in a reduction in the size of a protein meal. Once again, lesion studies have for a long time linked the lateral hypothalamus to hunger-stimulating processes and, more recently, have revealed this structure's critical function in the mediation of AMPH- and CA-induced hyperphagia (90).

It is likely that these hypothalamic monoamines interact closely in the control of energy and nutrient balance. Through this interaction, they apparently affect not only intake of a specific macronutrient, but also modulate the ratio, as well as the time-course pattern, of nutrient intake. The close proximity of the PVN and PFH, their direct anatomical association (45), and their active monoaminergic innervation, would appear to meet the essential requirements for a neurocircuit involved in the mediation of these complex functions. In monitoring need for carbohydrate and protein, it has been suggested that NE in the medial hypothalamus, and possibly CAs in the lateral hypothalamus, may be involved in regulating and responding to information concerning energy or carbohydrate level (62). Serotonin, in contrast, may function as a particularly responsive sensor of circulating amino acids, translating their blood levels and their ratio into neurotransmitter function (138, 139). Activation of these systems may enable an animal to maintain nutrient balance over the normal course of the diurnal cycle, as well as respond to physiological challenges (e.g. food-deprivation, cold, stress) that place demands on energy resources.

IMPACT OF FOOD INGESTION, CIRCULATING NUTRIENTS AND HORMONES ON BRAIN NEUROTRANSMITTER SYSTEMS

There is extensive evidence to indicate that the macronutrients, selected by a normal animal to satisfy its needs, may themselves influence brain mechanisms that regulate food intake. Ingestion of food has been shown to alter plasmo amino acid patterns, that in turn influence the entry of tyrosine and tryptophan into the brain and, thus, the synthesis of CAs and 5-HT, respectively (84, 138). Consumption of a large carbohydrate meal at the beginning of the night causes a substantial release of insulin and results in an increase in concentration of plasma tryptophan, relative to other neutral amino acids, thus producing an increase in the level of brain tryptophan and 5-HT (37, 137). Protein ingestion, in contrast, decreases brain tryptophan uptake and, consequently, decreases 5-HT synthesis (38). Similar effects are observed in humans (39, 95). There is additional evidence that both protein and carbohydrate meals increase brain tyrosine but that protein ingestion produces the greater effect (36). This suggests the possibility that precursor events may also influence the synthesis of hypothalamic NE, EPI and DA, with a protein meal enhancing their production due to increased tyrosine levels and a carbohydrate meal reducing their production. This proposal is strengthened by the evidence that a carbohydrate-rich nutrient loaded into the stomach of rats inhibits endogenous NE release in the medial hypothalamus, specifically in the PVN (98). Furthermore, in humans, a similar relationship, between the ingestion of pure protein and an increase in tyrosine levels, has recently been demonstrated (95).

A link of this nature, between food ingestion and brain monoamine systems, may similarly exist for other substances in the blood, including glucose and such hormones as insulin and CORT which are important in energy metabolism. Both of these hormones have been found to be closely associated with feeding behavior, to exhibit circadian variation, and to have an impact on neurotransmitter function in the brain. For example, insulin release and tissue sensitivity to insulin in the rat are higher at night than during the day (102, 103). The release of this hormone occurs in association with food intake (34) and, through its effect on tryptophan, increases the synthesis of 5-HT in the brain (138, 139). Additional evidence indicates that insulin may act synergistically with NE in stimulating feeding (33) and, similar to NE, preferentially increases consumption of carbohydrate (55, 119). This association may, in part, reflect the impact of insulin on NE turnover and release in the medial hypothalamus (93, 106) and also the impact of medial hypothalamic NE on the release of insulin (34).

Studies indicate that CORT, similar to insulin, can enhance ingestion of energy-rich nutrients, influence neurotransmitter systems, and show a distinct circadian variation. It is well known that daily CORT levels peak prior to the onset of the active eating cycle (57), suggesting that this rise may have a role in natural feeding behavior. Additional support for a role of CORT in feeding processes is indicated by the evidence that various forms of hyperphagia and obesity depend on this glucocorticoid for their full expression (24, 25, 31, 56). Recent findings have demonstrated that in addition to affecting 5-HT synthesis and receptors in the brain (22), CORT may have a specific impact on noradrenergic function, in particular

α_2 receptors in the medial hypothalamus. Through studies of adrenalectomized animals and of circadian rhythms in intact animals, it has been demonstrated that circulating CORT has direct impact on α_2-type receptors, specifically in the PVN (9, 49, 51, 72). With a short latency, CORT dramatically upregulates these receptors; this modulation occurs in a dose-dependent and steroid-specific manner, is apparent in the normal circadian rhythm of PVN α_2 receptors and responsiveness to NE activation, and is absent in adrenalectomized animals. Through this hormone-neurotransmitter interaction, it is believed that CORT plays an important role in permitting NE to express fully its stimulatory action on feeding. Adrenalectomy abolishes NE-induced food intake (75, 110), and also decreases spontaneous food intake, particularly at night (7, 10, 24, 25, 49, 51).

Although the role of blood glucose concentration in providing information to the brain has not been clearly defined, a number of studies have suggested a basis for linking this substance with neurotransmitter function. For example, it appears that a small decrease in blood glucose concentration precedes meal taking in the rat, and with food consumption, blood glucose rises (82, 86). This is of particular interest in light of recent evidence demonstrating an inverse relationship between hypothalamic NE turnover and plasma glucose concentration (123). Furthermore, the binding of (^{3}H) AMPH to hypothalamic membranes also appears to be dramatically affected in association with circulating glucose, as well as with levels of food deprivation and refeeding (46). In other studies, administration of agents that decrease cellular glucose utilization are shown to enhance hypothalamic NE turnover (93) and, similar to NE injection, to stimulate carbohydrate feeding (54, 55, 119). A circadian variation in cerebral glucose utilization, reaching a peak during the dark cycle, may also be related to feeding processes (30).

Together, these findings indicate that circulating substances affected by food ingestion, may themselves alter neurotransmitter synthesis in the brain. The hypothalamic monoamine systems appear to be particularly responsive, thus providing an avenue of communication, between the blood and the brain, in the control of eating patterns.

NORMAL FEEDING PATTERNS AND DIET SELECTION IN INTACT ANIMALS

The ability of intact animals to regulate protein and energy intake in relation to need, has been demonstrated to occur on a daily basis (97), within the day (52, 58, 131), and even within a meal (83). This capacity to alter patterns of food selection becomes especially apparent under conditions that require rapid adjustments in energy intake, such as during increased activity (29), food deprivation (89, 104, 130), and the active period of the diurnal cycle (52, 58, 131). The circadian pattern of eating, for example, places particular demands on the freely-feeding nocturnal rat, who consumes most (80-90%) of its food, in several discrete meals, during the dark cycle (3). At the beginning of this dark period, when food-seeking behavior and ingestion are most pronounced, a specific pattern of food intake can be seen. Work from this laboratory (131), in freely-feeding animals provided with pure macronutrients, has revealed that during the first 1-2 hours of the night, intact animals normally exhibit an initial preference for large carbohydrate meals. This pattern is shortly followed by a shift towards increased protein intake, which is then followed by a return to carbohydrate feeding. A similar nutrient shift, in rats given high-carbohydrate premeals, has been reported by Li and Anderson (83). In that study, rats that were fed high-protein meals emphasized carbohydrate in the next meal. The reverse pattern was observed with carbohydrate premeals, confirming that the consumption of these two macronutrients is closely interrelated.

Towards the end of the dark cycle, meals are found to contain a higher percent of protein composition, as compared to the meals taken during the early hours of the night (131). This differentiation between feeding patterns at the beginning versus end of the nocturnal period is consistent with recent reports of a circadian rhythm in protein-energy intake (52, 58). In those studies, rats demonstrated their ability to alter meal composition, depending on the time of day. That is, when provided with a choice of two diets, containing either 0% or 60% protein, the animals increased their selection of the non-protein diet during the night. They also tended to exhibit an increased protein preference at the end of the dark period (58).

WORKING HYPOTHESIS OF HYPOTHALAMIC MONOAMINE FUNCTION

As described earlier, the hypothalamic monoaminergic neurotransmitters which are shown to be affected by the ingestion of food, are believed themselves to actively participate and interact in coordinating the patterns of carbohydrate and protein meals that occur during the normal feeding cycle. Figure 1 illustrates our working hypothesis for these events.

It is proposed that, under conditions of decreased energy availability (e.g. at the start of the active period), an increase occurs in medial hypothalamic (PVN) α_2-noradrenergic activity, in association with a decline in 5-HT turnover and a rise in circulating CORT and insulin. Simultaneously, an increase in catecholaminergic activity in the perifornical lateral hypothalamus may also occur. Together, these neurotransmitter changes, through effects respectively on satiety and hunger mechanisms, are expected to result in potentiated carbohydrate feeding, along with a simultaneous inhibition of protein ingestion. Since brain 5-HT synthesis, relative to CA synthesis, is increased after carbohydrate ingestion, a subsequent switch in preference for protein then occurs as a consequence of increased satiety for carbohydrate. With protein ingestion, the

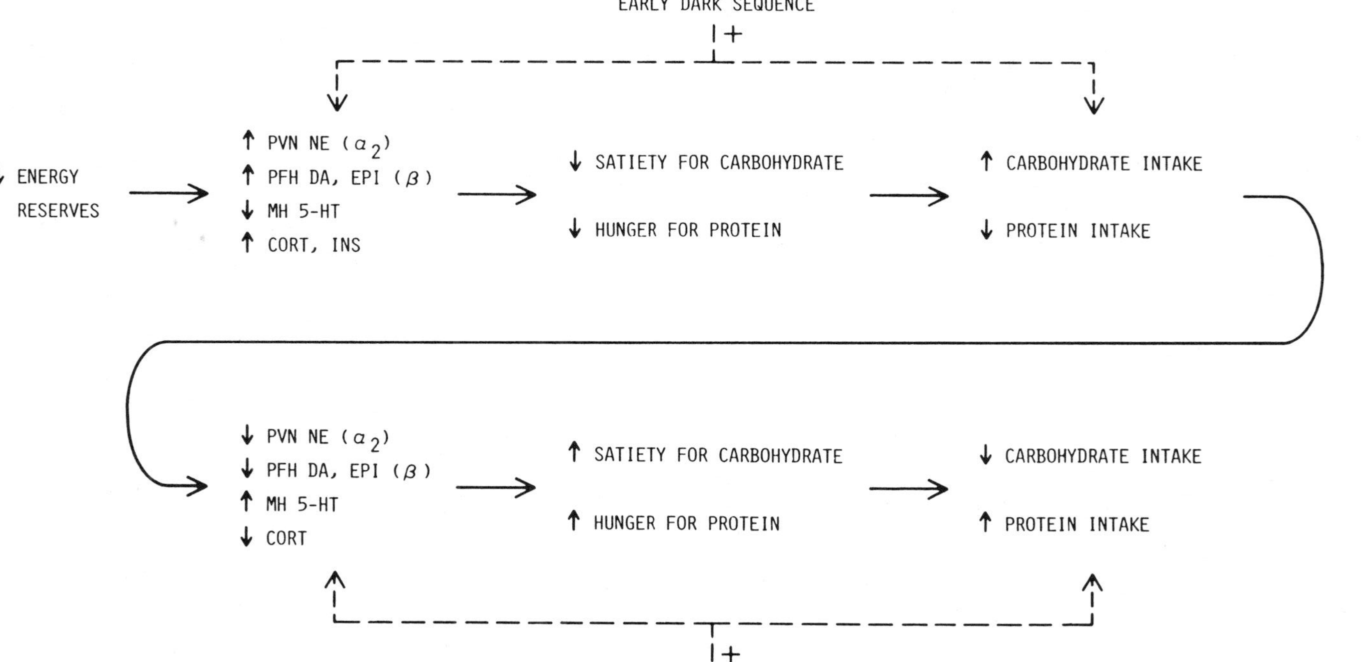

FIG. 1 A schematic representation of hypothalamic monoamine systems and their function in control of meal patterns and macronutrient selection, during the early and late parts of the dark cycle. Abbreviations : CORT, corticosterone; EPI, epinephrins; DA, dopamine; NE, norepinephrine; 5-HT, 5-hydroxytriptamine; INS, insulin; MH, medial hypothalamus; PFH, perifornical lateral hypothalamus; PVN, hypothalamic paraventricular nucleus.

neurochemical profile then shifts, once again, to an increase in hypothalamic CA synthesis and a decrease in 5-HT synthesis, followed by an enhanced preference for carbohydrate.

Superimposed on this pattern of alternating carbohydrate and protein meals appears to be an additional rhythm observed in the rat (Fig. 1), in which carbohydrate ingestion is favored in the early hours of the dark cycle and protein ingestion is favored in the late hours of the dark cycle (58, 131). This rhythm is consistent with the evidence that food ingested during the first half of the dark is used to fulfill immediate energy requirements as well as to promote lipogenesis; this is in contrast to later in the night, when nutrient and energy stores are to a large extent replenished and feeding is geared towards storage and subsequent utilization of nutrients during the light cycle (4, 82). Based on the evidence described above, and on the finding that brain 5-HT turnover may rise towards the end of the night (88), it is proposed that medial hypothalamic NE, and its α_2 receptors, are most active, in conjunction with CORT and insulin, during the early part of the dark cycle, whereas medial hypothalamic 5-HT activity peaks during the later part of the dark cycle.

MONOAMINE ACTIVATION DURING FOOD DEPRIVATION AND STRESS

In addition to their role in control of normal feeding patterns under stable environmental conditions, it is likely that hypothalamic monoamines may also become activated in an unstable environment, such as when food is scarce and unpredictable or when the organism is stressed. There is evidence to suggest that the monoamines, under these conditions, are involved in the compensatory eating behavior that is required for energy and nutrient repletion. For example, in response to deprivation or stress in the rat, there is a marked increase in hypothalamic or PVN NE turnover, as well as in circulating CORT and insulin (e.g., 31, 40, 50, 87, 107, Leibowitz and Diaz, unpublished data). Changes in receptor activity have also been revealed, with a rapid and highly site-specific down-regulation of α_2 receptors in the PVN after food deprivation, in contrast to a significant increase in β-adrenergic as well as dopaminergic receptors within the lateral hypothalamus, specifically the PFH (48, 50). Food deprivation also affects binding of (^{3}H) AMPH to hypothalamic membranes, an effect rapidly reversed by refeeding (46).

In association with these and other endocrine and neurotransmitter changes that occur after food deprivation or stress, there are a variety of behavioral changes which include an increase in meal size and an increase in feeding specifically of energy-rich food, rather than of protein (8, 89, 94, 130). This modification in macronutrient selection has been observed after 24hr, as well as 5-day, fasts (104, 119), and also when food is removed for only a 2hr period, specifically at the start of the dark cycle (131). After this very short deprivation in the early dark, rats exhibit a rapid and complete compensatory feeding response, overeating carbohydrate and fat, and to a lesser extent protein, during the next hour when food is returned. It is of interest that, at the end of the dark cycle, in contrast to the beginning, animals subjected to a similar brief deprivation period fail to exhibit an adequate compensatory feeding response in the final hour of the dark (131). These results are consistent with Le Magnen's findings (82), that a short delay in food presentation at the beginning of the dark cycle, as opposed to other times of the circadian period, produces the greatest decline in blood glucose, which in turn has been positively correlated with hypothalamic NE turnover (123). They also agree with data indicating that α-adrenergic receptors in the PVN respond, through down-regulation, to deprivation in the early dark period but not to deprivation in the late period (50).

It is particularly noteworthy that circulating CORT peaks during the first few hours of the early dark and then sharply declines thereafter (57). Thus, this distinction between the early and late dark, in terms of the impact of food deprivation on blood glucose, CORT-dependent α-adrenergic receptors, compensatory feeding and macronutrient selection, may be attributed, in part, to the circadian pattern of CORT release (62). In support of this proposal is the evidence that PVN-lesioned and adrenalectomized rats which have low levels of CORT, exhibit clear disturbances in their ability to compensate, and in particular overeat carbohydrate, in response to short- and long-term episodes of food deprivation (118, 119, Bhakthavatsalam and Leibowitz, unpublished data). Furthermore, adrenalectomized rats show the greatest deficit in spontaneous feeding during the early hours of the dark period and respond to systemic CORT injection by immediately increasing their ingestion specifically of carbohydrate and fat (10).

It is important to note that the complex regulation of nutrient selection may involve additional neurotransmitters, such as the hypothalamic peptides. Although a large number of peptides are found to modulate feeding, two classes are distinctive, in terms of their particular effectiveness at low doses and in discrete brain areas; their ability to potentiate rather than suppress feeding; and their specific impact on macronutrient selection (62). These potential modulators of feeding are the opioid peptides, which through μ, Δ, and κ receptors, act specifically within the hypothalamus to potentiate protein and fat intake (63, 96), and the pancreatic polypeptides (neuropeptide Y and peptide YY), which also act within the hypothalamus to stimulate specifically carbohydrate intake (125, 126). There is substantial evidence that these peptides alter monoamine effects on food intake and that the monoamines themselves have impact on the peptidergic systems. Thus, it may be expected that, within the hypothalamus, interactions between peptides and monoamines may occur to control meal patterns and diet selection during natural feeding processes.

ACKNOWLEDGMENTS

This work was supported by NIMH grant MH 22879 and by funds from the Whitehall Foundation.

REFERENCES

1. Anderson, H.G., Li, E.T.S., and Glanville, N.T., (1984): *Brain Res. Bull.*, 12:167-173.
2. Aravich, P.F., and Sclafani, A., (1983): *Behav. Neurosci.*, 97:970-983.
3. Armstrong, S., (1980): *Neurosci., Biobeh. Rev.*, 4:27-53.
4. Armstrong, S., Clarke, J., and Coleman, G., (1978): *Physiol. Behav.* 21:785-788.
5. Ashley, D.V.M., Coscina, D.V., and Anderson, G.H., (1979): *Life Sci.*, 24:973-984.
6. Barrett, J.E., (1982): *Pharmacol. Biochem. Behav.*, 17:1049-1053.
7. Bellinger, L.L., Williams, F.E., and Bernardis, L.L., (1979): *Proc. Soc. Exp. Biol. Med.*, 161:62-66.
8. Bertiere, M.L., Mame Sy, T., Baigts, F., Mandenoff, A., and Apfelbaum, M., (1984): *Pharmac. Biochem. Behav.*, 20:675-679.
9. Bhakthavatsalam, P., and Leibowitz, S.F., (1985): *Am. J. Physiol.*, in press.
10. Bhakthavatsalam, P., and Leibowitz, S.F., (1985): *Proc. East. Psychol. Assoc.*, 56-38.
11. Blundell, J.E., (1979): In: *Serotonin in Health and Disease V5 Clinical Applications*, edited by W.B. Essman, pp. 403-450. Spectrum, New York.
12. Blundell, J.E., (1981): In: *Theory in Pyschopharmacology*, edited by S.J. Cooper, Vol. 1, pp. 234-276. Academic Press, London.
13. Blundell, J.E., (1983): In: *Nutrition and Brain*, edited by R.J. Wurtman and J.J. Wurtman, p. 163-221. Raven Press, New York.
14. Blundell, J.E., (1984): *Neuropharmacology*, 23:1537-1551.
15. Blundell, J.E., Latham, C.J., and Leshem, M.B., (1976): *J. Pharm. Pharmac.*, 28:471-477.
16. Blundell, J.E., and Latham, C.J., (1978): In: *Central Mechanisms of Anorectic of Drugs*, edited by S. Garattini and R. Samanin, pp. 83-109. Raven Press, New York.
17. Blundell, J.E., and Latham, C.J., (1980): *Pharmac. Biochem. Behav.*, 12:717-722.
18. Blundell, J.E., Latham, C.J., Moniz, E., McArthur, R.A., and Rogers, P.J., (1979): *Curr. Med. Res. Opin.*, 6: Suppl. 1., 34-54.
19. Blundell, J.E., and McArthur, R.A., (1979): Br. J. Pharmacol. 67:436P-438P.
20. Blundell, J.E., and Rogers, P.J., (1980): *Appetite* 1:151-165.
21. Blundell, J.E., Tombros, E., Rogers, P.J., and Latham, C.J., (1980): *Progr. Neuro-Psychol.*, 4:319-326.

22. Bohus, B., De Kloet, E.R., and Veldhius, H.D., (1982): In: *Adrenal Actions on Brain*, edited by D. Ganten and D. Pfaff, pp. 108-148. Springer-Verlag, New York.
23. Booth, D.A., (1968): *J. Pharmac. exp. Ther.*, 160:336-348.
24. Bray, G.A., (1978): *Proc. Nutr. Soc.*, 37:301-309.
25. Bray, G.A., (1985): *Fed. Proc.*, in press.
26. Breisch, S.T., Zemlan, F.P., and Hoebel, B.G., (1976): *Science*, 192:382-384.
27. Burton, M.J., Cooper, S.J., and Popplewell, D.A., (1981): *Br. J. Pharmac.*, 69:621-633.
28. Collier, G., and Bolles, R., (1968): *J. Comp. Physiol. Psychol.*, 65:379-383.
29. Collier, G., Leshner, A.I., and Squibb, R.L., (1969): *Physiol. Behav.*, 4:83-86.
30. Crane, P.D., Braun, L.D., Cornford, E.M., Nyerges, A.M., and Oldendorf, W.H., (1980): *J. Neurochem.*, 34:1700-1706.
31. Dallman, M.F., (1984): *Am. J. Physiol.*, 246:R1-R12.
32. Davies, R.F., Rossi, J., Panksepp, J., Bean, N.J., and Zolovick, A.J., (1983): *Physiol. Behav.*, 30:723-730.
33. Davis, J.R., and Keesey, R.E., (1971): *J. Comp. Physiol. Psychol.*, 77:394-402.
34. de Jong, A., Strubbe, J.H., and Steffens, A.B., (1977): *Am. J. Physiol.*, 233:E380-E388.
35. Diaz, J., Ellison, G., and Masouka, D., (1974): *Psychopharmacologia*, 37:67-79.
36. Fernstrom, J.D., and Faller, D.V., (1978): *J. Neurochem.* 30:1531-1538.
37. Fernstrom, J.D., and Wurtman, R.J., (1971): *Science*, 174:1023-1025.
38. Fernstrom, J.D., and Wurtman, R.J., (1972): *Science*, 178:414-416.
39. Fernstrom, J.D., Wurtman, R.J., Hammarstrom-Wiklund, Rand, W.M., Munro, H.N., and Davidson, C.S., (1979): *Am. J. Clin. Nutr.*, 32:1912-1922.
40. Fuxe, et.al., (1983): *Acta Physiol. Scand.*, 117:421-
41. Goldman, C.K., Marino, L., and Leibowitz, S.F., (1985): *Eur. J. Pharmacol.*, in press.
42. Grinker, J.A., Drewnowski, A., Enns, M., and Kisseleff, H., (1980): *Pharmac. Biochem. Behav.*, 12:265-275.
43. Grinker, J., Marinescu, C., and Leibowitz, S.F., (1982): *Soc. Neurosci.Abstr.*, 8:604.
44. Grossman, S.P., Grossman, L., and Halaris, A., (1977): *Pharmac. Biochem. Behav.*, 6:101-106.
45. Hatton, G.I., Cobbett, P., and Salm, A.K., (1985): *Brain Res. Bull.*, 14:123-132.
46. Hauger, R., Hulihan-Giblin, B., Angel, I., Luu, M.D., Janowsky, A., and Paul, S.M., (1985): *Brain Res. Bull.*, in press.
47. Hoebel, B.G., and Leibowitz, S.F., (1981): In: *Association for Research in Nervous and Mental Disease*, edited by H. Weiner, M.A. Hofer and A.J. Stunkard, V59. p. 103. Raven Press, New York.

48. Jhanwar-Uniyal, M., Dvorkin, B., Makman, M.H., and Leibowitz, S.F., (1980): *Soc. Neurosci. Abstr.*, 6:2.
49. Jhanwar-Uniyal, M., Factor, A.D., Bailo, M., Roland, C.R., and, Leibowitz, S.F., (1985): *Proc. East. Psychol. Assoc.*, 56:36.
50. Jhanwar-Uniyal, M., Fleischer, F., Levin, B.E., and Leibowitz, S.F., (1982): *Soc. Neurosci. Abstr.*, 8:711.
51. Jhanwar-Uniyal, M., Roland, C.R., and Leibowitz, S.F., (1985): *Brain Res.*, submitted.
52. Johnson, D.J., Li, E.T.S., Coscina, D.V., and Anderson, G.H., (1979): *Physiol. Behav.*, 22:77-78.
53. Kanarek, R.B., Ho, L., and Meade, R.G., (1981): *Pharmacol. Biochem. Behav.*, 14:539-542.
54. Kanarek, R.B., Marks-Kaufman, R., and Lipeles, B.J., (1980): *Physiol.Behav.*, 25:779-782.
55. Kanarek, R.B., Marks-Kaufman, R., Ruthazaer, R., and Gualtieri, L., (1983): *Pharmacol. Biochem. Behav.*, 18:47-50.
56. King, B.M., Banta, A.R., Tharel, G.N., Bruce, B.K., and Frohman, L. Al, (1983): *Am; J. Physiol.*, 245:E194-E199.
57. Krieger, D.T., and Hauser, H., (1978): *Proc. Natl. Acad. Sci. U.S.A.*, 75:1577-1581.
58. Leathwood, P.D., and Arimanana, L., (1978) *Proc. 7th. Int. Conf. Physiol. Food and Fluid Intake*, Warsaw; July 7-10, 1980
59. Leibowitz, S.F., (1975): *Brain Res.*, 84:160-167.
60. Leibowitz, S.F., (1978): *Pharmacol. Biochem. Behav.* 8:163-175.
61. Leibowitz, S.F., (1980): In: *Handbook of the Hypothalamus. V1, Part A, Behavioral Studies of the Hypothalamus*, edited by P.J. Morgane and J. Panksepp, pp. 299-437. Marcel Dekker, New York.
62. Leibowitz, S.F., (1985): *Fed. Proc.*, in press.
63. Leibowitz, S.F., (1985): In: *Academy of Behavioral Medicine Research*, in press.
64. Leibowitz, S.F., Arcomano, A., and Hammer, N.J., (1978): *Prog. Neuropsychopharm.*, 2:349-358.
65. Leibowitz, S.F., and Brown, L.L., (1980): *Brain Res.* 201:315.
66. Leibowitz, S.F., Brown, O., and Tretter, J.R., (1982): *Proc. East. Psychol. Assoc.*, 53:136.
67. Leibowitz, S.F., Brown, O., Tretter, J.R., and Kirschgessner, A., (1985): *Pharmac. Biochem. Behav.*, in press.
68. Leibowitz, S.F., Hammer, N.J., and Chang, K., (1981): *Physiol. Behav.*, 27:1031-1040.
69. Leibowitz, S.F., Hammer, N.J., and Chang, K., (1983): *Pharmac. Biochem. Behav.*, 19:945-950.
70. Leibowitz, S.F., Jhanwar-Uniyal, M., and Levin, B.E., (1981): *Soc. Neurosci. Abstr.*, 7:928.
71. Leibowitz, S.F., Jhanwar-Uniyal, M., and Levin, B.E., (1983): *Brain Res.*, 266:348.
72. Leibowitz, S.F., Jhanwar-Uniyal, M., and Roland, C.R., (1984): *Soc. Neurosci. Abstr.*, 10:294.
73. Leibowitz, S.F., and Miller, N.E., (1969): *Science*, 165:609-611.
74. Leibowitz, S.F., and Papadakos, P.J., (1978): *Soc. Neurosci. Abstr.*, 4:452.

75. Leibowitz, S.F., Roland, C.R., Hor, L., and Squillari, V., (1984): *Physiol. Behav.*, 32:857-864.
76. Leibowitz, S.F., Roossin, P., and Rosenn, M., (1984): *Pharmac. Biochem. Behav.*, 21:801-808.
77. Leibowitz, S.F., and Rossakis, C., (1978): *Eur. J. Pharmacol.*, *53:69-81.*
78. Leibowitz, S.F., and Rossakis, C., (1978): *Neuropharmacology*, 17:691-702.
79. Leibowitz, S.F., and Rossakis, C., (1979): *Brain Res.*, 172:101-113.
80. Leibowitz, S.F., and Rossakis, C., (1979): *Brain Res.* 172:115-130.
81. Leibowitz, S.F., Weiss, G.F., Yee, F., and Tretter, J.R., (1985): *Brain Res. Bull.*, in press.
82. LeMagnen, J., (1981): *Behav. Brain Sci.* 4:561-607.
83. Li, E.T.S., and Anderson, G.H., (1982): *Physiol. Behav.*, 29:779-783.
84. Li, E.T.S., and Anderson, G.H., (1983): *Nutr. Abstr. Rev. Clin. Nutr.*, 53:169-181.
85. Lichtenstein, S., Constantine, M., and Leibowitz, S.F., (1984): *Brain Res. Bull.*, 13:591-595.
86. Louis-Sylvestre, J., and LeMagnen, J., (1980): *Neurosci. Biobehav. Rev.*, 4:(Suupl. 1), 13-15.
87. Martin, G.E., and Myers, R.D., (1975): *Am. J. Physiol.*, 229:1547-1555.
88. Martin, K., and Redfern, P., (1984): In: *Biological Rhythms and Medication : Proceedings of the First International Montreux Conference of Chronopharmacology*, edited by A. Reinberg, M. Smolensky and G. Labrecque.
89. McArthur, R.A., and Blundell, J.E., (1982): *Appetite*, 3:153-162.
90. McCabe, J.T., Bitran, D., and Leibowitz, S.F., (1985): *Pharmacol. Biochem. Behav.*, (in press).
91. McCabe, J.T., DeBellis, M.D., and Leibowitz, S.F., (1984): *Brain Res.*, 309:85-104.
92. McCabe, J.T., and Leibowitz, S.F., (1984): *Brain Res.*, 311:211-224.
93. McCaleb, M.L., Myers, R.D., Singer, G., and Willis, G., (1978): *Am. J. Physiol.*, 236:R312-R321.
94. McDonald, D.G., Stern, J.A., and Hahn, W.W., (1963): *J. Appl. Physiol.*, 18:937-942.
95. Moller, S.E., (1985): *J. Neural Trans.*, 61:183-191.
96. Morley, J.E., Levine, A.S., Yim, G.K.W., and Lowy, M.T., (1983): *Neurosci. Biobehav. Rev.*, 7:281-305.
97. Musten, B., Peace, D., and Anderson, G.H., (1974): *J. Nutr.*, 104:563-572.
98. Myers, R.D., and McCaleb, M.L., (1980): *Science*, 209:1035-1037.
99. Needleman, H.L., and Waber, D., (1976): *Lancet*, 2:580.
100. Orthen-Gambill, N., and Kanarek, R.B., (1982): *Pharmac. Biochem. Behav.*, 16:203-209.

101. Paykel, E.S., Muelter, P.S., and de la Vergue, P.M., (1973): *Brit. J. Psychiat.*, 123:501-507.
102. Penicaud, L., and LeMagnen, J., (1980): *Neurosci. Biobehav. Rev.*, 4: (Suppl. 1), 39-42.
103. Peret, J., Macaire, I., and Chanez, M., (1973): *J. Nutr.*, 103:866-874.
104. Piquard, F., Schaefer, A., and Haberey, P., (1978): *Physiol. Behav.*, 20:771-778.
105. Ritter, R.C., and Epstein, A.N., (1975): *Proc. Natn. Acad. Sci. U.S.A.*, 72:3740-3743.
106. Ritter, R.C., and Neville, M., (1977): *Fed. Proc.*, 35:642.
107. Ritter, S., Plezer, N.L., and Ritter, R.C., (1978): *Brain Res.*, 149:399-411.
108. Robinson, R.G., McHugh, P.R., and Bloom, F.E., (1975): *Psychopharmacol. Commun.*, 1:37-50.
109. Rogers, P.J., and Blundell, J.E., (1979): *Psychopharmacology*, 66:159-165.
110. Roland, C.R., Bhakthavatsalam, P., and Leibowitz, S.F., (1985): *Neuroendocrinology*, in press.
111. Roland, C.R., Oppenheimer, R.L., Chang, K., and Leibowitz, S.F., (1985): *Psychoneuroendocrinology*, in press.
112. Rossi, J.III, Zolovick, A.J., Davies, R.F., and Panksepp, J., (1982): *Neurosci. Biobehav. Rev.*, 6:195-204.
113. Rowland, N., and Engle, D.J., (1977): *Pharmac. Biochem. Behav.*, 7:295-301.
114. Saller, C.F., and Stricker, E.M., (1976): *Science*, 192:385-387.
115. Samanin, R., (1983): In: *Biochemical Pharmacology of Obesity*, edited by P.B. Curtis-Prior, pp. 339-356, Elsevier.
116. Sawchenko, P.E., Gold, R.M., and Leibowitz, S.F., (1981): *Brain Res.*; 225:249-269.
117. Sclafani, A., and Aravich, P.F., (1983): *Am. J. Physiol.*, 244:R686-R694.
118. Shor-Posner, G., Azar, A., Filart, R., and Leibowitz, S.F., (1985): *Brain Res. Bull.*, submitted.
119. Shor-Posner, G., Azar, A.P., Insinga, S., and Leibowitz, S.F., (1985): *Physiol. Behav.*, in press.
120. Shor-Posner, G., Grinker, J.A., Marinescu, C., and Leibowitz, S.F., (1985): *Physiol. Behav.*, in press.
121. Silverstone, T., (1982): In: *Drugs and Appetite*, edited by T. Silverstone, p. 93. Academic Press, New York.
122. Silverstone, T., and Kyriakides, M., (1979): *Curr. Med. Res. Opinion*, 6:(Suppl. 1), 180-187.
123. Smythe, G.A., Grunstein, H.S., Bradshaw, J.E., Nicholson, M.V., and Compton, P.J., (1984): *Nature*, 308:65-67.
124. Stachowiak, M., Bialowas, J., and Jurkowski, M., (1978): *Acta Neurobiol. Exp.*, 38:157-165.
125. Stanley, B.G., Daniel, D.R., Chin, A.J., and Leibowitz, S.F., (1985): *Peptides*, in press.
126. Stanley, B.G., and Leibowitz, S.F., (1984): *Life Sci.*, 35:2635-2642.

127. Strecker, E.R., Steinfels, G.F., and Jacobs, B.L., (1983): *Brain Res.*, 260:317.
128. Stricker, E.M., and Zigmund, M.J., (1984): In: *Neurology and Neurobiology*, edited by E. Usdin, A. Carlsson, A. Dahlstrom and J. Engel, Vol. 8B, p. 259. Alan R. Liss Inc., New York.
129. Swanson, L.W., and Sawchenko, P.E., (1983): *Ann. Rev. Neurosci.*, 6: 269.
130. Tagliaferro, A.R., and Levitsky, D.A., (1982): *Physiol. Behav.*, 29:747-750.
131. Tempel, D.L., Bhakthavatsalam, P., Shor-Posner, Dwyer, D., and Leibowitz, S.F., (1985): *Proc. East. Psychol. Assoc.*, 56:10.
132. Van der Gugten, J., and Slangen, J.L., (1977): *Pharmac. Biochem. Behav.*, 7:211-219.
133. Weiss, G.F., and Leibowitz, S.F., (1985): *Brain Res.*, in press.
134. Willis, G.L., Smith, G.C., Pavey, G.M., (1984): *Neurosci. Lett. Suppl.*, 15:65.
135. Wurtman, J.J., and Wurtman, R.J., (1977): *Science*, 198:1178-1180.
136. Wurtman, J.J., and Wurtman, R.J., (1981): In: *Anorectic Agents-Mechanisms of Actions and Tolerance*, edited by S. Garattini and R. Samanin, pp. 169-182. Raven Press, New York.
137. Wurtman, R.J., Fernstrom, J.D., (1976): *Biochem. Pharmacol.*, 25:1691-1696.
138. Wurtman, R.J., Hefti, F., and Melamed, E., (1981): *Pharmacol. Rev.*, 32:315-335.
139. Wurtman, R.J., and Wurtman, J.J., (1984): In: *Eating and its Disorders*, edited by A.J. Stunkard and E. Stellar, pp. 77-86. Raven Press, New York.
140. Zigmond, M.J., Heffner, T.G., and Stricker, E.M., (1980): *Prog. Neuro-psychopharmacol.*, 4:351-362.

Pharmacology of Eating Disorders: Theoretical and Clinical Developments, edited by M. O. Carruba and J. E. Blundell. Raven Press, New York © 1986.

Behavioural Pharmacology of Feeding: Relevance of Animal Experiments for Studies in Man

John E. Blundell and Andrew J. Hill

Biopsychology Group, Psychology Department, University of Leeds, Leeds, LS2 9JT, United Kingdom

THEORETICAL AND CLINICAL CONSIDERATIONS

Research in the behavioural pharmacology of feeding can be roughly divided into two domains according to the primary purpose underlying the research. In the theoretical domain drugs are used as tools to investigate the mechanisms responsible for the control of food consumption, whilst in the practical arena drugs are developed to treat abnormalities of eating and disorders of body weight regulation. Of course there is normally a good deal of overlap between these two enterprises. However in both domains extensive use is made of animal models; that is experimental procedures in which food consumption can be measured and from which the mechanism of action of a drug or its capacity to adjust food intake and/or body weight can be assessed. In the last 25 years a vast array of data has been generated by studies on the effect of drugs on food intake in experimental animals. Hundreds of chemical compounds have been reported to adjust food consumption (11, 67) and many produce long term changes in body weight. This ready alteration of eating in animals can be contrasted with the difficulty of developing effective drug treatments for human feeding and weight disorders. For example, in the case of anti-obesity drugs, a survey of more than 10,000 patients in some 350 studies involving 11 anorexic compounds indicated that the drugs produced an advantage over placebo of 0.56 lb of weight lost per week (74) and the reviewer regarded this as clinically trivial. It should be pointed out that such weight losses, if maintained for long periods of time, would be far from insignificant. However, the studies in the survey lasted for a maximum of 20 weeks, and it is known that in the treatment of obesity creating small initial weight losses is not difficult; the problem is to maintain weight loss (79, 12). Consequently, in the behavioural pharmacology of feeding there appears to be a puzzle; drugs adjust with ease the food consumption of animals yet apparently fail to provide effective therapeutic aids in man.

The situation described above frequently encourages clinicians to express doubts about the relevance of animal studies to the understanding of human feeding. Indeed it is relatively simple to provide justification for such doubts. On the one hand, data from animal studies are obtained from subjects kept isolated in cages in experimental laboratories, frequently maintained on food deprivation schedules and periodically allowed to eat briefly from a single composite food. On the other hand, eating in man is usually a social behaviour, subjects are not forcibly prevented from eating, a wide variety of foods are available, and eating is influenced by a large number of cultural and economic factors. It is apparent that many animal studies employ a highly stylized experimental situation which contrasts with the complexity and variability of human feeding. These differences question whether animal models used for the investigation of drug actions provide appropriate bases for extrapolating the outcome to human situations. What strategies can be adopted to upgrade the dialogue between animal and human studies ?

SYSTEMS AND INTERACTIONS

There are two important ways in which animal experiments and human clinical problems can be brought closer together; these are conceptual and methodological. The conceptual revision requires an updating of the classical view of the control of food intake. Contemporary views (66, 61) have developed from the dual-centre theory proposed by Stellar (77) and Brobeck (30) more than 20 years ago but have retained the principle of hypothalamic integrating centres. The notion of facilitatory and inhibitory centres can be expanded in two ways. First, the highly sensitive hypothalamic sites can be viewed as part of a much broader fabric of neural networks within the brain (47). Second, the brain itself can be incorporated within a more extensive system (Figure 1) which embraces the influences of social, behavioural and physiological processes. This system illustrates how shifts in food consumption (increases or decreases) could arise from pharmacological manipulations at many points. For example, eating may be altered by drugs acting directly on the brain (the highly localized and sensitive hypothalamic sites or other parts of the network to which these loci are linked), on gastro-intestinal functions, on fat metabolism, or on energy expenditure. Moreover, this systems view illustrates how the effect of drugs at the various sites could be modulated (suppressed or amplified) by the activity of other elements of the system. For example the effect of a drug acting on the brain could be altered by changing the characteristics (taste, texture, ease of access) of the available food, or by adjusting some aspect of the environment (introducing alternative activities or changing from an isolated to group situation). The recognition that a drug acts upon a system rather than upon a single controller or master switch has three important consequences. First, even though the drug may act at a particular locus the outcome of drug administration will be variable - depending upon the state of the rest of the system. Second, the use of a systems view to consider the effect of drugs in animal studies means that

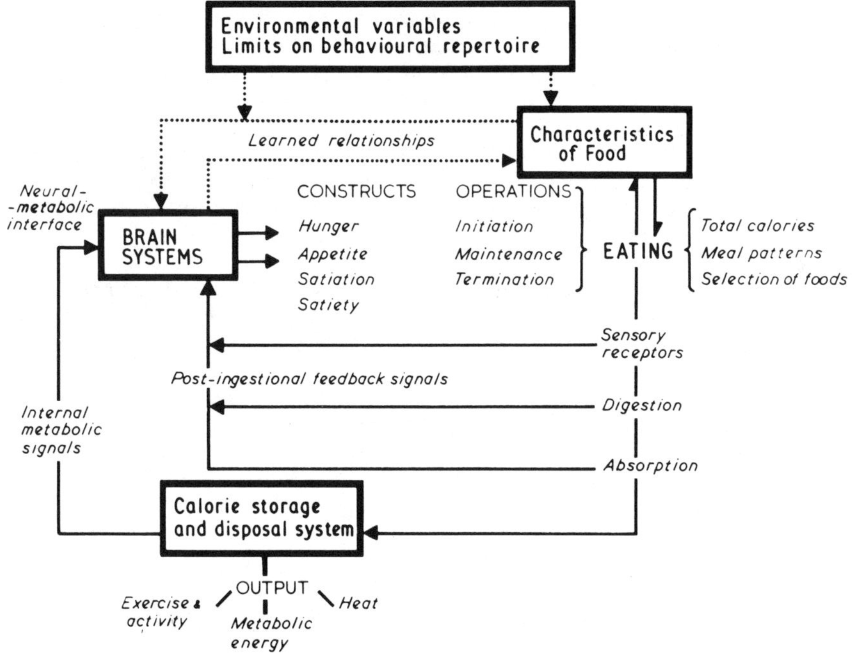

FIG. 1. Conceptualization of a bio-psychological system for interpreting the effects of drugs on feeding.

many more variables and the interactions between them can be utilised in developing an interpretation of drug action (22). This additional complexity of the systems approach brings animal studies conceptually closer to experiments on man. Third, inspection of the elements in the conceptual system set out in Figure 1 draws attention to qualitative as well as quantitative features of feeding. Whereas many traditional studies in the behavioural pharmacology of feeding have dealt only with quantitative shifts in food consumption (17-20), the systems view forces a recognition of the qualitative aspects of food stimuli and of feeding behaviour itself (8). This again develops common ground for animal and human studies and illustrates how the conceptual reorientation of a systems approach draws attention to certain methodological improvements which could enhance the external validity of animal experiments.

METHODOLOGICAL ISSUES: NEW EXPERIMENTAL MODELS

The techniques which have defined the orthodox approach to the measurement of food intake in animals for many years may possess inherent deficiencies which hinder their usefulness. The combined use of severe deprivation periods and short food tests represent a procedure which may be highly insensitive to certain drug effects - masking the action of a weak drug and exaggerating the effect of more powerful compounds (53). In addition this procedure may create circumstances for the appearance of abnormal behaviour and may modify drug action in an unknown way by altering brain chemistry (44). The major weaknesses of the traditional approach is that it provides only a single measure of eating (weight of food consumed), is purely quantitative, may be physiologically anomalous (4), and largely neglects the ecological context. These features keep animal experiments within narrow limits and serve to maintain a conceptual distance between studies on animals and man.

In recent years a number of new test models have become available for evaluating the effect of drugs on feeding. These models make use of neurochemical procedures, physiological manipulations and behavioural strategies. One major feature in the development of procedures to induce eating and which can be used in addition to food deprivation to bring about short-term hyperphagia. Some of these procedures are set out in Table 1.

Naturally one primary purpose of using techniques for promoting hyperphagia is to elaborate the mechanisms underlying the action of anorexic drugs. In addition, in expanding the range of test situations, they begin to embrace certain factors which are often thought to be the cause of overeating and obesity in man - namely exposure to stress and the availaility of sweet palatable foods.

However, considering wider aspects of the behavioural pharmacology of feeding beyond the domain of experimental hyperphagia and the testing of anorexic drugs, there are certain methodological features which appear to have the greatest value for upgrading animal experiments and improving their ecological validity.

These are :

a) The use of free-feeding animals in addition to severe food deprivation schedules and cyclic feeding regimes.

b) The employment of foods characterised by their variety and palatability as opposed to the uniform consistency of laboratory chow.

c) The provision of two or more diets varying in macronutrient composition (thereby allowing self-selection) as apposed to the single composite diet.

d) The evaluation of qualitative changes in feeding through the macro and micro- analysis of behaviour sequences as opposed to the single measure of the weight of food consumed.

Illustrations of the usefulness of these procedures in the analysis of drug action are set out below.

TABLE 1. Experimental procedures useful for testing the effects of anorexic agents on overeating by rats.

Techniques for inducing overeating	Drug investigated
Addition of sucrose to diet	Naloxone
Cafeteria foods	Naloxone, naltrexone, amphetamines, fenfluramine
Electrical stimulation of lateral hypothalamus	Amphetamine, fenfluramine
Noradrenaline injections into paraventricular nucleus	Fenfluramine
Ventro-medial hypothalamic lesions	Amphetamine, fenfluramine, chlorphentermine
Hypothalamic knife cuts	- - -
Muscimol injections into medial raphe nuclei	Amphetamine, fenfluramine
Lesions of ventral noradrenergic bundle	Amphetamine, fenfluramine, diethylpropion
Injections of diazepam	Naloxone, amphetamine
Injections of yohimbine	Naloxone
2-Deoxy-d-glucose administration	Naloxone, fenfluramine, amphetamine
Insulin injections	Naloxone, fenfluramine, amphetamine
Stress-induced (tail-pinch) arousal	Amphetamine, fenfluramine, naloxone.

CASE STUDIES IN THE BEHAVIOURAL PHARMACOLOGY OF FEEDING

Micro-structural analysis of feeding behaviour

In pharmacological experiments on feeding one distinction which is often blurred is that between food intake and feeding behaviour. Food intake is a quantitative term which refers to the mass of nutrients consumed whereas feeding behaviour draws attention to the qualitative aspects of an animal's movements as it satisfies its nutritional requirements. A measure of food intake can be reduced to a single number but feeding behaviour can only be described by reference to changes in state or to sequences of actions. For many animals feeding is an episodic activity and even the eating episodes themselves show discontinuities in behaviour. Using a continuous observation procedure Wiepkema (82) categorized and measured the particular episodes of eating, called bouts, the intervals of non-eating, and the relationship between these variables. In this way qualitative changes in behaviour can be objectively represented. For example, following a period of food deprivation Wiepkema found that the mean number of feeding bouts did not change; however the duration of these bouts was notably increased whilst the duration of the inter-bout intervals was decreased (83). This analytical technique can be used to characterise the effect of pharmacological manipulation on feeding. In turn the drug-induced adjustments to the micro-structure of feeding behaviour can help to elucidate the way in which a drug enhances, or more commonly suppresses, food intake.

For example, in a recent development of the technique used by Wiepkema the behaviour of rats during a one-hour period was exhaustively recorded in six categories: eating, drinking, grooming, locomotor activity, resting and others (16). From these records together with the food weighing it is possible to derive the following parameters: total food intake (g), duration of time spent eating (min), number of eating bouts (n), size of bouts (g), duration of bouts (min) and the local rate of eating (g/min). It is worth noting that the measure of eating rate is a local value calculated only from the rat's actual eating time and is quite different from an overall rate which can be simply computed by dividing the weight of food consumed by the duration of the testing period. The purpose of measuring these particular parameters is to permit the detection of certain subtle differences between the actions of drugs not revealed by a simple measure of the amount of food consumed. This can be demonstrated by an experiment which compared the effects of equi-anorectic doses of amphetamine, fenfluramine, mazindol and diethylpropion. Although these compounds produced a similar suppression of food intake they differed on a number of micro-structural parameters (17). In particular it was revealed that amphetamine markedly increased the latency to the initiation of eating, and actually caused rats to markedly increase the rate of consumption. On the other hand, fenfluramine brought about a noticeable slowing of the rate of eating. It has since been demonstrated that this slow rate of eating is reliably displayed by neuroleptics such as pimozide and α -flupenthixol, by serotonin re-uptake blockers such as ORG 6582 (78) and Lilly 110140 (43), and by compounds such as 5-hydroxytryptophan which are believed to enhance activity in serotonin systems (19, 20). However, it is clear that the slow rate of eating need not invariably *cause* the reduction in food intake. For example, pimozide does not necessarily produce anorexia - when the rate of eating is slowed the animals compensate by increasing the time spent eating resulting in no deficit in food intake. On the other hand, with a serotonergic drug such as fenfluramine rats do not compensate for the slow eating rate by increasing eating time. Consumption is curtailed independently of the rate of eating (21). These measures of feeding have also been used successfully in an abbreviated feeding test to examine the actions of chlordiazepoxide (33) and spiperone (34). In addition microstructural analysis has provided a useful tool for investigating the involvement of β -receptors in amphetamine anorexia (84) and for understanding the action of amphetamine following chronic antidepressant treatment (85).

More recentlty, analysis of the fine structure of eating behaviour has been used to investigate the mode of action of the opioid receptor blockers - naloxone and naltrexone (52). In many ways the anorexic action of naloxone is quite ambiguous - the inhibition of food intake is mild, dose-response curves are frequently shallow and total suppression of eating is extremely difficult to achieve even with very high doses. The micro-analysis procedure has revealed that naloxone appears to have both facilitatory and inhibitory effects on eating, with a mild stimulating effect on the initiation of consumption being overridden by an enhancement of satiation. This dual effect of naloxone on the appetitive and consummatory phases of eating could account for its unusual characteristics as an anorectic agent. The profile of naloxone is quite dissimilar to that of fenfluramine or amphetamine. These examples illustrate the power of micro-structural analysis to discriminate between anorectic compounds and to elucidate their modes of action.

Macro-analysis of feeding patterns

A technique closely associated with micro-analysis (described above) involves the recording and measurement of long-term feeding patterns in *free-feeding* rats never forcibly subjected to periods of food deprivation. The application of continuous monitoring techniques to the investigation of pharmacological manipulation of food intake is a natural outcome of the endeavour to improve the ecological validity of testing procedures and has revealed interesting and unexpected effects inaccessible to studies involving deprived rats.

The major advantage of the continuous monitoring procedure is the identification of the meal as the unit of feeding. From this basic variable can be computed the parameters of meal size, meal duration, meal frequency, inter-meal interval, intra-meal eating rate, ratios of meal size to meal interval and various other measures which describe the pattern of feeding behaviour. Increases in technical sophistication of monitoring equipment and the use of computers for data logging and analysis have greatly improved the ease and precision of measuring the parameters of meal patterns (22).

The procedure appears to have been used in drug studies about 17 years ago (28) when the active drug (amphetamine) was delivered via the rat's drinking water. A more recent study which compared the effects of amphetamine and fenfluramine demonstrated that these drugs displayed quite different profiles when meals were monitored continuously over 24-hour periods in non-deprived rats (25, 23). Interestingly, the effect of fenfluramine was characterised by a reduction in meal size which suggested that the drug was acting to promote the process of satiation and therefore cause an early termination of eating. This effect has now been confirmed many times (17, 31, 36, 37, 45). This type of analysis provides qualitative information about feeding behaviour over long periods of time and permits alterations in behavioural parameters to be matched against the time course of drug concentration in blood (9, 10, 14). The procedure has been particularly useful in disclosing the changes in the feeding profile brought about by fenfluramine and thereby suggesting a role for serotonin in the process of satiation.

However, the strength of a sensitive procedure like meal pattern analysis depends upon the capacity to distinguish between the actions of different pharmacological agents. Consequently, it is important to point out that drugs do give rise to quite distinctive behavioural profiles. It has already been noted that amphetamine and fenfluramine can readily be separated. In addition, the dopamine receptor blockers give rise to quite different profiles characterised by a slow rate of eating and a large increase in meal size (17). The profiles of tryptophan (53) and 5-hydroxytryptophan (18, 19, 20) can be distinguished, whilst the opioid antagonists naloxone (60) and naltrexone (52) produce a profile different to serotoninergic agonists and dopamine antagonists.

Accordingly, macro-analysis of meal patterns advances research on the pharmacology of feeding in a number of ways :

a) the sensitivity of the technique permits distinctions to be made between different compounds with similar effects on the total weight of food consumed,

b) throws light on the mode of action of drugs and allows assessments to be made under normal physiological conditions,

c) provides information on the way in which drugs influence different aspects of the feeding process through the mechanisms of hunger, appetite, satiation and satiety.

All of these considerations improve the ecological validity of animal experiments and increase their relevance as guides to the possible effects of drugs in man.

Variety and palatability of food

Traditionally, pharmacological studies on feeding have used laboratory rats allowed to consume only the bland and balanced diet of laboratory chow. However, rats are omnivorous animals which have surely evolved to exploit many different food sources through techniques of foraging and hoarding. Accordingly, it is likely that under more natural circumstances rats would normally encounter a number of different types of food differing in taste, texture and nutrient density. The tendency of rats to eat more of a tasty and varied diet has been experimentally exploited to produce a form of dietary-induced obesity (72, 73). The use of novel and varied food items in anorexic drug research has led to a number of interesting research possibilities including the possibility of distinguishing between drug effects on hunger and appetite (7, 27) and assessing the action of drugs on the hedonic value of food (9, 10). It has also become clear that not all anorexic drugs suppress intake equally when offered different types of food. The use of varied diets in drug research is essential to investigate the processes underlying the action of anorexic drugs and to increase confidence in generalizing from laboratory to clinical studies.

The use of varied and palatable diets has encouraged interest in a form of experimental obesity which appears to have features in common with the development of obesity in man. Accordingly, the effectiveness of anorexic drugs to inhibit intake of highly palatable food and to retard or suppress the occurrence of dietary induced obesity becomes of crucial importance. It has been demonstrated that the opiate receptor blocker naloxone exerts a greater suppressive effect on the consumption of snack food diet than of laboratory chow, at least during the dark (3). This effect also occurs with naltrexone, and appears to indicate a more potent anorexic effect when the diet induces hyperphagia. However, this effect is not unique to opiate blockers. Interestingly, amphetamine is less potent with a varied diet than with laboratory chow but the action of naloxone is matched by fenfluramine (29). Moreover, fenfluramine has been shown to suppress the level of dietary-induced obesity (51). In addition, a further more detailed study has investigated the action of the dextro isomer of fenfluramine (dextrofenfluramine) on the development and the maintenance of dietary-induced obesity. It is known that dietary-induced obesity can be partitioned into a dynamic and plateau phase (70); that is the process of actively getting fat and then the more static situation of maintaining the level of achieved obesity. Accordingly, in two separate experiments dextrofenfluramine was administered continuously to rats for 76 days during the dynamic phase of obesity or for 36 days once a plateau phase of obesity had been reached. The design of the study is set out in Figure 2 and provides a scheme for assessing the effects of

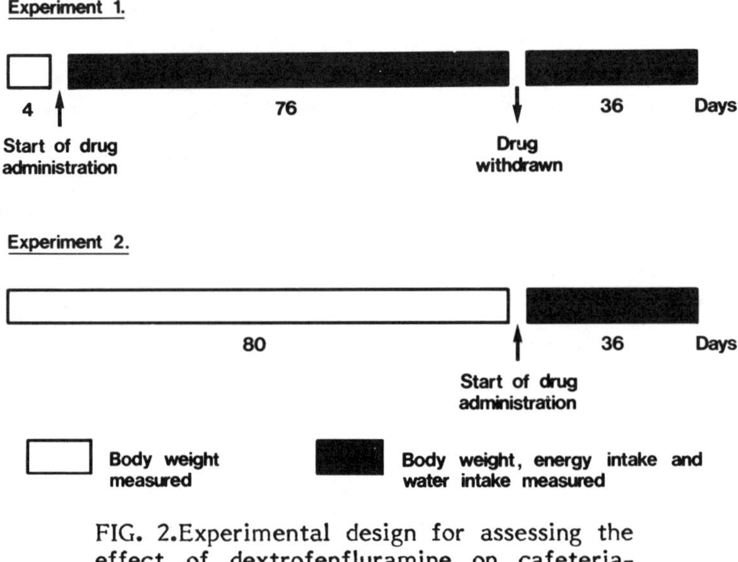

FIG. 2.Experimental design for assessing the effect of dextrofenfluramine on cafeteria-induced feeding during the dynamic and plateau phases of obesity.

pharmacological agents on the dietary model of obesity. The results disclosed an interesting pattern of effects. First, dextrofenfluramine caused a significant reduction of food intake in both cafeteria-fed rats and in the chow-fed control group and this was accompanied by a marked loss of body weight (Table 2). However, the potency of the drug (i.e. its capacity to suppress body weight compared with placebo treatment) was much greater in the plateau phase of obesity (Exp. 2) than in any of the other groups. In other words, although dextrofenfluramine will suppress body weight over considerable periods of time in cafeteria or chow fed animals, it appears to be most effective in animals which have already been made obese.

The studies outlined above can be regarded as useful landmarks in the behavioural pharmacology of feeding. The action of drugs has been evaluated in animals eating a varied and palatable diet. These characteristics greatly increase the relevance of animal experiments and illustrate that drugs can be evaluated under laboratory conditions which resemble more closely natural circumstances.

TABLE 2. Effect of dextrofenfluramine on weight loss during dynamic (Experiment 1) and plateau (Exp. 2) phases of dietary-induced obesity.

	Experiment 1		Experiment 2
Diet	36 days	76 days	36 days
Cafeteria	0.28 (0.04)	0.16 (0.03)	0.75 (0.05)*
Chow	0.25 (0.03)	0.14 (0.02)	0.18 (0.06)

The figures in the body of the table are the mean (S.E.) body weight losses for the treated animals compared with placebo treated controls. The values indicate the body weight (g) lost per day per mg/kg of drug administered. $*t = 6.72$, $p<.001$.

Self-selection of macronutrients

A considerable body of evidence indicates that omnivorous animals, feeding from a variety of food sources, possess the ability to select and to qualitatively monitor their intake of certain nutrients (64, 71). For example, rats allowed to select from a cafeteria array of separate dietary components such as protein, fat, carbohydrate, vitamins and minerals are able to maintain a balanced intake of essential elements (68). In addition, this dietary self-selection can be influenced by the ambient temperature (54), changing hormonal states (55), activity level (32) and the availability of water (35, 65). Indeed, it appears that dietary self-selection is a fundamental characteristic of feeding behaviour in animals which becomes more clearly apparent when functional demands are placed on the system.

Until recently, this phenomenon had been ignored in pharmacological investigations of feeding in which animals are generally maintained on a single composite diet containing a balanced mixture of essential nutrients. However, interest in pharmacological aspects of voluntary self-selection has been promoted by theoretical developments concerning the role of neurotransmitter systems in the regulation of protein and carbohydrate intake. It has been proposed that the concentration of the transmitter serotonin in the brain is dependent upon the ratio of tryptophan to neutral amino acids in the plasma (42). The nature of the diet exerts a major influence over this plasma ratio, and it has been demonstrated in rats that a high carbohydrate meal can lead to increase in brain tryptophan and serotonin (40). It has therefore been proposed that serotonin-containing brain neurons may function as "ratio-sensors" - the rate of neurotransmitter synthesis in these neurons varying with the nutrient composition of the diet. Although there exists some opposition to this idea (63), it has been argued that serotonin neurons could discriminate between the metabolic effects of various diets (41). One implication of this process is that the feedback effect from neurotransmitter synthesis to feeding behaviour may involve qualitative rather than quantitative adjustments in food intake. This means that neurotransmitter activity will influence an animal's choice of nutrients. In keeping with this idea Ashley and Anderson (5) have demonstrated that in the weanling rat the ratio of tryptophan to neutral aminoacids in the plasma is related to the amount of protein self-selected by the rat. In turn this has led to the suggestion that serotonin neurons participate in feeding not by regulating total caloric intake but by adjusting protein (1, 2) or by controlling the balance of protein and carbohydrate in the diet (42).

This hypothesis lends itself readily to test by pharmacological agents and allows drugs to be used as tools to further probe the complex structure of feeding. Moreover, experimenters are obliged to allow animals to voluntarily self-select their intake of particular dietary components. This demand has led to the development of an experimental procedure in which animals are faced with two or more food containers holding varying concentrations of the major macro-nutrients protein, carbohydrate and fat. In a typical two-container design animals are allowed to choose between isocaloric diets containing 5 and 45%, or 15 and 55%, or 0 and 60% protein diets. Accordingly, by moderating their eating from a particular source animals can adjust their elective consumption of protein and carbohydrate. In one of the first pharmacological studies using this paradigm it was demonstrated that different anorexic drugs exerted distinctive effects on the pattern of selection (86). Fenfluramine and fluoxetine which increase the synaptic activity of serotonin, displayed a protein sparing effect in weanling rats; that is, they reduced total food intake but actually increased the proportion of protein consumed. In contrast amphetamine gave rise to an equal suppression of protein and total caloric intake. In an extension of this study using adult animals and allowing the rats to feed freely, fenfluramine maintained but did not spare protein intake whilst amphetamine brought about a severe suppression of protein consumption (26, 59). Recently, it has been shown that the depletion of brain serotonin by systemic injections of para-chloro-phenyl-alanine, intraventricular administration of 5,7-dihydroxytryptamine or by electro-thermal lesions of the medial raphe nuclei lead to a selective decrease in protein intake (6). In turn, this work is complemented by the finding that drugs which are believed to enhance central serotonergic transmission selectively suppress carbohydrate consumption by rats (87). Under certain circumstances pharmacological manipulation of serotonin metabolism can adjust the selection of macro-nutrients by rats although it is currently not clear whether the primary effect is on protein or carbohydrate intake (87).

More recently the phenomenon of nutrient selection has been complicated by the finding that clonidine, an α -adrenergic agonist, enhances food consumption and appears to specifically stimulate protein intake (58). This effect was interpreted as an action upon presynaptic receptors and it was suggested that central noradrenergic neurons participate in the mechanisms controlling appetites for protein. Accordingly, it seems that both serotonin and noradrenaline systems may be involved in the control of protein-carbohydrate intake. However, this picture is further complicated by the report that injections of clonidine actually increase the preference for carbohydrate following peripheral or central administration (39). Since similar effects have been obtained after noradrenaline injections into the paraventricular nucleus (81), these findings tend to implicate central noradrenaline systems in the control of carbohydrate rather than protein consumption.

Using a different design in which pure samples of protein carbohydrate and fat are offered in the selection test, it has been reported that insulin (50) and gonadal hormones (48) influence diet selection. Moreover, whilst morphine led to an increase in fat intake (57), amphetamine selectively depressed consumption of this commodity (49). These data suggest that fat, protein and carbohydrate may be under the control of complex neurochemical relationships in the brain.

Accordingly, the dietary self-selection model provides an experimental arena for the deeper investigation of pharmacological agents. This, in turn, throws light upon the mechanism of action of drugs and, at the same time, creates a further point of contact between animal and human studies.

IMPLICATIONS

The case studies outlined above have a number of implications both for understanding the mechanism of action of drugs on food consumption and also for using these findings as a basis for research in man. Firstly, it is clear that the observed effect of a drug depends upon the experimental circumstances. These circumstances embrace the physiological state of the animals (deprived or fed), the structural configuration of the environment (food in cage-hopper or reached by negotiating a runway), the characteristics of the food (palatability, macronutrient composition etc.) ad the availability of choices (single composite diet or opportunity to select from several). For example, the physiological state of the animal can markedly influence the effect of amphetamine. In deprived rats the anorectic action of amphetamine is invariably observed but when injected into free feeding rats anorexia can not only be suppressed but actually reserved to give rise to a mild hyperphagia (17, 90). Moreover, if rats are trained to obtain food by traversing a runway instead of receiving food in the home cages the action of certain drugs can be markedly modified. Indeed the anorexic effect of an ED50 dose of amphetamine can be almost totally suppressed when the environment is reshaped by introducing a runway (52, 80). On the other hand the action of serotoninergic drugs can also be drastically modulated. When animals are fed a high carbohydrate diet all anorectic drugs produce a powerful response but with a low carbohydrate diet the anorectic effet of fenfluramine and MK-212 has been reported to be lost (62). In other words drugs may be regarded as anorectic with certain diets but not others. In addition, a number of experiments have illustrated how the anorectic potency of a drug may vary with the palatability of the diet; in particular both naloxone and fenfluramine appear to be more potent anorectics against the hyperphagia induced by good tasting food whilst other drugs such as amphetamine and hydroxycitrate are less potent.

Considering the proposition that the pharmacological control of feeding may be best understood by conceptualizing a bio-psychological system, the above findings indicate that drugs producing effects with the system in one particular state may give rise to quite different outcomes when elements in the system are altered. Consequently drugs influencing feeding do not appear to act upon a single controller of total caloric intake, food volume or energy. The action of a drug is not independent of the nutritional composition of food, the sensory qualities of the food, difficulty of obtaining the food etc. Rather different drugs create distinctive dispositions which are subject to a variety of modulating influences.

One further implication is that the qualitative adjustments in feeding revealed by new techniques provide means of disclosing the processes through which a drug may alter eating under particular circumstances. For example, it may be adduced that a drug acts primarily upon a process like hunger or satiation, or upon a process regulating carbohydrate intake, or a process reflecting the operation of appetite. Consequently, these findings provide an indication of relevant variables to be measured in studies in man.

RESEARCH IN MAN

When experiments on rats are restricted by the use of long periods of food deprivation, a single composite diet and a brief food intake test, it is difficult to do studies in man which resemble the animal model yet retain the credibility and relevance to the complexities of human eating. However, the use of varied and palatable food, choice of macronutrients and the micro-analysis of behaviour provide devices which can be used directly in man and which preserve, to an extent, the meaningfulness of human feeding circumstances. In addition, the greater sensitivity of such procedures makes possible the detection of milder, more subtle changes induced by drugs. This is necessary since whereas the ED50 dose of a drug is commonly employed in animal studies, the much smaller doses used in man usually decrease intake by only 15-20%. Consequently, animal and human studies can be carried out parallel. The range of techniques employed in man (15, 46) together with their use in pharmacological studies have recently been reviewed (13). The use of micro-analysis of the structure of eating behaviour has been used to investigate the effects of amphetamine and fenfluramine (69) and the findings were remarkedly similar to those in animals. Amphetamine inhibited the onset of eating and increased eating rate whilst fenfluramine shortened the duration of the meal and markedly slowed the rate of eating. Based on the idea of an automated eatometer used in animal studies, Silverstone & Fincham (75) developed an automated food dispenser for experiments in man. The technique has been used to investigate the action of various anorectic drugs on eating profiles (76). Researchers have also introduced the dimension of choice into human feeding experiments, usually monitoring the selection of proteins and carbohydrates by monitoring actual consumption (24, 88, 89) or by assessing expressed preferences (27). These findings indicate that serotoninergic compounds tend to produce a suppression of carbohydrate intake or a relative sparing of protein in a manner milder but similar to that displayed in animals.

CONCLUSIONS

The last 10 years have seen major developments take place in the pharmacology of feeding. Advances have been made in three areas :

a) Methodology - new experimental techniques have been introduced to provide a much more detailed analysis of feeding and to improve the meaningfulness and ecological validity of laboratory studies.

b) Theory - more sophisticated models and systems have been constructed to promote new lines of research and to assimilate and explain the experimental findings.

c) Clinical studies - the advances in methodology and theory have provided a more relevant base from which to explore various aspects of eating disorders. The effects on eating of nutritional composition, sensory qualities and stressors have provided route for the investigation of issues common to animal and human studies.

REFERENCES

1. Anderson, G.H. (1977): *Adv. Nutr. Res.*, 1: 145-166.

2. Anderson, G.H. (1979): *Can. J. Physiol. Pharmacol.*, 57: 1043-1057.

3. Apfelbaum, M. and Mandenoff, A. (1981): *Pharmacol. Biochem. Behav.*, 15: 89-91.

4. Armstrong, S. (1980): *Neurosci. Biobehav. Rev.*, 4: 27-53.

5. Ashley, D.V.M. and Anderson, G.H. (1975): *J. Nutr.*, 105: 1404-1411.

6. Ashley, D.V.M., Coscina, D.V., and Anderson, G.H. (1979): *Life Sci.*, 24: 973-984.

7. Blundell, J.E. (1979): In: *Nutrition and Lifestyles*, edited by M. Turner, pp. 21-42. Applied Sci. Pub., London.

8. Blundell, J.E. (1981): In: *Progress in Theory in Psychopharmacology*, edited by S.J. Cooper, pp. 233-266. Academic Press, London.

9. Blundell, J.E. (1982): *Alimentazione, Nutrizione, Metabolismo*. 3: 7-19.

10. Blundell, J.E. (1982): *Rev. Pure Appli. Pharmacol. Sci.*, 3 : 381-462.

11. Blundell, J.E. (1984): In: *Eating and Its Disorders*, edited by A.J. Stunkard and E. Stellar, pp. 39-65. Raven Press, New York.

12. Blundell, J.E. (1984): *Postgrad. Med. J.*, 60 (Suppl. 3): 36-48.

13. Blundell, J.E. (1985): In: *Psychopharmacology and Food*, edited by M. Sandler and T. Silverstone, Oxford University Press.

14. Blundell, J.E., Campbell, D.B., Leshem, M.B. and Tozer, R. (1975): *J. Pharm. Pharmacol.*, 27: 187-192.

15. Blundell, J.E. and Hill, A.J. (1985): In: *Modern Concepts of the Eating Disorders: Research, Diagnosis, Treatment*, edited by B.J. Blinder, E. Friedman, B.F. Chaitin, and R. Goldstein, Spectrum, New York.

16. Blundell, J.E. and Latham, C.J. (1977): *Proceedings of 6th International Congress on Physiology of Food and Fluid Intake*, Paris.

17. Blundell, J.E., and Latham, C.J. (1978): In: *Central Mechanisms of Anorectic Drugs*, edited by S. Garattini and R. Samanin, pp. 83-109. Raven Press, New York.

18. Blundell, J.E. and Latham, C.J. (1979): In: *Chemical Influences on Behaviour*, edited by S. Cooper and K. Brown, pp. 201-254. Academic Press, London.

19. Blundell, J.E. and Latham, C.J.(1979): *Pharmacol. Biochem. Behav.*, 11: 431-437.

20. Blundell, J.E. and Latham, C.J. (1979): *Br. J. Pharmacol.*, 66: 482.

21. Blundell, J.E. and Latham, C.J. (1980): *Pharmacol. Biochem. Behav.*, 12: 717-722.

22. Blundell, J.E. and Latham, C.J. (1982): In: *Drugs and Appetite*, edited by T. Silverstone, pp. 41-80. Academic Press, London.

23. Blundell, J.E., Latham, C.J. and Leshem, M.B. (1976): *J. Pharm. Pharmacol.*, 28: 471-477.

24. Blundell, J.E., Latham, C.J., McArthur, R.A., Moniz, E. and Rogers, P.J. (1979) *Cur. Med. Res. Opin.*, 6: 34-54.

25. Blundell, J.E. and Leshem, M.B. (1975): In: *Recent Advances in Obesity*, edited by A. Howard, pp. 368-371. Newman, London.

26. Blundell, J.E. and McArthur, R.A. (1979): *Br. J. Pharmacol.*, 67: 436-438.

27. Blundell, J.E. and Rogers, P.J. (1980): *Appetite*, 1: 151-165.

28. Borbely, A. and Waser, P.G. (1966): *Psychopharmacology*, 9: 373-381.

29. Bowden, C., White, K. and Tutwiler, G. (1983): *Proceedings of IV Int. Cong. on Obesity*, New York, p. 35A.

30. Brobeck, J.R. (1960): *Recent Prog. Horm. Res.*, 16: 439-459.

31. Burton, M.J., Cooper, S.J. and Popplewell, D.A. (1981): *Br. J. Pharmacol.*, 72: 621-633.

32. Collier, G., Leshner, A.I. and Squibb, R.L. (1969): *Physiol. Behav.*, 4: 79-82.

33. Cooper, S.J. and Francis, R.L. (1979): *Psychopharmacology*, 62: 253-259.

34. Cooper, S.J., Sweeney, K.F. and Toates, F.M. (1979): *Psychopharmacology*, 63: 301-305.

35. Corey, D.T., Walton, A. and Wiener, N.I. (1978): *Physiol. Behav.*, 20: 547-552.

36. Davies, R.F. (1976): *Ph. D. Thesis*, McGill, Montreal.

37. Davies, R.F., Rossi, J., Panksepp, J., Bean, N.J. and Zolovick, A.J. (1983): *Physiol. Behav.*, 30: 723-730.

39. Fahrbach, S.E., Tetter, J.R., Aravich, P.F., McCabe, J. and Leibowitz, S.F. (1980): *Proceedings of the Society for Neuroscience,* 10th annual meeting, Cincinnati Nov. 9-14. Abstract Vol 6. p. 784.

40. Fernstrom, J.D. and Wurtman, R.J. (1972): *Science,* 178: 414-416.

41. Fernstrom, J.D. and Wurtman, R.J. (1973): In: *Serotonin and Behaviour,* edited by J. Barchas and E. Usdin, pp. 121-128. Academic Press, New York.

42. Ferstrom, J.D. and Wurtman, R.J. (1974): *Sci. Am.,* 230: 84-91.

43. Fuller, R. W. and Wong, D.T. (1977): *Fed. Proc.,* 36: 2154-2158.

44. Glick, S.D., Waters, D.H. and Milloy, S. (1973): *Res. Comm. Chem. Path. Pharmacol.,* 6: 775-778.

45. Grinker, J.A., Drewnowski, A., Enns, M., and Kissileff, H. (1980): *Pharmacol. Biochem. and Behav.,* 12: 265-275.

46. Hill, A.J. and Blundell, J.E. (1982/83): *J. Psychiat. Res.,* 17: 203-212.

47. Hoebel, B.G; (1984): In: *Eating and its Disorders,* edited by A.J. Stunkard and Stellar, pp. 15-23. Raven Press, New York.

48. Kanarek, R.B. and Beck, J.M. (1980): *Physiol. Behav.,* 24: 381-386.

49. Kanarek, R.B., Ho, L. and Meade, R.G. (1981): *Pharmacol. Biochem. Behav.,* 14: 539-542.

50. Kanarek, R.B., Marks-Kaufman, R. and Lipeles, B.J. (1980): *Physiol. Behav.,* 25: 779-782.

51. Kirby, M.J., Pleece, S.A. and Redfern, P.H. (1978): *Br. J. Pharmacol.,* 64: 442.

52. Kirkham, T.C. and Blundell, J.E. (1984): *Appetite,* 5: 45-52.

53. Latham, C.J. and Blundell, J.E. (1979): *Life Sci.,* 24: 1971-1978.

54. Leshner, A.I., Collier, G.H. and Squibb, R.L. (1971): *Physiol. Behav.,* 6: 1-3.

55. Leshner, A.I., Siegel, H.I. and Collier, G. (1972): *Physiol. Behav.,* 8: 151-154.

56. Mandenoff, A., Fumeron, F., Apfelbaum, M. and Margules, D.L. (1982): *Science*, 215: 1536-1538.

57. Marks-Kaufman, R. and Kanarek, R.B. (1980): *Pharmacol. Biochem. Behav.*, 12: 427-430.

58. Mauron, C., Wurtman, J.J. and Wurtman, R.J. (1980): *Life Sci.*, 28: 781-791.

59. McArthur, R.A. and Blundell, J.E. (1983): *Appetite*, 4: 113-124.

60. McLaughlin, C.L. and Baile, C.A. (1984): *Physiol. Behav.*, 32: 755-761.

61. Morley, J.E. (1980): *Life Sci.*, 27: 355-368.

62. Moses, P.L. and Wurtman, R.J. (1984): *Life Sci.*, 35: 1297-1300.

63. Neckers, L.M., Biggio, G., Moja, E. and Meek, J.L. (1977): *J. Pharmacol. Exp. Ther.*, 201: 110-116.

64. Overmann, S.R. (1976): *Psychol. Bull.*, 83: 218-235.

65. Overmann, S.R. and Yang, M.G. (1973): *Physiology and Behav.*, 11: 781-786.

66. Panksepp, J. (1975): *Pharmacol. Biochem. Behav.*, 3: Suppl. 1, 107-119.

67. Peters, G., Besseghir, K.P., Kaserman, H.P. and Peters-Haefeli, L. (1979): *Pharmacol. Ther.*, 5: 485-503.

68. Richter, C.P. (1943): *Harvey Lect.*, 38: 63-103.

69. Rogers, P.J. and Blundell, J.E. (1979): *Psychopharmacology*, 66: 159-165.

70. Rogers, P.J. and Blundell, J.E. (1984): *Neurosci. Biobehav. Rev.*, 8: 441-453.

71. Rozin, P. (1976): In: *Advances in the Study of Behaviour VI*, edited by J. Rosenblatt, R. Hinde, C. Berr and E. Shaw, pp. 1121-76. Academic Press, New York.

72. Sclafani, A. (1978): In: *Recent Advances in Obesity Research II*, edited by G. Bray, pp. 123-132. Newman, London.

73. Sclafani, A. and Springer, D. (1976): *Physiol. Behav.*, 17: 461-471.

74. Scoville, B. (1976): In: *Obesity in Perspective* Pt. 2, edited by G.A. Bray, pp. 441-443. US Government Printing Office, Washington, D.C.

75. Silverstone, J.T. and Fincham, J. (1978): In: *Central Mechanisms of Anorexic Drugs,* edited by S. Garattini, and R. Samanin, pp. 375-382. Raven Press, New York.

76. Silverstone, T. and Kyriakides, M. (1982): In: *Drugs and Appetite,* edited by T. Silverstone, pp. 93-123. Academic Press, London.

77. Stellar, E. (1954): *Psychol. Rev.,* 61: 5-23.

78. Sugrue, M.F., Goodlet, I. and Mireylees, S.E. (1976): *Eur. J. Pharmacol.,* 40: 121-130.

79. Stunkard, A.J. (1978): *Int. J. Obes.,* 2: 237-248.

80. Thurlby, P.L. and Samanin, R. (1981): *Pharmacol. Biochem. Behav.,* 14: 799-804.

81. Tretter, J.R. and Leibowitz, S.F. (1980): *Proceedings of the Society for Neuroscience,* 10th annual meeting, Cincinnati, Nov. 9-11, p. 532.

82. Wiepkema, P.R. (1971): *Behaviour,* 39: 266-273.

83. Wiepkema, P.R. (1971): *Proc. Nutr. Soc.,* 30: 142-149.

84. Willner, P. and Towell, A.D. (1982): *Pharmacol. Biochem. Behav.,* 17: 252-262.

85. Willner, P. and Towell, A.D. (1982): *Soc. Neurosci. Abstr.,* 8: 358.

86. Wurtman, J.J. and Wurtman, R.J. (1979): *Life Sci.,* 24: 895-904.

87. Wurtman, J.J. and Wurtman, R.J. (1979): *Curr. Med. Res. Opin.,* 6 (Suppl. 1): 28-33.

88. Wurtman, J.J. and Wurtman, R.J. (1981): In: *Anorectic Agents Mechanisms of Action and Tolerance,* edited by S. Garattini and R. Samanin, pp 169-182. Raven Press, New York.

89. Wurtman, J.J., Wurtman, R.J., Growdon, J.H., Henry, P., Lipscomb, A. and Zeisel, S.H. (1982): *Int. J. Eating Disorders.,* 1: 2-15.

90. Wynn, P., Williams, S.F., and Herberg, L.J. (1982): *Psychopharmacology.,* 78: 336-341.

Pharmacology of Eating Disorders: Theoretical and Clinical Developments, edited by M. O. Carruba and J. E. Blundell. Raven Press, New York © 1986.

Stress-Induced Feeding Disorders

*John E. Morley, † § ¶ Allen S. Levine, and ‡ Mark L. Willenbring

**Education and Clinical Center, VA Medical Center, Sepulveda, California; †Neuroendocrine Research Unit and ‡Department of Psychiatry, VA Medical Center, Minneapolis, Minnesota; and Departments of §Medicine, ¶Food Science and Nutrition, and ‡Psychiatry, University of Minnesota, Minneapolis - St. Paul, Minnesota*

Psychological stress in animals and humans has been associated with a variety of behavioural abnormalities, including disturbances in feeding. The particular form of eating disturbance can be quite varied, depending on the particular stressor. As way of explanation, Robbins and Fray (141) have suggested that many different stressors can induce similar internal stimulus states, so that the organism may respond to a stressor in an apparently irrelevant way. For example, laboratory studies in animals have indicated that "stress" can lead to either increased or decreased food consumption. Both the type and duration of the stressor appear to play a role in determining the effect on food intake. Thus, mild tail pinching produces overeating in the rat, while immobilization stress or exposure to a novel environment leads to anorexia (37, 128). In humans we found that 47% of males and 37% of females report increasing their food consumption under stress, whereas 40% of males and 58% of females decrease their eating when under stress (131). In addition, 68% of females and 40% of males report eating when they are bored.

One of the major problems in evaluating the literature on stress and feeding relates to the definition of stress. Is social isolation a stress ? How about noise, divorce, a car accident, problem solving with a deadline ? Hans Selye (153) whose name is synonymous with the word stress defined stress as "the nonspecific response of the body to demand". Thus, the normal homeostatic state is altered due to a new level. In addition, we often assume that stress equals distress; however, stress can also be positive and invigorating and then we term this eustress. Running five miles is extremely distasteful to some and represents distress while many other individuals claim that this test of endurance is invigorating. Recent studies have shown that some, but not all runners, increase endogenous opioid levels after exercising (30) perhaps explaining the elusive "joggers high" seen in a small percentage of individuals. Alternatively, it has been suggested that some joggers may be suffering from a forme fruste of anorexia nervosa (183) although this has been strongly contested.

Just as different stressors produce different effects on eating behaviour, different types of stress procedures produce differing effects on neurotransmitter metabolism in the central nervous system. In the present chapter we will review our rapidly expanding knowledge of the neuropharmacology of stress-induced feeding disorders.

STRESS-INDUCED OVEREATING

"A stomach full of food also soothes by draining the blood away form a disgruntled and maladaptive brain".

-- Selye, 1956

Stress-Induced Eating in Wild and Laboratory Animals (Figure 1)

A variety of animals in the wild will engage in displacement feeding when under stress. Animals when approaching danger may indulge in a bout of grooming or preening before deciding to "flee or fight" (19, 92). Tinbergen and others (53, 138, 171) have described eating during boundary disputes in a wide variety of birds. Kruijt (67) showed that during fights between male jungle fowl, pecking at the ground was more than four times as common in winners than losers, whilst the converse ratio was found for preening. Barbary doves experimentally frustrated in drinking or courtship behaviour will peck at small objects on the ground (95). This experiment suggested that this pecking was related to the feeding system because: (i) total time spent pecking was increased in the presence of grain; (ii) food deprivation increased pecking time in the presence of grain, and (iii) time spent pecking was partly replaced by time spent at a specific food retrieving activity in birds trained to obtain food in this way. Also, cichlid fish have been reported to bite at the substratum (sand and stones) during intervals between fighting (58) and stickleback given electric shocks engage in hurried feeding similar to that following food deprivation (172). Sexual behaviour of rats is often associated with sporadic eating (15).

Other stresses also have been reported to induce eating in animals. Drew (38) reported that the sound of rapid jets of water or a buzzer in combination with light could produce feeding in satiated rats. Kupferman (68) has suggested that acoustic stimuli can elicit a complex series of behaviours, including chewing, approach to food, and eating in rats, guinea pigs and rabbits. He further suggested that the behaviour was related to the intensity of the sound: lower intensities elicited chewing while higher intensities produced eating. Anecdotal reports have suggested that handling may stimulate eating and that a saline injection may induce latency to feed in animals

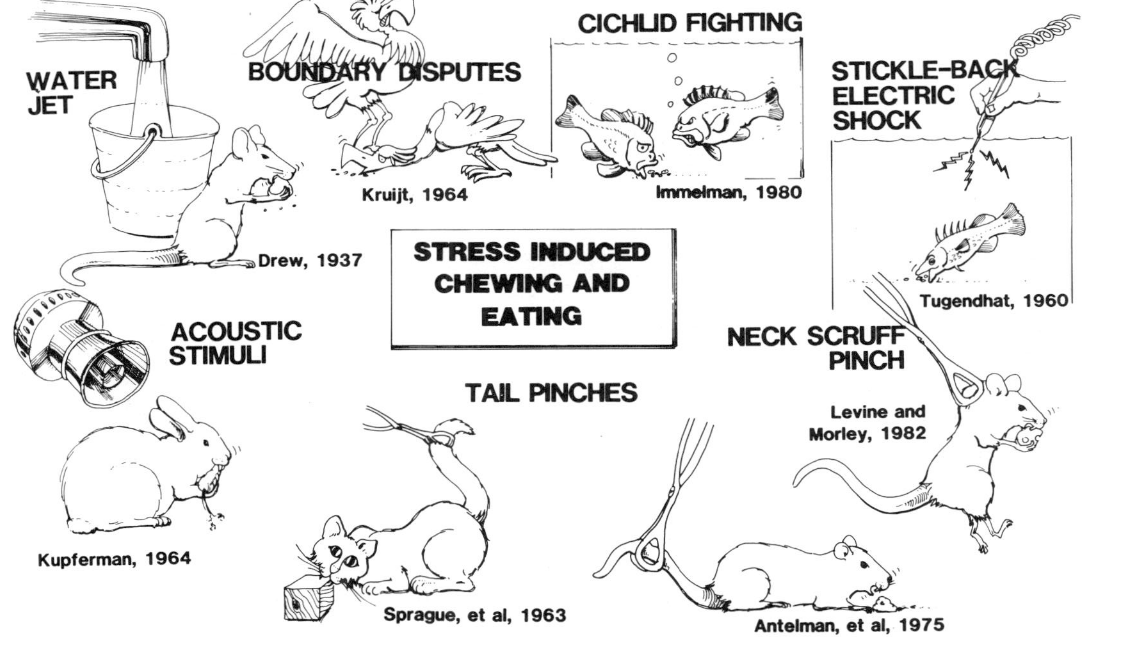

FIG. 1. A variety of examples of environmental and laboratory stressors capable of producing stress-induced eating.

housed in isolation (22, 179). Handlings rat also produces brief periods of drinking which has been shown to be secondary to abrupt alterations in circulating salt concentrations related to the handling of stress (34). Rats which are raised in isolation eat more (particularly during the day) and gain excess weight (103, 154). Electric shock has been reported to increase chewing in monkeys and rabbits (62, 68). In rats, a number of studies have suggested that electric shock may facilitate some aspects of feeding (164, 166, 173, 174).

In 1963, studies by Sprague, et al. (163) showed that mild tail pinch in normal cats and in cats with midbrain lesions induced biting of a wooden block and swallowing of wet paper or food. In 1975, Antelman and his colleagues (7, 8) reported that a sustained mild tail pinch in the rat could induce a variety of oral behaviours including gnawing, eating and licking in almost every animal tested (Figure 2). Although Rowland and Antelman (144) have reported that chronic tail pinch may lead to obesity, careful perusal of their data suggests that the weight gain must have been due to fluid filling the gut following forced feeding rather than true weight gain. Levine and Morley (78) in an analagous experiment using solid food found, in fact, that the rats tended to loose weight during chronic tail pinch. Levine and Morley (84) have shown that a mild tail pinch stimulus to other parts of the rat will induce a similar set of behaviours. Tail pinch also induces chewing and eating in mice (86) and has been shown to decrease the latency of feeding in the mollusk, Apylsia (69).

Other laboratory models of stress-induced overeating have recently been recognized. These include overeating of high fat foods following a cold swim stress (176) and neck scruff pinch producing overeating in the Siberian hamster (Bartness, Morley and Levine, unpublished observations). A particularly interesting model of stress eating has been reported by Teskey, et al. (170). In this model a large mouse is allowed to attack a smaller mouse. When the smaller mouse displays the typical posture of defeat, the smaller mouse is then given access to food. The defeated mouse then displays a stress-induced hyperphagia.

Stress, Chewing and Feeding in Humans

The relationship of oral behaviours to stress has long been recognized by humankind. The onset of depression and anxiety was correlated with spasm and contractions of the muscles of mastication by St. Mattew: "and there shall be a weeping and gnashing of teeth". Before the introduction of anesthetics, it was common practice to give the patient something to bite during surgery. Finger nail biting is a well recognized behaviour in people under stress and we are all familiar with gum chewing during examinations. The incidence of bruxism (tooth grinding) is higher in anxious or stressed children (71, 72, 180).

FIG. 2. Typical behaviours observed following the application of mild pressure (tail pinch) to the tail of a rat.

Of particular interest in regard to the interrelationship of stress, chewing and feeding is the syndrome of bulimia (23, 24). This syndrome is characterized by episodic binge eating (bulimia = ox hunger (GK)) followed by, in most cases, vomiting (2, 99, 147). The syndrome may occur alone or in association with anorexia nervosa (41, 57, 64). Pyle, et al. (139) have stressed that the onset of bulimic behaviour tends to be precipitated by a traumatic event occuring during a period of voluntary dieting. In their series, 30 of the 34 patients recalled some traumatic events associated with the onset of bulimic behaviour, the most common being loss or separation from a significant person in their life. Twenty-four of their subjects reported that a major trigger of individual binges was unhappiness, while others referred to anxiety, frustration and anger. Although stress appears to be an important precipitating factor, only 6 of the 34 patients reported stress alleviation (i.e. being satisfied or relaxed) following episodes of binge eating. We could find no report in the literature commenting on whether stress alleviation occurs during the actual binge eating episodes which may last from 15 minutes to 8 hours (100).

Another situation in which stress appears to be directly related to oral behaviours is the Lesch-Nyhan syndrome. This is an incapacitating hereditary neurological disorder of childhood characterized clinically by choreoathetosis, spasticity, mental retardation and a compulsive self mutilation associated with a deficiency of the enzyme, hypoxanthine-guanine phosphoribosyltransferase (77, 134, 150, 151). Edwin Seegmiller (152) has reported that the oral stereotypy displayed by these children (compulsive biting of the fingers, lips and tongue) is markedly increased during periods of emotional upset and has suggested that this condition may represent an amplified version of the far more common compulsive biting of lips and fingernails produced in certain individuals by stressful situations.

Numerous clinical descriptions have been reported indicating that internal emotional factors such as anxiety play a role in overeating. In the early 1950's a study was reported in which obese college undergraduates were found to gain weight during exam periodes, whereas their lean dormitory peers lost weight or had no change in weight. In 1955, Stunkard and his colleagues (167) described what has become the well-known "night-eating syndrome". In their original description they defined the night-eating syndrome as having the following characteristics: (i) consumption of at least one-quarter of one's daily caloric intake following the evening meal; (ii) sleeplessness, at least until midnight, more than half the time, (iii) morning anorexia with breakfast including no more that a cup of coffee and a small glass of orange juice. The night-eating syndrome generally occurs during periods of "life stress". In one patient, during periods of anxiety she would awake each morning with no desire to eat. Her supper then was large and she continued to nibble at sweets the rest of the evening. She later was hospitalized for phlebitis and was more than happy to go to the hospital. The morning after her admission to the hospital she ate a normal breakfast, with a small lunch and supper and did not eat in the evening. She slept well and did not complain of hunger.

Stunkard, et al. (167) felt that the morning anorexia represented a specific organic deficit. We feel, however, that a psychological explanation may be more appropriate. In informal conversations with night eaters, they invariably suggest that the morning after anorexia is occasioned by their guilt related to their eating binge of the previous night.

Gloria Leon (76) also reported on stress-induced eating in a 1973 study in which she asked patients who had lost and maintained their weight for a one-year period a series of questions. She compared this group with a group who had regained the weight they had lost and with a control group of normal-weight individuals. The regainers stated that they ate in response to a variety of states of emotional arousal. The maintainers ate due to boredom and loneliness, whereas the control group ate because of hunger. In contrast, some investigators have suggested that eating appears to be independent of anxiety and other internal clues, but instead is related to external food signals such as desirable flavors.

An unpublished study by Maher (18) indicated that fat executives in high-stress jobs weighed the same as other fat executives in low-stress jobs. However, Maher's thin executives got thinner when placed under stress. Perhaps the overweight individuals simply failed to undereat when under anxiety.

Konner (65), a biological anthropologist, has invoked psychological principles, elucidated by Schachter, to explain the differing prevalence of obesity in various social groups. As he points out in advanced industrial countries rich people tend to be thin and poor people tend to be fat, whereas in the poor countries of the underdeveloped the reverse is the case. Poor people in poor countries are thin, "obesity being conspicuously absent during famine". However, rich people in poor countries become obese because, perhaps subconsiously, they are uncertain how long an ample food supply will last. Another stressor leading to increased eating is the general economic instability. Thus, the rich in poor countries are under constant stress which leads to the ideal of "fat is beautiful". Similarly the poor in industrialized countries suffer the constant threat of famine and also the condition of subordination, both of which enhance the syndrome of anxiety-induced overeating. Thus, in the absence of better and more specifically predictive explanations, Konner (65) feels that "it seems reasonable to postulate the anxiety theory as a provisional model for the obesity of the industrial poor and the agricultural rich".

Abramson and Wunderlich (1) designed a study in which they attempted to better estimate neurotic anxiety by using predictions of later social failure; that is, they told their subjects that they would have problems in marriage and in getting along with people in general. Their results indicated that the obese ate the same amount during shock or after a prediction of social failure. This once again supports the external cue hypothesis over the so-called psychosomatic hypothesis.

Thus, there appear to be two schools of thought, one stating that obese individuals eat due to internal cues such as hunger and emotions, and another stating that eating is independent of internal cues but is due to food-related or external cues. Bruch (28) suggests that obesity may be due to inappropriate learning during early development, in which the obese child may learn to respond to emotional rather than hunger cues. This child may feel that eating represents a way of coping during emotional stress, with food representing a means of reducing anxiety. The real problem in distinguishing which of the theories is correct resides in the definition of stress-induced eating. How does one reproduce what the stressed person may be feeling ? Slochower (158) argues that obese individuals must experience diffuse, unlabeled anxiety in order for stress-induced eating to occur. In order to reproduce such anxiety, Slochower designed an ingenious experiment in which subjects received both labeled or unlabeled arousal conditions. The subjects in this study heard what they thought was their heart rate, when in actuality they heard either low (70/min) or high (88/min) heart rates generated artificially. The labeled arousal group was then told that the heart rate appeared to be high but was actually due to the acoustics of the room. The other group, referred to as unlabeled, was not given any reason for the high heart rate. Following baseline heart rate measurements, the subjects were told that they would now participate in a thinking task. The experimenter brought in several objects for the task, including a tin of cashews. The subjects were told that they could think about and touch any of the objects and could eat the nuts. This task was completed in three minutes. The normal subjects were found to eat fewer cashew nuts during the high arousal, unlabeled condition, whereas the obese individuals demonstrated large increases in food intake. Slochower and Kaplan (159) have attempted to clarify why such a tendency for obese individuals to overeat during high arousal stress occurs. For this study they added a group (control) of subjects who were told that they could return their heart rate to its normal level by simply breathing in a given fashion. Obese participants ate most when they could not control nor explain their rapid heart rate. The overeating pattern was reduced markedly when they had a sense of control and when a labeled condition existed. Normal subjects were virtually unaffected by the label or control variables. Their eating was well correlated with their hunger level and negatively correlated with their anxiety level. The eating response seemed to be effective in decreasing anxiety in the obese. In considering therapeutic applications of their findings, Slochower and Kaplan (159) suggested that one aim of obesity treatment would be to aid the obese individual in developing an ability to label and modulate anxiety states without using food as the only alternative to the anxious state. They also indicated that the label manipulation had a relatively weaker effect when compared to the control manipulation.

It has been suggested that obese individuals might simply have a more sensitive level of arousal or emotionality. This would result in increased sensitivity to either internal or external stimuli. Ross (142) attempted to measure sensitivity to an external cue by varying intensity of illumination on a bowl of cashew nuts. The increased awareness due to a change in illumination resulted in significantly increased ingestion of the cashews by the obese. Meyer and Pudel (97) studied food intake in 100 subjects with the introduction of stressors such as flickering lights, noise, and insoluble puzzles. These stressors resulted in decreased eating in some subjects and increased eating in others. In general, obese adult women showed the largest increase in food ingestion. Nisbett found that obese individuals also have heightened sensitivity to taste (133). When offered a superior vanilla ice cream, obese individuals ingested more than normal or thin subjects. In contrast, all subjects consumed about the same amount of quinine adulterated ice cream.

Schachter et al. (149) conducted a series of manipulations during which time food intake was measured. In one experiment he pre-fed obese and lean subjects two roast beef sandwiches to satiate them. Following this they gave the subjects some plain crackers to taste as part of a marketing experiment. The investigators then produced anxiety by first giving the subjects a mild but unpredicted shock and then asking them if they had a heart condition. In the lean subjects a reduction in the number of crackers eaten occured following the shock. In contrast, the obese individuals did not alter their intake. In fact, even if the subjects were not pre-fed with the sandwiches, the obese subjects ate the same quantity of crackers following the shock. Schachter and his colleagues concluded that external cues were more important to obese subjects than internal hunger or emotional states. These investigators used shock which may not accurately represent the anxiety normally experienced by obese individuals.

We have recently examined the characteristics of stress over- and under-eaters (Willenbring, Levine, Morley, in preparation). From our studies we defined two major groups of stress responders (Table 1). The stress eater tended to also be a boredom eater and had a preference for high density, sweet foods. In addition, stress eaters were unhappy with their weight and yet appeared capable of maintaining their weight at a reasonable level. This may indicate that stress-eaters who are successful at weight control do so through constant awareness of eating behaviours. Obesity in this study tended to be associated with a low awareness of problem-eating behaviours. Interestingly, stress eaters did not display a high degree of current stress suggesting that stress eating may be stress alleviating. On the other hand, stress factors tended to have a high degree of current stress (as measured by the Symptom Checklist 90). Stress fasters expressed a preference for salty over sweet foods.

TABLE 1. Characteristics of stress eaters and stress fasters

STRESS EATERS	STRESS FASTERS
Boredom eating	Younger
Sweet preferences	Salt preference
Unhappy with weight	Not overweight
Liking for high density foods	Currently stressed
Not overweight	
Not currently stressed	

Previously, using the mild tail pinch model of stress-induced eating, we have found that stress induces a preference for chewing crunchy foods (85). In fact, the rats preferred wood chips to ground rat chows. Based on these animal studies, we tested the preference for crunchy (low water density, Aw = 0.3) compared to chewy (high water density, Aw = 0.7) bars in our population. A lower preference for the test food bar containing the greater water activity (and therefore chewier texture) was predicted by both being a stress eater and high stress. Based on these studies we suggest that stress eaters may be helped by the availability of a crunchy (low water density), low caloric chew bar. Such a bar should prove a useful adjunct in the therapy of stress eaters.

Do Endogenous Opioids Modulate Stress-induced Overeating?

Following the pioneering study by Holtzman (55) in which he showed that antagonism of opioid receptors with naloxone decreases feeding, a variety of studies have suggested a role for endogenous opioids in the modulation of food intake (see 129 for a review). Central administration of a variety of opioid peptides inclunding β -endorphin and dynorphin increase feeding in sated animals (48, 74, 96, 112, 117, 125). Recently much evidence has accumulated favoring a central role for the kappa opioid receptor and its endogenous ligand dynorphin in the regulation of food intake (88, 121, 127, 148). However, it seems likely, that, as is the case for analgesia, more than one opioid receptor may be involved in the regulation of feeding.

Margules has suggested that the endogenous opioid peptides play an important role in the network of physiological responses used by animals to deal with threats to metabolic homeostasis (93). As stress, in broadest sense, represents a threat to metabolic homeostasis it would not be surprising to find that opioid peptides played a role in the physiological and behavioural responses to stress. In fact, it has been suggested that the discovery of the opioid peptide system provided a logical neurochemical extension of Hans Selye's "general adaptation to stress syndrome" (3,109). The similarities between some aspects of "reward" (e.g. brain stimulation) and appetite have been noted (98) and the opioids provide a logical connection between these two systems.

Evidence for a role for the endogenous opioids in the initiation of stress induced feeding has come from studies conducted in three separate animal models of stress-eating. In our original study we found that naloxone decreased tail pinch induced eating in rats (105). In this study we also found that prolonged chronic tail pinch led to the production of naloxone precipitable withdrawal symptoms. This suggested that prolonged tail pinch stress caused rats to become addicted to their own endogenous opioids. In addition, Ornstein (136) has reported that tail pinch will suppress "wet dog" shakes in rats in a manner similar to morphine.

Others have also reported that naloxone will decrease tail pinch induced feeding (20, 105). Further studies have shown that naloxone's suppressive effects on tail pinch eating cannot be reversed by central administration of a variety of pharmacological agents known to enhance appetite (123). Naloxone also inhibits tail pinch induced eating in mice (86). Further, the suppressive effect of a number of peptides on stress induced eating is partially reversed by a long acting methionine enkephalin analog (80, 106, 110, 123). Dexamethasone, which abolishes stress-induced release of ACTH and β-endorphin (50, 143), also decreases tail pinch induced feeding (90). Although Antelman and Rowland (12) were unable to demonstrate an effect of naloxone on tail pinch induced eating in rats, they did find that naloxone facilitated the haloperidol attenuation of tail pinch induced oral behaviours.

Rats starved for 12 hours and then subjected to a ten minute swim stress at 4°C have a marked increase in fat intake compared to rats who have been starved for 12 hours only (176). Naloxone inhibits this stress induced hyperphagia with the high fat diet being inhibited more than any other diet. β-endorphin levels have been reported to increase in concentration in different levels of the brain during cold swim stress (16). These findings suggest a role for endogenous opioids in the preferential intake of palatable foods following cold swim stress.

In the defeated mouse model of stress-induced eating, it was found that the pattern of eating was similar to that observed after morphine injection (170). As in the other two models of stress induced eating, the hyperphagia observed in the defeated mouse was attenuated by naloxone administration (170).

We measured the levels of immunoreactive dynophin in rat brain following a ten minute tail pinch period (119). We found a significant decrease in ir-dynorphin levels in the cortex but not in the hypothalamus following tail pinch.

Neck scruff pinch [which also induces eating (84)] produces a cataleptic state that can be prevented by prior administration of naloxone (4). Catalepsy also occasionally occurs during tail pinch (111) and tail pinch has been shown to facilitate morphine induced catalepsy in mice and rats as well as to potentiate morphine-induced caudate spindles in freely moving rats (14, 17, 36, 52, 60, 165). Amir and Ornstein (5) have presented evidence suggesting that pinch induced catalepsy may represent a natural defensive response involving the blockage of central dopamine systems by endogenously released opioids.

If endogenous opioids were involved in tail pinch behaviours, one would expect tail pinch to produce analgesia. In early studies, Antelman and his colleagues (10) noted that tail pinch induced apparent indifference to pin prick. Tail pinch produces naloxone-irreversible analgesia when writhing is used as the nociceptive stimulus (45, 87). These experiments suggest that tail pinch induced analgesia involves both the opiate and non-opiate pain control system (178).

As pain is a well recognized activator of endogenous opiates (169) the demonstration that tail pinch involves nociception (pain) would be necessary but not sufficient evidence to infer involvement of opiate mechanisms. Although Antelman and his colleagues (10) have consistently argued that tail pressure when applied correctly is not painful, Rowland and Marques (136) have pointed out that, at the very least, tail pinch represents an annoying stimulus and that the "demarcation between pain and annoyance (or stress) is a fuzzy line at best". Evidence that nociception plays in integral role in tail pinch behaviours includes: (i) tail pinch behaviours are blocked by a local anesthetic ring block of the tail (85); (ii) painful stimuli applied to other parts of the body, such as foot and neck, induced feeding (84); and (iii) diabetic animals with increased tail flick latencies have a prolonged latency for induction of tail pinch behaviours (86).

Antelman has stressed the similarities between the neural effects of amphetamine and tail pinch (12), and, although dopamine is a prime candidate for the similarity, opioids cannot be discounted. For example, amphetamine tolerant guinea pigs exhibit supersensitivity to naloxone with respect to feeding behaviours (59). Bilateral administration of morphine into the substancia nigra produces amphetamine-like stereotypy movements (59). Long term amphetamine exposure leads to higher levels of β-endorphin in the hypothalamus in guinea pigs and acute infusions of dextro-amphetamine induce increases in plasma β-endorphin levels in humans (32, 182). These findings suggest that endogenous opioid peptides have a role in amphetamine-induced behaviours.

The studies reviewed in this section certainly provide a strong body of evidence favoring at least some role of endogenous opioids in stress induced eating. In view of the ability of opiates to stimulate dopamine turnover and release (31, 70) this system may well be dopamine interdependent as well (*vide infra*).

The Role of Other Neurotransmitters in Streess-induced Overeating

A number of studies have shown a role for central nervous system dopamine in the regulation of tail pinch behaviours. Tail pinch feeding is abolished by bilateral 6-hydroxydopamine injections into the substantia nigra (94) and dopaminergic antagonists block tail pinch induced feeding (7, 8). It appears that dopamine antagonists block both chewing and feeding behaviours whereas opioid antagonists only decrease the feeding component leaving the chewing behaviour relatively intact (86). In addition to studies with dopamine antagonists, it appears that serotonin agonists also decrease tail pinch behaviours (11, 13, 145). On the other hand, α -adrenergic antagonists produce no effect on tail pinch behaviours (9).

A number of neuropeptides have been demonstrated to modify tail pinch induced ingestive behaviours. Tail pinch induced food ingestion has been demonstrated to be suppressed by cholecystokinin (CCK) (81, 132), bombesin (114), thyrotropin releasing hormone (114) and its metabolite - histidyl-proline diketopiperazine (108), by calcitonin (116), somatostatin (82), and substance P (107) as well as the prostaglandins (PGE_2 and $PGF_{2\ alpha}$) (79). In all of these cases it appears as if the peptides directly inhibit the ingestive response to tail pinch without suppressing the chewing response as quantitated by measuring spillage (123).

CCK has been demonstrated to be widely distributed throughout the brain as well as the gastrointestinal tract (118). CCK was the first neuropeptide implicated as a putative short-term satiety hormone (42) which potently inhibits spontaneous, sham and starvation induced feeding in the rat after peripheral administration (35, 49). Further, the satiety effect of cholecystokinin is abolished by vagotomy, suggesting a peripheral site of action (122, 160).

It was thus of interest when Nemeroff (132) showed that CCK suppressed tail pinch-induced feeding after either parenteral or central administration. Close examination of their data indicate that the doses of CCK-8 given centrally to reduce tail pinch eating are at least as great as the peripherally effective doses. It is possible that leakage of centrally administered CCK to the periphery (137) may account for the phenomena.

There is an alternative reason why centrally administered CCK may suppress tail pinch induced feeding but not other forms of eating. CCK produces opiate dependent analgesia (184) and antagonizes the analgesia due to exogenously administered opiates. CCK produces hyperglycemia after central administration (113). This hyperglycemia can be reversed by adrenalectomy. Recent studies have demonstrated that glucose can profoundly alter the opiate receptor both *in vivo* and *in vitro*, resulting in a decreased response to some opiate agonists (33, 83, 115, 155, 156). Levine and Morley (81) showed that adrenalectomy reversed not only the hyperglycemic effect of central CCK-8 but also its inhibitory action on tail pinch feeding. Thus, it seems reasonable to postulate that the unique action of CCK on tail pinch induced feeding may be secondary to its effects on opiate-mediated pain and arousal systems because of the hyperglycemia it produces. Studies by Telegdy, et al. (168) support this concept, in that, they found that after intraperitoneal injection of CCK-8, only the sulfated form inhibited food intake whereas after central injection both the sulfated and non-sulfated form were equally effective. This data suggests that CCK inhibits tail pinch-induced feeding by separate mechanisms, depending on the route of administration. The suppression of feeding produced by peripheral CCK-8 (5 μg/kg) is reversed by the concomitant administration of a number of well-known appetite stimulants; namely, a long acting enkephalin analog, diazepam, muscimol, the GABA agonist, and

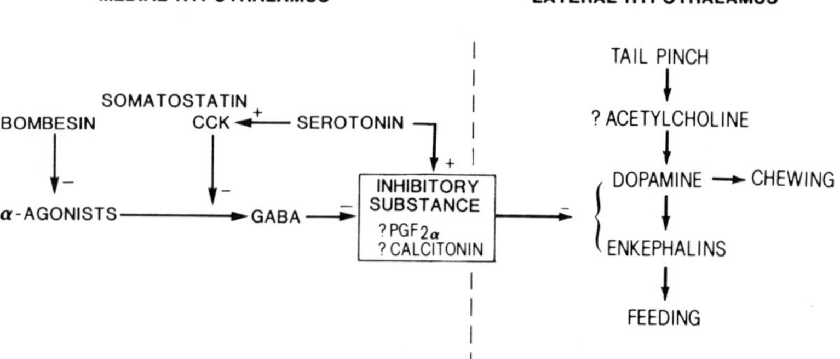

FIG. 3. Overview of the interactions of neurotransmitters involved in the regulation of stress-induced (tail pinch) behaviour. CCK = cholecystokinin; GABA = gamma amino butyric acid; PG = prostaglandins.

propranolol, the β -antagonist (123). Norepinephrine failed to reverse the suppressive effect of CCK-8 on tail pinch feeding.

Bombesin, a tetradecapeptide from frog skin, is also widely distributed throughout the mammalian gut and brain (6, 26). Bombesin suppresses tail pinch induced feeding equipotently after central and peripheral administration (114). This effect appears to be unrelated to the hyperglycemia it produces (114). Peripherally administered bombesin (5 μ g/kg) also has its suppressive effects reversed by the same substances that reverse the suppression of feeding by peripherally administered CCK-8 (123). In contrast to CCK-8, however, bombesin suppression of tail pinch feeding was also inhibited by norepinephrine.

Both CCK and bombesin inhibit tail pinch and normal feeding, suggesting common substrates could be involved. However, a critical difference was found in the ability of peripherally administered substance P to inhibit tail pinch but not starvation induced eating (107). A number of lines of evidence suggest that a balance between enkephalins and substance P may be the physiological basis of the "pain gate of Melzack and Wall" (39, 135).

Substance P has been shown to be capable of producing either analgesia or hyper-analgesia dependent on the dose administered and on the responsiveness of the animals to pain (39, 135). The effect of substance P on tail pinch induced feeding would be compatible with the concept that tail pinch feeding involves the activation of peripheral nociceptive fibers which relay via the small diameter pain fibers of the dorsal horn (54).

In an attempt to provide a cohesive model for the regulation of feeding, we have proposed a model involving monoamine-peptide interaction at the level of the central nervous system (104). The original model was based on neuropharmacological modeling techniques and applying the same principles to tail pinch eating we have developed a model to describe the neurotransmitter interactions involved in the initiation of tail pinch feeding (Figure 3). This model clearly represents an oversimplification of the situation and should be seen as a malleable matchstick diagram, which allows the design of future experiments. This model suggests that the key to tail pinch behaviours is the activation of a dopamine-opioid system. It is perceived that the dopaminergic system is predominantly responsible for initiating chewing (and other oral behaviours) while being facilitatory to the opioid system which is responsible for initiating the ingestive behaviour.

STRESS-INDUCED ANOREXIA

The most dramatic example of possibly stress-induced anorexia is that demonstrated in patients with anorexia nervosa. Anorexia nervosa is a syndrome occurring primarily in young women, characterized by self-starvation, laxative abuse, and hyperactivity. The starvation and weight loss are further associated with a variety of other pathophysiological changes, such as amenorrhea and lanugo hair. Anorexia and bulimia commonly occur together, or at different times in the same individual. How many of these physiological changes are secondary to the malnutrition and how many play a role in perpetuating the anorexia is uncertain.

Another common example of stress induced anorexia occurs in response to interpersonal loss. For example, the immediate trauma of widowhood (for man or woman) is commony associated with anorexia, especially in the elderly. In many cases food (as a symbol of life) becomes taboo at the time of bereavement. This symbolic role of food is well recognized by the "shivah" in Judaism and the "wake" in Irish Catholic homes where food is brought into the home of the bereaved family (91). Another example of stress anorexia in the elderly is when feelings of loneliness, isolation and desolation lead to a decreased food intake as a plea for attention. Once again it is the interaction of the psychological milieu with the *milieu intérieur* that leads to the activation of the anorexia syndrome. Grief induced anorexia is not, however, specific to the elderly as Spitz (162) observed that loss of primary caretakers (parents) for infants eight to ten months old can result in the infant developing "marasmus" - a gradual, steady, life threatening wasting away. Anorexia and weight loss are also comon in Major Depression, which shares many features of the acute grief reaction but is more prolonged and less clearly related to a stressor.

Corticotropin Releasing Factor (CRF) as a Mediator of Stress Anorexia

CRF is a 41 amino acid peptide which was first isolated from the ovine hypothalamus (161, 175). CRF stimulates the release of ACTH and β-endorphin from the pituitary and elevates plasma norepinephrine, epinephrine and glucose (27). Recently, both our group (89, 128) and Britton, et al. (25) have shown that centrally administered CRF is a potent reducer of nocturnal and starvation induced feeding. This effect occurs in hypophysectomized animals which suggests that it is not secondary to the effects of CRF on the pituitary (128). CRF's effect on feeding is also not dependent on intact adrenals (46). Besides its effect on nocturnal and starvation induced feeding, CRF also reduces feeding induced by a number of pharmacological agents including muscimol, norepinephrine, dynorphin, and insulin (89). Sauvagine, a peptide isolated from the skin of the frog *(Phyllomedusa sauvagei)*, has structural similarities to CRF and also stimulates the release of ACTH from the anterior pituitary (101). Sauvagine is a more potent inhibitor of feeding than is CRF (47).

CRF produces its decrease in feeding by shifting the animal to an increase in grooming (128). From the anthropomorphic point of view this is reminiscent of the excessive interest in their appearance demonstrated by some patients with anorexia nervosa. Further evidence for a role for CRF in anorexia nervosa comes from the demonstration that these patients have an "activated" hypothalamic-pituitary-adrenal axis which is suggestive of CRF excess (177). In addition, patients with anorexia nervosa respond poorly to exogenously administered CRF again suggesting an excess of CRF (43).

The effects of CRF on feeding have been localized to the paraventricular nucleus (PVN) of the hypothalamus (66). This is the area where norepinephrine acts to increase feeding and serotonin to decrease feeding (73). Norepinephrine appears to produce its effect by inhibiting the release of a satiety agent as lesions of the PVN lead to an increase in feeding (75). Norepinephrine appears to specifically increase carbohydrate intake (73) and we have found that CRF decreases carbohydrate intake while relatively sparing fat intake (Krahn, Morley, Gosnell, Romsos and Levine, Unpublished observations). Thus, CRF may well be the satiety agent that norepinephrine inhibits to produce its increase in feeding.

Pharmacological manipulations that increase the availability of or directly stimulate serotonin receptors decrease food intake while treatments that decrease serotonin release or inactivate its receptors increase food intake (21). There is evidence that serotonin releases CRF at the hypothalamic level (29). The effect of serotonin, like CRF, appears to be predominantly on carbohydrate intake (181). CRF continues to decrease feeding in rats rendered anorexic with the

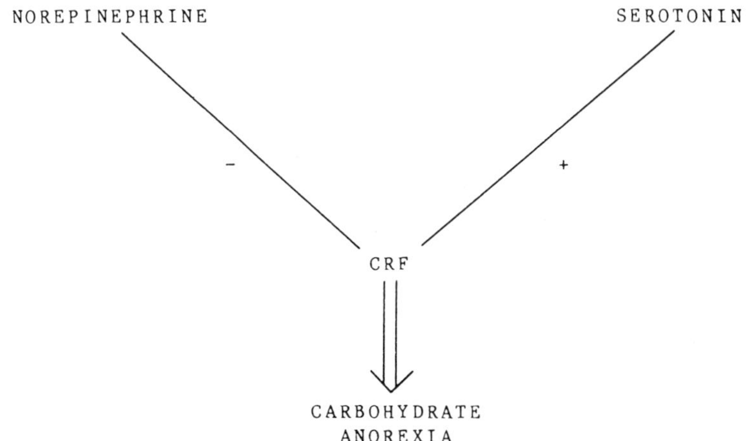

FIG. 4. The proposed interaction of norepinephrine and serotonin with CRF in the paraventricular nucleus.

serotoninenrgic agent, fenfluramine (Krahn, Gosnell, Levine and Morley, unpublished observations). These observations suggest that serotonin may produce its anorectic effect through the release of CRF. A disturbance in carbohydrate intake is a characteristic feature of anorexia nervosa (37). It has been reported that some patients with anorexia nervosa respond to treatment with the serotonin antagonist, cyproheptadine (44, 51). Based on these findings we can suggest that the feeding effects produced by norepinephrine and serotonin within the PVN involve an interaction with CRF (Figure 4).

A Model for the Neurotransmitter Abnormalities in Anorexia Nervosa

While the importance of psychosocial factors in the precipitation of anorexia nervosa is clearly recognized, it is our position that the full expression of the syndrome is secondary to the alteration in the neurotransmitters involved in the regulation of appetite. Thus, we see that the antecedent events as described by Slade (157), i.e. (i) the general setting conditions (constitutional factors) and (ii) specific psychological stimuli (environmental stressors) as being the precipitants that produce an altered neurotransmitter milieu resulting in the eating disorder developing into the perpetuating problem of anorexia nervosa. This altered neurotransmitter balance interacting with the malnutrition resulting from the downward spiraling of weight is also responsible for the production of the endocrinological changes associated with anorexia nervosa.

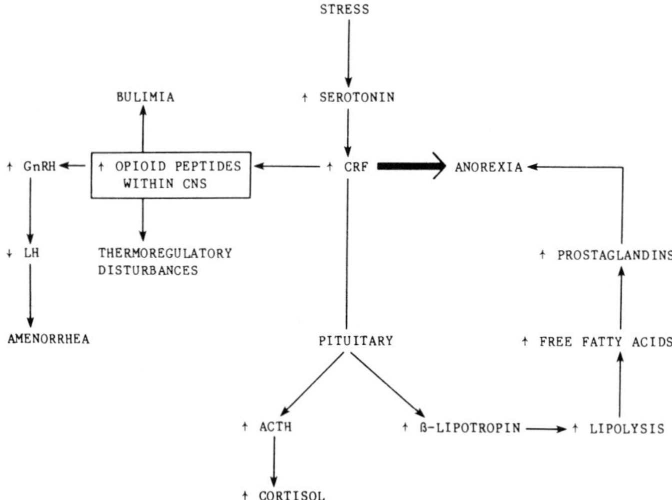

FIG. 5. Hypothetical model of the neurotransmitter interactions involved in the pathogenesis of anorexia nervosa. GnRH = gonadotropin releasing hormone; LH = luteinizing hormone; CRF = corticotropin releasing factor; CNS = central nervous system.

Kaye, et al. (61) have shown that there is an increase in opioid activity as measured in the CSF of patients with anorexia nervosa. This increase in opioid activity may be secondary to CRF stimulation of the arcuate nucleus. As endogenous opioids have been shown to play a role in stimulating food intake (120) the increase in opioid activity may explain why some patients with anorexia nervosa develop breakthrough bulemic binges. In addition, an increase in arcuate nucleus opioid activity has been shown to inhibit the release of gonadotropin releasing hormone, which in turn would lead to a decrease in luteinizing hormone (109). This would then lead to the amenorrhea associated with anorexia nervosa. Such an explanation would fit with Russel's argument (146) that anorexia nervosa is primarily a hypothalamic disorder. However, it must be recognized that a significant loss of weight or body fat (40) coupled with increased physical activity could equally explain the amenorrhea. The opioid increase could also play a role in the disturbances of thermoregulation seen in anorexia nervosa (124).

The increased activation of the proopiomelanocortin gene in the anterior pituitary by an increase in CRF could also play a role in the weight loss seen in anorexia nervosa. Firstly, peripheral administration of opioid peptides, acutely, leads to a decrease, rather than the expected increase, in food intake (128). Secondly,

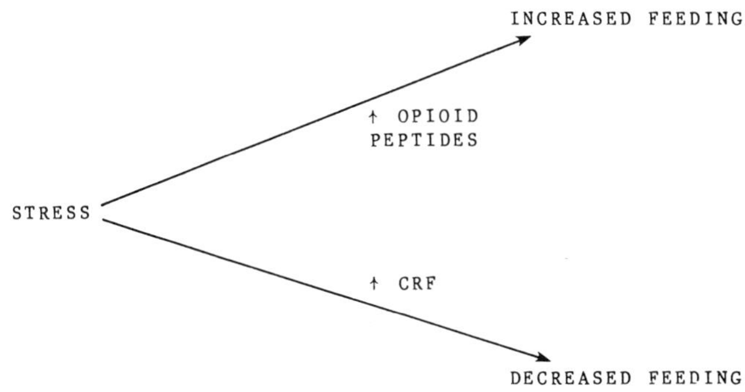

FIG. 6. Putative neuropeptides involved in stress induced eating disorders.

β-lipotropin has been shown to produce lipolysis in rabbits (140) which would lead to weight loss and also to increased free fatty acids. The increased circulating free fatty acids would provide a substrate for increased prostaglandin production. Prostaglandins are, themselves, potent inhibitors of feeding (79). Chronic morphine administration to rats causes weight loss, rather than weight gain, due to increased thermogenesis and alterations in fat metabolism (130). This further supports the possibility that circulating opioids may play a role in weight loss. Finally, in a British study in which patients with anorexia nervosa received the opioid antagonist, naltrexone, they gained weight without a noticeable increase in food intake (102). This weight gain was accompanied by a decrease in circulating fatty acids.

In our model of the neurotransmitter abnormalities associated with anorexia nervosa we suggest that non-specific environmental stressors act in the constitutionally predisposed individual to increase serotonin turnover in the PVN (Figure 5). This increased serotonin turnover then leads to release of CRF. This CRF then produces anorexia while at the same activating the portal-pituitary system with the resultant release of ACTH and β-endorphin.

CONCLUSION

Based on a large body of experimental evidence in animals it now appears that it is the interaction of a number of neurotransmitters that is responsible for the activation or deactivation of feeding mechanisms (126). Certain environmental stressors appear to activate one of the major feeding pathways viz. the opioid pathaway resulting in stress-induced overeating. Other environmental stressors activate the release of CRF leading to stress-induced undereating (Figure 6). This increased understanding of the role of neurotransmitters in the modulation of feeding could suggest a direction for the development of a logical pharmacological approach to the treatment of stress-induced eating disorders.

REFERENCES

1. Abramson, E.E., and Wunderlich, R.A. (1972): *J. Abnormal Psych.*, 79: 317-321.

2. American Psychiatric Association, (1980): *Diagnostic and Statistical Manual of Mental Disorders*, American Psychiatric Association, Washington, D.C.

3. Amir, S., Brown, Z.W., and Amit, Z. (1980): *Neurosci. Biobehav. Rev.*, 4: 77-86.

4. Amir, S., Brown, Z.W., Amit, Z., and Ornstein, K. (1981): *Life Sci.*, 28: 1189-1194.

5. Amir, S., and Ornstein, K. (1981): *Neurosci. Abstr.*, 7: 49.

6. Anastasi, A., Erspamer, V., and Bucci, A. (1971): *Experientia*, 27: 166-167.

7. Antelman, S.M., and Szechtman, H. (1975): *Science*, 189: 731-733.

8. Antelman, S.M., Szechtman, H., Chin, P., and Fisher, A.E. (1975): *Brain Res.*, 99: 319-337.

9. Antelman, S.M., Rowland, N.E., and Fisher, A.E. (1976): *Brain Res.*, 102: 346-350.

10. Antelman, S.M., and Caggiula, A.R. (1977): *Animal Models in Psychiatry and Neurology*, p. 277, Pergamon Press, New York.

11. Antelman, S.M., Caggiula, A.R., Eichler, A.J., and Lucik, R.R. (1979): *Curr. Med. Res. Opin.*, 6: 73-82.

12. Antelman, S.M., and Rowland, N. E. (1981): *Science*, 214: 1149-1151.

13. Antelman, S.M., Rowland, N.E., and Kocan, D. (1981): In: *Anorectic Agent Mechanisms of Action and Tolerance*, edited by S. Garattini and R. Samanin, p. 43. Raven Press, New York.

14. Ariyanayagum, A.D., and Handley, S.L. (1975): *Psychopharmacology*, 41: 165-167.

15. Barrett, S.A. (1958): *J. Psychosom. Res.* , 3: 1-11.

16. Barta, A., and Yashpal, K. (1981): *Prog. Neuropsychopharmacol.*, 5: 595-598.

17. Beecham, I.J., and Handley, S.L. (1975): *Psychopharmacology*, 41: 165-167.

18. Beller, A.S. (1977): *Fat and Thin : A Natural History of Obesity*, McGraw-Hill Book Company, New York.

19. Bendra, D., and Spinner, N. (1958): *J. Exp. Anal. Behav.*, 1: 341-347.

20. Bertiere, M.C., Mome, Sy T., Baigts, F., Mandenoff, A., and Apfelbaum, M. (1984): *Pharmacol. Biochem. Behav.*, 20: 675-679.

21. Blundell, J.E. (1977): *Int. J. Obes.*, 1: 15-42.

22. Booth, D.A., and Campbell, C.S. (1975): *Physiol. Behav.*, 15: 523-535.

23. Boskind-Lodahl, M. (1975): *Bulimarexia*, Ph. D. Thesis, Cornell.

24. Boskind-Lodahl, M. J. (1976): *Women in Culture and Society*, 2: 342-356.

25. Britton, D., Koob, G., Rivier, J., and Vale, W. (1982): *Life Sci.*, 31: 363-367.

26. Brown, M.R., Allen, R., Villareal, J., Rivier, J., and Vale, W. (1978): *Life Sci.*, 23: 2721-2728.

27. Brown, M.R., Fisher, L.A., Rivier, J., Spiess, J., Rivier, C., and Vale, W. (1982): *Life Sci.*, 30: 207-210.

28. Bruch, H. (1973): *Eating Disorders: Obesity, Anorexia Nervosa, and Person Within*, Basic Books, New York.

29. Buckingham, J.C. (1980): *Pharmacol. Biochem. Behav.*, 31: 253-274.

30. Carr, D.B., Bullen, B.A., Skinnar, G.S., Arnold, M.A., Rosenblatt, M., Beitus, I.Z., Martin, J.B., and McArthur, J.W. (1981): *N. Engl. J. Med.*, 305: 560-562.

31. Chesselet, M.F., Cheramy, A., Reisine, T.D., Glowinski, J. (1981): *Nature*, 291: 320-322.

32. Cohen, M.R., Nurnberger, J.J., Pickar, D., Gershon, E., and Bunney, W.E. (1981): *Life Sci.* , 29: 1243-1247.

33. Davis, W.M., Miya, T.S., and Edwards, L.D. (1956): *J. Am. Pharm. Assoc.*, 45: 60-62.

34. Deaux, E., and Kakolewski, J.W. (1970): *Science*, 169: 1226.

35. Della-Fera, M.A., and Baile, C.A. (1979): *Science*, 206: 471-473.

36. Dereyck, M., Schallert, T., and Teitelbaum, P., (1980): *Brain Res.*, 201: 143-172.

37. Donohoe, T.P. (1984): *Life Sci.* 34: 203-218.

38. Drew, G.C., (1937): *Proc. Zoological Soc. Lond.*, 107: 95-106.

39. Frederickson, R.C., Bargis, V., Harrell, C.E., and Edwards, J.D. (1978): *Science*, 199: 1359-1361.

40. Frisch, R.E. (1984): *Biol. Rev.*, 59: 161-188.

41. Garfinkel, P.E., Moldofsky, H., and Garner, D.M. (1980): *Arch. Gen. Psychiatry*, 37: 1036-1040.

42. Gibbs, J., Young, R.C., and Smith, G.P. (1973): *Nature*, 245: 323-325.

43. Gold, P.N., Chousos, G., Kellner, C., Post, R., Roy, A., Augennos, P., Schulte, H., Oldenfield, E., and Loriaux, D.L. (1984): *Am. J. Psychiatry* 141: 619-627.

44. Goldberg, S.C., Halmi, K.A., Eckert, E.D., Casper, R.C., and Davis, J.M. (1979): *Br. J. Psychiatry*, 134: 67-70.

45. Goldman, R.G., Elson, J.F., and Lytle, L.D. (1980): *Fed. Proc. Am. Soc. Biol.*, 39: 602.

46. Gosnell, B.A., Morley, J.E., and Levine, A.S. (1983): *Peptides*, 4: 807-812.

47. Gosnell, B.A., Morley, J.E., and Levine, A.S. (1983): *Pharmacol. Biochem. Behav.*, 19: 771-775.

48. Grandison, L., and Guidotti, A. (1977): *Neuropharmacology*, 16: 533-536.

49. Grinker, J.A., Schneider, B.S., Ball, G., Cohen, A., Strohmayer, A., and Hirsh, J. (1980): *Fed. Proc.*, 39: 1234A.

50. Guillmein, R., Vargo, T., Rossier, J., Minnick, S., Ling, N., Rivier, C., Vale, W., and Bloom, F. (1977): *Science*, 197: 1367-1369.

51. Halmi, K.A., Eckert, E.D., and Falk, J.R. (1983): *Psychopharmacol. Bull.*, 19: 103-105.

52. Heft, M., Daniels, G., Buller, A., and Riley, A. (1981): *Neurosci. Abstr.*, 7: 854.

53. Hinde, R. (1952): *Behaviour*, Suppl. 2: 1-199.

54. Hokfeldt, T., Johansson, O., Ljungdahl, A., Lundberg, J.M., and Schutzberg, M. (1980): *Nature,* 284: 515-521.

55. Holtzman, S.G. (1974): *J. Pharmacol. Exp. Ther.,* 189: 51-60.

56. Howell, S.C., and Lowb, M.G. (1969): *Gerontologist,* 9: 46-52.

57. Hsu, C.K. (1980): *Arch. Gen. Psychiat.,* 37: 1041-1046.

58. Immelman, K. (1980): *Introduction to Ethology,* Plenum Press, New York.

59. Iwamoto, E.T., and Way, E.L. (1977): *J. Pharmacol. Exp. Ther.,* 203: 347-359.

60. Katz, R.J. (1980): *Prog. Neuropsychopharmacol. Biol. Psychiatry,* 4: 309-312.

61. Kaye, W.H., Pickar D., Ebert, M.H., and Naber, D. (1982): *Am. J. Psychiatry,* 139: 643-645.

62. Kelly, D.D. (1973): *J. Exp. Anal. Behav.,* 20: 93-104.

63. Kennedy, L., (1978): Cited in Antelman, S.M. and Caggiula, A.R. (1978): In: *Animal Models in Psychiatry and Neurology,* edited by I. Hanin and E. Usdin, p. 227, Pergamon Press, New York.

64. King, A. (1963): *Br. J. Psychiatry,* 109: 470-479.

65. Konner, M. (1982): *The Tangled Wing,* Harper & Row, New York.

66. Krahn, D.D., Gosnell, B.A., Levine, A.S., Morley, J.E. (1984): *Soc. Neurosci. Abstr.,* 10: 302.

67. Kruijt, J.P. (1964): *Behaviour,* 12: 1-201.

68. Kupferman, I. (1964): *Nature,* 201: 324.

69. Kupferman, I. and Weiss, K.R. (1981): *Behav. Neural. Biol.,* 32: 126-132.

70. Kuschinsky, K., and Hornykiewicz, O. (1972): *Eur. J. Pharmacol.,* 19: 119-122.

71. Lefer, L. (1971): *Postgrad. Med.,* 49: 171-175.

72. Lefer, L. (1975): *Comparative Textbook of Psychology,* William Wilkins, Baltimore.

73. Leibowitz, S.F. (1980): In: *Handbook of the Hypothalamus, Volume 3,* Edited by P. Morgane and J. Panksepp, pp. 299-437. Marcel-Dekker, New York.

74. Leibowitz, S.F., and Hor, L. (1982): *Peptides,* 3: 421-428.

75. Leibowitz, S.F., Hammer, N.J., and Chang, K. (1983). *Pharmacol. Biochem. Behav.,* 19: 945-950.

76. Leon, G.R., and Chamberlain, K. (1973): *J. Cons. Clin. Psych.,* 40: 474-477.

77. Lesch, M. and Nyhan, W.L. (1964): *Am. J. Med.,* 36: 561-570.

78. Levine, A.S., and Morley, J.E. (1981): *Am. J. Physiol.,* 241: R72-R76.

79. Levine, A.S., and Morley, J.E. (1981): *Pharmacol. Biochem. Behav.,* 15: 735-738.

80. Levine, A.S., and Morley, J.E. (1981): *Pharmacol. Biochem. Behav.,* 15: 735-738.

81. Levine, A.S., and Morley, J.E., (1981): *Reg. Peptides,* 2: 353-357.

82. Levine, A.S., and Morley, J.E. (1981): *Brain Res.,* 222: 187-191.

83. Levine, A.S., Morley, J.E., Brown, D.M., and Handwerger, B.S. (1981): *Physiol. Behav.,* 28: 987-989.

84. Levine, A.S., and Morley, J.E. (1982): *Physiol. Behav.* 28: 565-567.

85. Levine, A.S., and Morley, J.E. (1982): *Appetite* 3: 135-138.

86. Levine, A.S., Morley, J.E., Wilcox, G., Brown, D.M., and Handwerger, B.S. (1982): *Physiol. Behav.* 28: 39-43.

87. Levine, A.S., Wilcox, G.F., Grace, M., and Morley, J.E. (1982): *Physiol. Behav.,* 28: 959-962.

88. Levine, A.S., and Morley, J.E. (1983): *Life Sci.,* 32: 781-785.

89. Levine, A.S., Rogers, B., Kneip, J., Grace, M., and Morley, J.E. (1983): *Neuropharmacology,* 22: 337-339.

90. Lowy, M.T., and Yim, G.K.W. (1980): *Life Sci.,* 27: 2553-2558.

91. Mandelbaum, D.G. (1959): In: *The Meaning of Death,* edited by H. Feifel, pp. 189-217. McGraw-Hill Book Co., New York.

92. Manning, A. (1972): *An Introduction to Animal Behavior* Addison-Wesley Publishing Co., Reading.

93. Margules, D.L. (1979): *Neurosci. Biobehav. Rev.*, 3: 155-162.

94. Marshall, J.F., Richardson, J.S., and Teitelbaum, P. (1974): *J. Comp. Physiol. Psychol.*, 87: 808-830.

95. McFarland, D.J. (1965): *Anim. Behav.*, 13: 293-300.

96. McLean, S., and Hoebel, B.G. (1982): *Peptides* 4: 287-292.

97. Meyer, J.E., and Pudel, V.E. (1977): *Psychosom. Med.*, 39: 153-157.

98. Miller, N.E. (1967): *Handbook of Physiology: Section 6, Alimentary Canal*, p. 51, American Physiological Society, Washington, D.C.

99. Mitchell, J.E., and Pyle, R.L. (1982): *Int. J. Eating Disorders* 1: 61-73.

100. Mitchell, J.E., Pyle, R.L., and Eckert, E.D. (1981): *Am. J. Psychiatry*, 138: 835-836.

101. Montecucchi, P.C. and Henchen, A. (1981): *Int. J. Pep. Prot. Res.*, 18: 113-120.

102. Moore, R., Mills, I.H., and Forster, A. (1981): *J. Roy. Soc. Med.*, 74: 129-131.

103. Morgan, M.J. (1973): *Anim. Behav.*, 21: 429-442.

104. Morley, J.E. (1980): *Life Sci.*, 27: 355-368.

105. Morley, J.E., and Levine, A.S. (1980): *Science*, 209: 1259-1261.

106. Morley, J.E., and Levine, A.S. (1980): *Life Sci.*, 27: 1269-274.

107. Morley, J.E., and Levine, A.S. (1980): *Eur. J. Pharmacol.*, 67: 309-311.

108. Morley, J.E., and Levine, A.S. (1980): *Life Sci.*, 27: 269-274.

109. Morley, J.E. (1981): *Metabolism*, 30: 195-209.

110. Morley, J.E., and Levine, A.S. (1981): *Pharmacol. Biochem. Behav.*, 14: 149-151.

111. Morley, J.E., and Levine, A.S. (1981): *Science*, 214: 1150-1151.

112. Morley, J.E., and Levine, A.S. (1981): *Life Sci.*, 29: 1901-1903.

113. Morley, J.E., and Levine, A.S. (1981): *Life Sci.*, 28: 2187-2190.

114. Morley, J.E., and Levine, A.S. (1981): *Pharmacol. Biochem. Behav.*, 14: 149-151.

115. Morley, J.E., Levine, A.S., Hess, S.A., Brown, D.M., and Handwerger, B.S. (1981): *Soc. Neurosci. Abstr.*, 7: 854.

116. Morley, J.E., Levine, A.S., and Prasad, C. (1981): *Brain Res.*, 210: 475-478.

117. Morley, J.E. (1982): *Diagn. Med.*, 5: 39-47.

118. Morley, J.E. (1982): *Life Sci.*, 30: 479-493.

119. Morley, J.E., Elson, M.K., Levine, A.S., and Shafer, R.B. (1982): *Peptides*, 3: 901-906.

120. Morley, J.E., and Levine, A.S. (1982): *Am. J. Clin. Nutr.*, 35: 757-761.

121. Morley, J.E., Levine, A.S., Grace, M., and Kneip, J. (1982):*Life Sci.*, 31: 2617-2626.

122. Morley, J.E., Levine, A.S., Kneip, J., and Grace, M. (1982):*Life Sci.* 30: 1943-1947.

123. Morley, J.E., Levine, A.S., Murray, S.S., Kneip, J., and Grace, M. (1982):*Am. J. Physiol.* 243: R159-R163.

124. Morley, J.E., Levine, A.S., Oken, M.M., Grace, M., and Kneip, J. (1982):*Peptides* 3: 1-6.

125. Morley, J.E., and Levine, A.S. (1983):*Peptides* 4: 797-800.

126. Morley, J.E. and Levine, A.S. (1983):*Lancet* , i: 398-401.

127. Morley, J.E., Levine, A.S., Grace, M., Kneip, J., and Zeugner, H. (1983):*Eur. J. Pharmacol.*, 93: 265-269.

128. Morley, J.E., Levine, A.S., and Rowland, N.E. (1983):*Life Sci.* 32: 2169-2182.

129. Morley, J.E., Levine, A.S., Yim, G.K.W., and Lowy, M.T. (1983): *Neurosci. Biobehav. Rev.* 7: 281-305.

130. Morley, J.E., Bartness, T.J., Gosnell, B.A., and Levine, A.S. (1984): In:*International Review of Neurobiology*, edited by R.J. Bradley. Academic Press, San Diego, CA.

131. Morley, J.E., Levine, A.S., and Willenbring, M.L. (1984): *Clin. Neuropharmacol.* 7: 702-703.

132. Nemeroff, C.B., Osbahr, A.J., Bissette, G., Jahnke, G., Lipton, M.A., and Prange, A.J. (1978):*Science* 200: 793-794.

133. Nisbett, R. (1968):*Science*, 159: 1254-1255.

134. Nyhan, W.L. (1972):*Arch. Int. Med.*, 130: 186-192.

135. Oehme, P., Hilse, E., Morgenstern, E., and Gores, E. (1980): *Science* 208: 305-307.

136. Ornstein, K. (1981):*Physiol. Behav.* 27: 13-17.

137. Passaro, E., Debas, H., Oldendorg, W., and Yamada, T. (1982): *Brain Res.*, 241: 338-340.

138. Peckwell, G.B. (1931):*Trans. Acad. Sci. St. Louis* 27: 1-160.

139. Pyle, R.L., Mitchell, J.E., and Eckert, E.D. (1981): *J. Clin. Psychiatry*, 42: 60-64.

140. Richter, W.O., Kerscher, P., and Schwandt, P. (1984): *Neuropeptides*, 4: 167-173.

141. Robbins, T.W., and Fray, P.J. (1980): *Appetite*, 1: 103-133.

142. Ross, L. (1974): In: *Obese Humans and Rats*, edited by Schachter, S. and Roden, J., pp. 43-51. Erlbaum, Potomac, MD.

143. Rossier, J., French, E., Rivier, C., Shibasaki, T., Guillemin, R., and Bloom, F.E. (1980): *Proc. Natl. Acad Sci. USA*, 77: 666-669.

144. Rowland, N.E., and Antelman, S.M. (1976): *Science*, 191: 310-312.

145. Rowland, N.E., Antelman, S.M., and Kocan, D. (1982): *Eur. J. Pharmacol.*, 81: 57-66.

146. Russell, G.F.M. (1977): *Psychol. Med.*, 7: 363-367.

147. Russell, G. (1979): *Psychol. Med.* 9: 429-448.

148. Sanger, D.J. and McCarthy, P.S. (1981): *Psychopharmacology*, 74: 217-220.

149. Schachter, S., Goldman, R., and Gordon, A. (1968): *J. Pers. Soc. Psychol.* 10: 91-97.

150. Seegmiller, J.E., Rosenbloom, F.M., and Kelley, W. (1967): *Science* 155: 1682-1684.

151. Seegmiller, J.E. (1969-70): *Harvey Lect.*, 65: 175-192.

152. Seegmiller, J.E. (1980): *Metabolic Control and Disease*, p. 777. W.B. Saunders Co., Philadelphia.

153. Selye, H. (1976): *The Stress of Life*, McGraw-Hill Book Co., New York.

154. Shelley, H.P. (1965): *Psychosomatic Sci.*, 3: 521-522.

155. Simon, G.S., and Dewey, W.L. (1981): *J. Pharmacol. Exp. Ther.*, 218: 318-323.

156. Simon, G.S., and Dewey, W.L. (1981): *J. Pharmacol. Exp. Ther* 218: 324-329.

157. Slade, P. (1982): *Br J. Clin. Psychol.*, 21: 167-180.

158. Slochower, J. (1976): *Psychosom. Med.*, 38: 131-139.

159. Slochower, J. (1980): *Appetite*, 1:75-79.

160. Smith, G.P., Jerome, C., Cushin, B.J., Eterno, R., and Simansky, K.J. (1981): *Science*, 213: 1036-1037.

161. Spiess, J., Rivier, J., Rivier, C., and Vale, W. (1981): *Proc. Natl. Acad. Sci. USA*, 78: 6517-6521.

162. Spitz, R. (1965): *The First Year of Life*, International University Press, New York.

163. Sprague, J.M., Levitt, M., Robson, K., Lui, C.N., Stellar, E., and Chambers, W.N. (1963): *Arch. Ital. Biol.*, 101: 225.

164. Sterritt, G.M. (1962): *J. Comp. Physiol. Psychol.*, 55: 226-229.

165. Stille, G., and Sayers, A. (1975): *Pharmakopsychology*, 8: 105.

166. Strongman, K.T. (1965): *Quart. J. Exp. Psychol.*, 17: 255-272.

167. Stunkard, A.J., Grace, W.J., and Wolff, H.G. (1955): *Am. J. Med.*, 19: 78-86.

168. Telegdy, G., Kadar, T., Kovacs, K., and Penke, B. (1984): *Life Sci.*, 35: 163-170.

169. Terenius, L. (1978): *Ann. Rev. Pharmacol. Toxicol.*, 18: 189.

170. Teskey, G.C., Kavaliers, M., and Hirst, M. (1984): *Life Sci.*, 35: 303-316.

171. Tinbergen, N. (1937): *Ardea*, 26: 222-223.

172. Tugendhat, B. (1960): *Science*, 132: 896-897.

173. Ullman, A.D. (1951): *J. Comp. Physiol. Psychol.*, 44: 575-581.

174. Ullman, A.D. (1952): *J. Comp. Physiol. Psychol.*, 45: 490-496.

175. Vale, W., Spiess, J., Rivier, C., and Rivier, J. (1981): *Science*, 213: 1394-1397.

176. Vaswani, K., Tejwani, G.A., and Mousa, S. (1983): *Life Sci.*, 32: 1983-1986.

177. Walsh, B.T. (1980): *Psychiat. Clin. North Am.*, 3: 299-312.

178. Watkins, L.R., and Mayer, D.J. (1982): *Science*, 216: 1185-1192.

179. Wesley, F. (1978): *New Scientist*, 80: 57-58.

180. Willis, S.E. II, (1964): *New Dimensions in Psychosomatic Medicine*, pp. 1768, Little Brown & Co., Boston.

181. Wurtman, R.J. (1982): *Sci. Amer.*, 246: 50-59.

182. Wuster, M., Schule, B., and Herz, A. (1980): *Brain Res.*, 189: 403-411.

183. Yates, A., Leehey, K., and Shisslak, M. (1983): *N. Engl. J. Med.*, 308: 251-255.

184. Zetler, G. (1980): *Neuropharmacology*, 19: 415-422.

Pharmacology of Eating Disorders: Theoretical and Clinical Developments, edited by M. O. Carruba and J. E. Blundell. Raven Press, New York © 1986.

Regulation of Body Weight and Its Implications for the Treatment of Obesity

Albert J. Stunkard

Department of Psychiatry, University of Pennsylvania, Philadelphia, Pennsylvania 19014

A decade ago, it could be said that "Most people will not enter treatment for obesity; of those who do enter such treatment most will drop out of it; of those who remain in treatment most will not lose very much weight and of those who lose weight, most will regain it. Furthermore, most will pay a high price for trying" (22).

The treatment of obesity has improved since that gloomy pronouncement. Nevertheless, it is still true that drop-out rates remain high, weight losses are modest, and the maintenance of these losses infrequent. One thing, however, has changed during the past years. The explanation for this sorry state of affairs has undergone a 180 degree change of direction and today we understand far better than we did before why it is so hard to treat obesity. The change in our understanding is one from a primarily psychogenic explanation of obesity to a primarily somatogenic one. It now appears that these problems are a result of the regulation of body weight.

THE REGULATION OF BODY WEIGHT

Normal Weight Animals and Humans

For many years discussions of the origins of obesity started with what seemed a truism: obesity results from a disorder in the regulation of body weight. Nothing seemed more obvious. The wild fluctuations in the body weights of obese persons posed a sharp contrast to the remarkable stability of the weights of experimental animals, and of many humans of normal weight. This contrast was even more striking when the remarkable regulatory ability of experimental animals was examined.

When the body weight of experimental animals was altered by a variety of experimental manipulations it predictably followed by a return to its previous level when the source of the perturbation was removed. For example, rats made obese by force-feeding (2), or by insulin injections (11), will subsequently lower their body weight to control levels when the manipulations are stopped. Similarly, rats made underweight by food restriction will increase their body weight to control levels when permitted to return to *ad libitum* feeding (9). Furthermore, they respond to changes in the caloric density of their diet by increasing or decreasing food intake so as to maintain a stable body weight (1). The evidence for regulation of body weight in these animals is thus based not only upon their ability to maintain a constant body weight under usual conditions, but to defend that body weight against attempts to raise or lower it.

Migration and hibernation provide particularly compelling illustrations of the remarkable ability of some animals to regulate their body weight. These animals not only maintain a constant body weight under usual circumstances, but they can also perform extraordinary feats of anticipatory regulation. Prior to its 600 mile flight across the Caribbean Sea, the ruby-throated hummingbird undergoes a period of premigratory hyperphagia which produces fat stores sufficient to provide energy for this long flight, plus a reserve sufficient for excess flying time in the event of adverse wind conditions (18). Similarly, golden-mantled ground squirrels undergo a period of prehibernatory hyperphagia that produces fat stores sufficient to provide energy for several winter months plus a reserve sufficient for their survival during an unexpectedly prolonged winter (19).

The regulation of body weight in organisms of normal weight is not confined to animals. Two experiments with humans indicate that people of normal weight can also regulate body weight with considerable accuracy. A classic experiment by Keys and his colleagues during World War II investigated the effects of severe caloric deprivation upon young adult male volunteers (13). Restriction of their caloric intake to 50 % of its normal value for 24 weeks reduced the body weight of these volunteers to 75 % of its usual value. When they were subsequently allowed to eat as much as they wished, their body weight increased to its preexperimental level and stopped there.

A complementary experiment investigated the effects of excessive food intake upon a similar group of young adult male volunteers of normal weight (20). These men consumed diets containing two to three times their usual caloric intake until their body weight reached 125 % of its initial value. Thereafter, when they were permitted to eat as much as they wished, these men restricted their food intake and their body weights fell to their preexperimental levels.
Evidently, the precise regulation of body weight of so many animals also characterizes humans of normal weight.

Fat Rats

Study of the regulatory capacities of obese animals soon followed demonstration of the regulatory capacity on non-obese animals. The very first study dealt a severe blow to the regulatory disorder theory of obesity. When rats made obese by hypothalamic lesions were tested for their ability to regulate body weight, it was found that they too regulated body weight ! Figure 1 depicts one of the first demonstrations of the regulation of body weight by a hypothalamic obese rat (11). After its body weight had reached an asymptote at its high postoperative level, force-feeding produced further increases in weight. When force-feeding was discontinued, body weight returned to its previous level. Similarly, Figure 1 shows that weight lost by starvation was promptly regained when the animal was given free access to food.

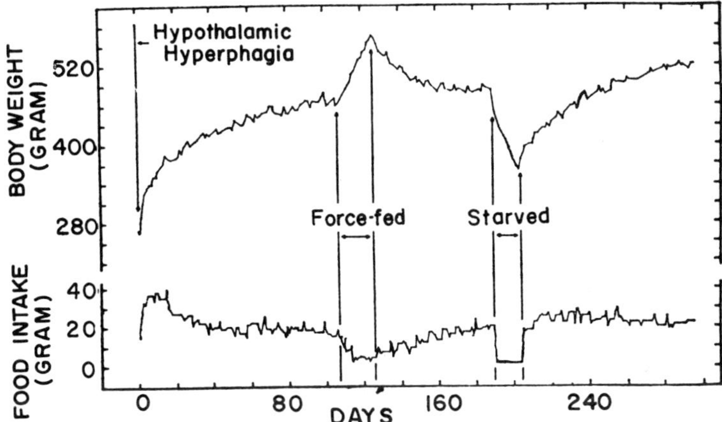

FIG. 1. Effects of force-feeding and starvation on food intake and body weight of a rat with ventromedial hypothalamic lesions. (Adapted from Hoebel and Teitelbaum, 1966).

Body weight is thus regulated in the hypothalamic obese rat (11) and in other, genetic, (4) strains of obesity. But, if regulation is not impaired, why are these animals obese ? One suggestion is that their obesity results from an elevation in the set point about which body weight is regulated (17). Hypothalamic obese rats, according to this view, are not fat simply because they overeat; they overeat in order to become fat.

An ingenious experiment tested this theory (11). Figure 2 shows the production of obesity by insulin injections in Rat Number 3. When its weight had reached 475 grams, the ventromedial hypothalamus was destroyed. In contrast to the usual result of such damage, there was no increase in body weight, suggesting that the lesion simply elevated the setpoint to the level of body weight that had already been reached. The existence of a set point at about 475 grams was further substantiated by the consequences of a period of starvation and weight loss. When the rat was allowed free access to food, its body weight returned promptly to its previous level. Indeed, the rate of weight gain from its starvation-induced nadir was approximately the same as that of Rat Number 4, which shows the more usual course of hypothalamic obesity in which weight gain promptly follows hypothalamic damage.

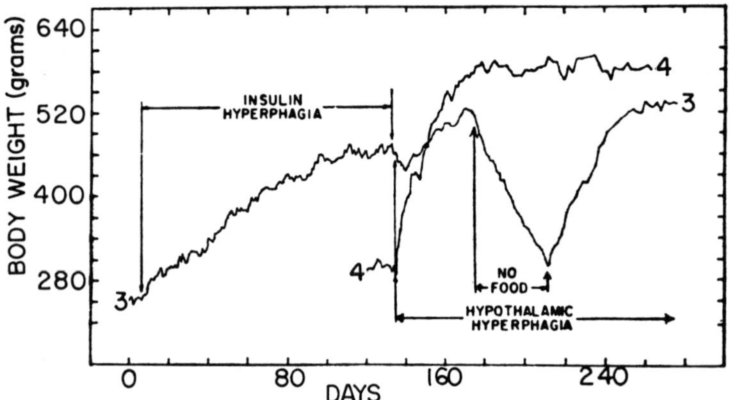

FIG. 2. Failure of a rat to increase body weight following ventromedial hypothalamic lesions when obesity had already been produced by chronic insulin injection. The usual course of increase in body weight following such lesions is seen in the second rat. Food intake not shown. (Adapted from Hoebel and Teitelbaum, 1966).

Thin Rats

Hypothalamic lesions, this time in the lateral hypothalamus (LH), can also render rats *underweight.* Two experiments by Keesey and his colleagues show the mirror image of the results with obese rats: a return of body weight to baseline after it has been artificially raised, and lowered (12). When LH-lesioned rats are force-fed, their body weight increases. When they are permitted to feed *ad libitum*, body weight promptly returns to its usual lower level. The primary effect of the LH lesions is apparently upon the body weight set point. As with hypothalamic obese animals, changes in food intake appears to be secondary to establishment of this new level of regulation.

Further evidence for the regulation of body weight in LH-lesioned animals is provided by a parallel experiment with food deprivation (12). Restriction of food intake lowers the weight of LH-lesioned animals. When allowed free access to food, their body weight promptly returns to its earlier level. The pattern of weight change of the LH-lesioned animals closely parallels that of the non-lesioned animals subjected to the same level of deprivation. Both regain at the same rate and take the same number of days to reach their predeprivation level. The only difference between the LH-lesioned and the normal animals is in the level of the body weights which each defended.

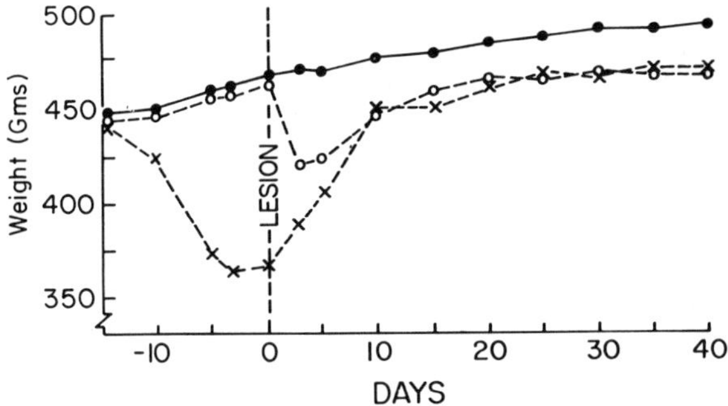

FIG. 3 Body weight of control and lateral-hypothalamic-lesioned rats as a function of weight at time of lesioning. Solid circles refer to rats fed *ad libitum*. Open circles refer to rats fed *ad libitum* prior to lesioning. Xs refers to rats whose body weight had been reduced to 80 % of control values by partial starvation prior to lesioning. (Redrawn from Keesey et al., 1976).

These experiments indicate that LH-lesioned animals regulate their body weight and they are compatible with the theory that lateral hypothalamic lesions lower a body weight set point. They do not, however, test the theory in the same manner as the experiment illustrated in Figure 2 tested parallel theory that ventromedial hypothalamic lesions elevate a body weight set point. Such a test would require that body weight be lowered to the level to be achieved by the lateral hypothalamic lesion and then finding that the lesion produces no further weight loss. Precisely this outcome is depicted in Figure 3. It shows the changes in body weight produced by lateral hypothalamic lesions in rats of normal weight and in those in which body weight had been reduced by food deprivation. Following the lesion, the body weight of the normal weight animals fell to 93% of its previous value and then returned to a steady state. Following the lesion, the body weight of the food-deprived animals, however, showed a dramatic and paradoxical *increase*, a most unusual response to lateral hypothalamic lesions. When their body weight climbed to 93% of control values, it returned to a steady state. Lesions of the lateral hypothalamus apparently establish a new and lower body weight set point; changes in food intake appear to be secondary to the establishment of this new level of regulation.

Anorectic Agents

Levitsky and his colleagues have shown that anorectic agents apparently act precisely like lateral hypothalamic lesions; they primarily lower a body weight set point and only secondarily suppress appetite (14). Their experimental paradigm closely paralleled that of Keesey's. They first deprived rats of food so as to reduce their body weight. The anorectic agent fenfluramine was then administered to these rats and to a control group whose body weight had remained at its baseline value.

Figure 4 shows that fenfluramine given to rats at their normal body weight brings about the usual response of a decrease in body weight. Thereafter, weight increased slowly, parallel to that of the control rats, but at a lower level. By contrast, rats which had previously lost weight showed no drug-induced suppression of appetite. Instead, their food intake and body weight *increased* during the first few days on fenfluramine. When their body weight reached that of rats which had received fenfluramine at normal body weight, weight gain decreased to the same slow rate. It was as if their weight increased to the level set by that particular dose of fenfluramine. When fenfluramine was discontinued, the body weights of both groups of fenfluramine-treated rats rapidly increased toward control levels. These effects are not confined to fenfluramine, but occur also with d-amphetamine, an agent whose pharmacological and behavioral actions differ radically from those of fenfluramine (14).

These experiments with anorectic agents are remarkably similar to Keesey's experiments with brain lesions, illustrated in Figure 3. They differ only in the reversibility of the manipulation. Surgical lowering of the set point is irreversible; pharmacological lowering is reversible. In each case, food intake is determined by pressures to reach a new set point. When this new set point is higher than the current weight, the usual anorectic response to both lateral hypothalamic lesions and to anorectic agents reversed. Under both circumstances, animals overeat !

Hervey and Parabiosis

Additional support for the regulation of food intake and the existence of body weight set points is provided by Hervey's study of

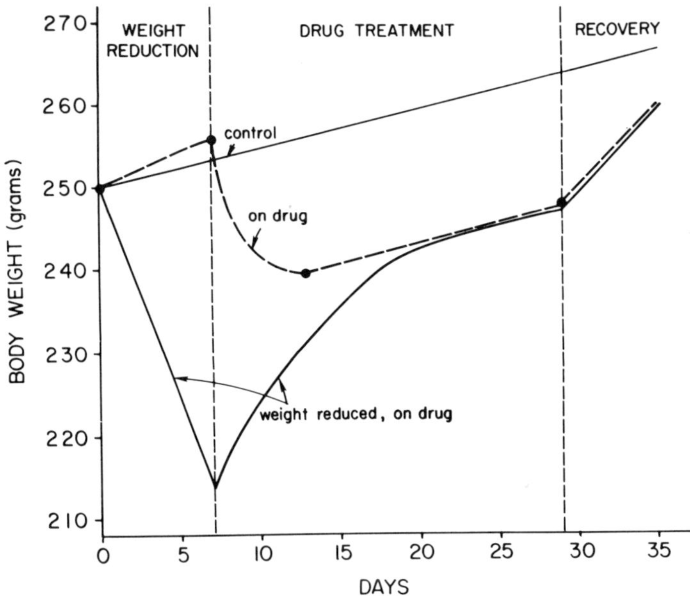

Fig. 4. Increase in body weight during administration of "appetite suppressant" medication. Following a period of weight reduction, rats gained weight when fed *ad libitum* even though receiving fenfluramine. When body weight reached that of rats which had received fenfluramine without prior weight reduction, rapid weight gain ceased. Body weights of both groups of rats rapidly returned towards control values when fenfluramine was discontinued. (Adapted from Levitsky et al., 1981).

parabiotic rats (10). He rendered rats parabiotic by opening the peritoneal cavities and suturing the cut edges of muscle and peritoneum to form artificial Siamese twins. The circulation of the members of the pair were sufficiently crossed to permit the exchange of plasma between the two at a rate of about one per cent per minute. Under normal circumstances, each rat regulated its body weight. One rat was then made hyperphagic and obese by lesions in the ventromedial hypothalamus. The other rat responded in a dramatic manner; it drastically curtailed its food intake. In some cases the non-lesioned partner even died of starvation. While body fat increased from 12 % to 50 % in the obese rats, it fell from 12 % to less than two per cent in their "twins".

The initial interpretation of this finding was that satiety factors produced in the lesioned animal crossed into the unlesioned animal and decreased its food intake. A corollary interpretation is that the total body weight, or body fat, of the two animals was regulated. If the body fat of one animal increased, that of the other animal decreased in compensation.

Faust and Body Fat

Increasing body fat in one of a pair of parabiotic rats led to a decrease in the other. Decreasing body fat in a rat by lipectomy, conversely, leads to a compensatory increase in body fat. Some of the strongest evidence for the regulation of body fat comes from studies of lipectomy. Liebelt and his colleagues were the first to show that surgical removal of body fat in rats and mice was followed by compensatory growth of the remaining adipose tissue (15).

Faust and his colleagues determined the mechanism of this compensatory growth of adipose tissue following lipectomy and, in the process, learned how body fat is linked to the control of eating behaviour (7). They showed that the increase in body fat following lipectomy was accomplished by an increase in the size of individual fat cells; there was no increase in fat cell number. After lipectomy, particularly when receiving a palatable high fat diet, rats increased their food intake, their body weight and the size of their fat cells. When the size of the fat cells reached a maximum, however, food intake decreased and weight gain ceased, even if the lost body fat had not been totally restored. The regulation of body fat is evidently determined by, and secondary to, the regulation of the size of individual fat cells. If the capacity of these cells to store fat is exceeded, regulation of total body fat following lipectomy does not occur. So, in the final analysis, the regulation of body weight (and body fat) depends upon the regulation of fat cell size, and the critical determinant of a body weight set point is the set point for fat cell size.

Fantino and Hoarding

An important new contribution to our understanding of the regulation of body weight has recently been made by Fantino's study of hoarding behaviour (5, 6). Hoarding constitutes a specialized and

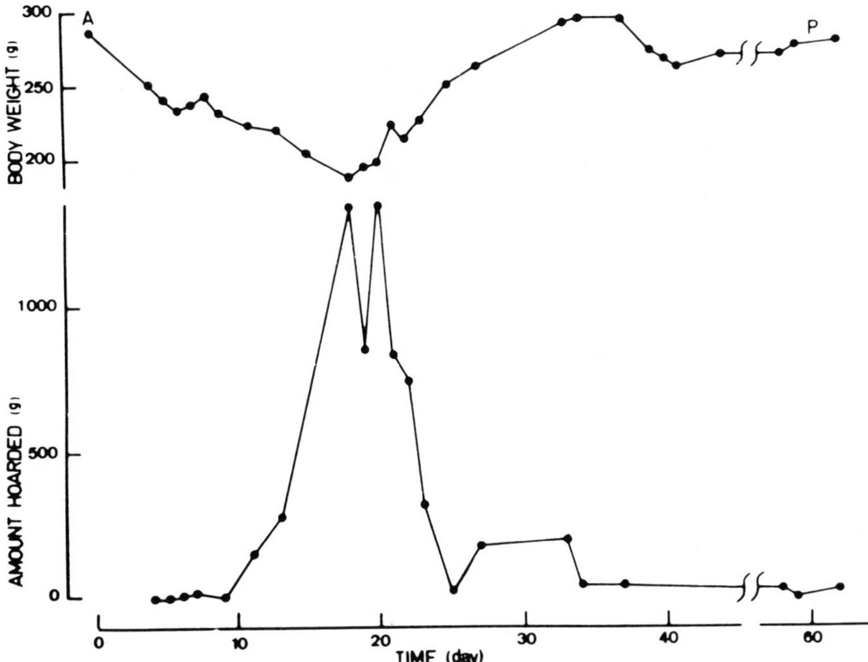

FIG. 5. Effect of losing and gaining weight upon hoarding behaviour in a single rat (After Fantino and Cabanac, 1980).

remarkably quantifiable response to food deprivation and weight loss. Until the introduction of the study of hoarding behaviour, information about body weight set points could be deduced only from the body weight itself. This limitation has meant that information about set points can be determined only when the body weight is in equilibrium, and tells us nothing about quantitative departures from the set point. Such quantitative information can readily be obtained, however, from the measurement of hoarding behaviour at various levels of body weight below the set point.

Figure 5 shows the remarkable responsiveness of the hoarding behaviour of rats to decreases in body weight (5). The loss of 30 % of body weight is associated with intense hoarding behaviour and the intensity of this behaviour decreases in proportion to the restoration of body weight. Rats do not hoard food when they are fed *ad libitum*, but begin to do so as soon as they lose weight from food deprivation. The amount hoarded is directly proportional to the amount of weight lost, and, with severe weight loss, can reach enormous quantities (sometimes as much as two kilograms in three hours).

According to the hoarding model, the body weight set point is that weight at which the amount hoarded reaches zero in the

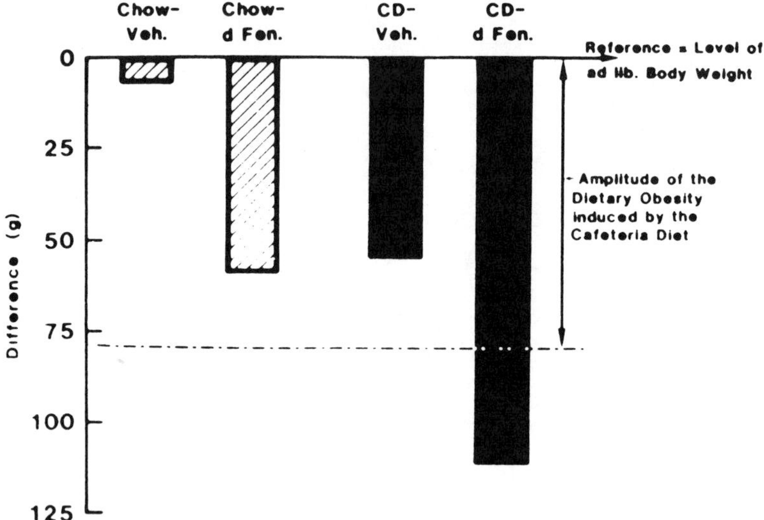

FIG. 6. Difference (g) between the mean *ad libitum* body weight and the set point for energy regulation (required for the initiation of hoarding) following treatment with desxtro-fenfluramine on chow and cafeteria diets.

regression of amount hoarded on body weight. Hoarding behaviour responds with exquisite sensitivity to decreases in body weight below the set point defined in this manner.

Fantino and his colleagues have used the hoarding model to study two factors known to modify food intake and body weight: the cafeteria diet, which induces dietary obesity and the appetite suppressant dextrofenfluramine. Animals received either a diet of laboratory chow or the highly palatable cafeteria diet and either a placebo or dextrofenfluramine. The results are shown in Figure 6 which plots the difference in grams between the body weight of the animals while feeding *ad libitum* and the set point as determined by the hoarding model. In the chow-fed, placebo-treated rats, hoarding behaviour began following a weight loss of less than 10 grams, suggesting that the body weight of these rats was at its set point when food deprivation began. By contrast, hoarding behaviour of the chow-fed and dextrofenfluramine-treated rats did not begin until they had lost at least 60 grams. The hoarding model thus suggests that fenfluramine lowered a body weight set point, just as Levitsky's earlier experiment had done.

A different picture is provided by rats fed a cafeteria diet. These rats did not begin to hoard until they had lost at least 50 grams of body weight. The hoarding model suggests that the body weight of the cafeteria-diet rats is at least 50 grams above its set point.

Figure 6 also shows that the cafeteria-diet rats are at least 75 grams overweight in comparison to their chow-fed controls. Part of the excess weight of the cafeteria-diet rats is apparently above the set point and is thus not regulated, while another part is below the set point and *is* regulated. Administering fenfluramine to cafeteria-diet rats significantly increased the extent of their weight loss before hoarding occurs, much as with chow-fed rats.

It appears as if the highly palatable cafeteria diet induced a dietary obesity which included both a regulated and a non-regulated component. How much of the obesity is regulated and how much is not regulated may depend on the duration of the diet. Dietary obesity is totally reversible after a short time on a cafeteria diet, whereas it may become permanent after a longer time on a cafeteria diet. The mechanism of this transformation has been established. Both Mandenoff et al. (16) and Faust et al. (8) have shown that a short period of cafeteria diet induces an increase in fat cell size whereas longer periods on such diets result also in an increase in fat cell number. Once the number of fat cells has increased, the obesity becomes irreversible, and subject to regulation at an elevated body weight set point.

IMPLICATIONS FOR THE TREATMENT OF OBESITY

Four problems encountered in the treatment of obesity above, can be interpreted in terms of set point theory: dropping out of treatment, symptoms during treatment, limited weight losses, and regaining of weight lost in treatment. All of these problems can be interpreted as results of the attempts to oppose a powerful physiological regulation. Two other implications of the theory can be drawn from a recent large-scale controlled clinical trial. One involves pharmacotherapy, the other involves behaviour therapy.

The trial was undertaken to determine the relative effectiveness of behaviour therapy and pharmacotherapy, the two leading treatments for obesity. It assessed the effects of behaviour therapy alone, pharmacotherapy (with fenfluramine) alone, and their combination in 98 obese women during 6 months of treatment and at a one-year follow-up (3). These three conditions were compared with each other and with two control groups, a waiting list control and a "doctor's office medication control group" which received traditional office treatment for obesity. The patients averaged 63 % overweight, their median age was 47 and all were of middle socioeconomic status.

Figure 7 shows that the patients in all treatment groups lost significantly more weight than those in the waiting list control group, who gained 1.3 kg. Weight losses of the pharmacotherapy (14.5 kg) and combined-treatment patients (15.3 kg) did not differ significantly and both exceeded the weight losses of the behaviour therapy patients (10.9 kg, $p < 001$). Patients in the doctor's office medication control group lost only 6.0 kg, significantly less than the 14.5 kg lost by the pharmacotherapy patients ($p < 0.05$) even though the drug dosage in the two groups was the same.

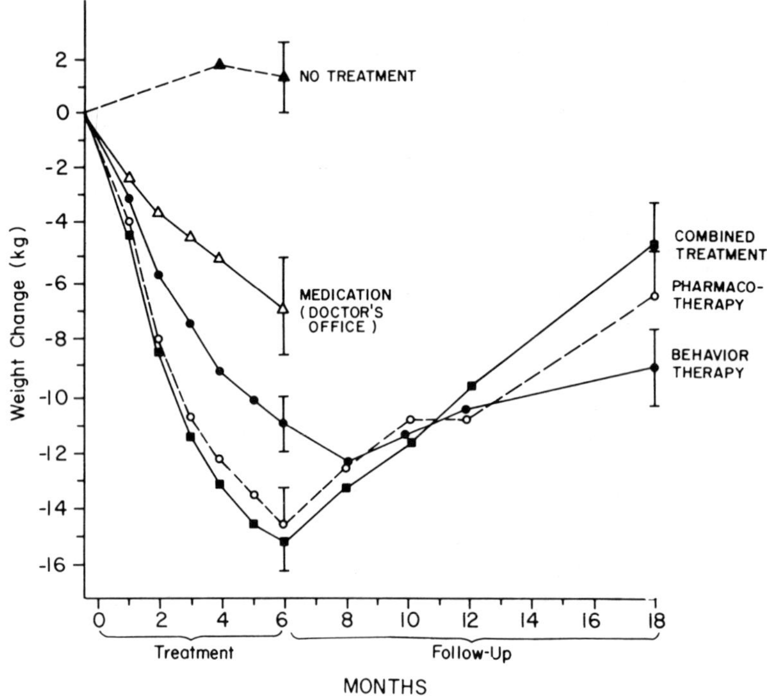

FIG. 7. Weight changes during six-month treatment and 12-month follow-up. The three major treatment groups lost large amounts of weight during treatment: behaviour therapy, 10.9 kg; pharmacotherapy, 14.5 kg; and combined treatment, 15.3 kg.
Behaviour therapy group regained weight slowly, pharmacotherapy and combined-treatment groups, rapidly.
No-treatment group gained weight; doctor's office medication group lost 6.0 kg. Vertical line represent 1 SEM.

A one year follow-up of all of the patients in the three major treatment conditions showed a striking reversal in the relative efficacy of the treatments. Far less weight was regained by behaviour therapy patients than by pharmacotherapy and combined-treatment patients. At one year, behaviour therapy patients had regained only 1.9 kg, for a net weight loss from the beginning of treatment of 9.0 kg By contrast, pharmacotherapy patients had regained 8.2 kg for a net loss of only 6.3 kg and the combined-treatment patients regained even more weight (10.7 kg), for an even smaller net loss (4.6 kg). The long-term results strongly favored behaviour therapy alone over the two conditions that utilized pharmacotherapy.

The implications of set point theory for the results of pharmacotherapy are clear. As we have noted, laboratory research has shown that both racemic fenfluramine (14) and the dextrofenfluramine given alone (6) acts primarily by lowering a body weight set point and only secondarily by suppressing appetite. When fenfluramine was discontinued in the trial, the body weight set point of the patients returned to its pre-treatment level. Powerful biological pressures to gain weight to this higher level were thus released, resulting in the rebound in body weight.

These practical results, supported by the results of laboratory research suggest a radical revision of prescribing practices for "appetite-suppressant" medication: do not use it unless you are prepared to use it indefinitely.

Important implications can be drawn also from the effects of behaviour therapy. The maintenance of weight loss following treatment confirms the efficacy of this modality, and raises the question of how behaviour therapy acts. Does it, for example, lower a body weight set point ? The answer is not obvious, and includes at least three possibilities.

1) Behaviour therapy may lower a body weight set point. A promising candidate for such a mechanism is the increase in physical activity which is emphasized in behavioural weight loss programs. Whether increased physical activity can actually lower a body weight set point is currently the subject of vigorous research. Should this research show that physical activity can lower a body weight set point, it would provide a strong rationale for a treatment measure that is still in part a matter of faith.

Another candidate for a lowering of a set point by behaviour therapy is modification of dietary habits. Behavioural programs attempt to lower the high fat content of the typical American diet. If high fat diets promote obesity in humans, as they do in experimental animals, lowering the fat content of the diet may well lower a set point.

2) Behaviour therapy may have no effect upon the body weight set point. It may help patients to maintain their body weight below its set point simply by providing the skills to live in a state of semi-starvation. The intensity of this starvation may vary, depending upon

the tolerance for fluctuations below the body weight set point. If, for example, body weight is very tightly regulated, a reduction of 10.9 kg below a set point, as in the present study, may be an onerous task. It is quite possible, however, that there is considerable tolerance about the set point and that a loss of 10.9 kg would produce only modest pressures to restore weight to its higher, regulated, level.

3) A third mechanism of action of behaviour therapy is one rendered more plausible by Fantino's research. Lowering the fat content of the diet may act to control obesity by limiting that component of dietary obesity that Fantino has shown to be not regulated (or not yet regulated). This component is the one that results from an increase in fat cell size, before any increase in fat cell number has occured. This third mechanism has intuitive appeal. Furthermore it fits the experience of many graduates of behavioural programs who have lost weight and maintained their weight losses without evidence that they are coping with semi-starvation.

These three mechanisms may not be mutually exclusive and more than one of them may be at work in successful weight control programs.

CONCLUSIONS

There is strong reason to believe that body weight is regulated, for it not only remains at a relatively constant level, but is also defended at that level against environmental challenges. Regulation occurs not only among animals of normal weight, as has long been believed, but also among obese animals. They are obese, it is argued, because the set point about which their body weight is regulated is elevated.

There is strong and growing evidence for regulation of body weight. It includes studies of animals made obese by lesions in the ventromedial hypothalamus as well as animals made thin by lesions in the lateral hypothalamus. Studies of appetite suppressant medication provide evidence for regulation via its apparent mechanism of action in lowering a body weight set point. Studies of parabiotic rats and of lipectomized animals support the idea of regulation by demonstrating compensatory decreases and increases in body fat in response to experimentally-induced changes in body fat. The study of hoarding in animals provides a quantitative model for estimating body weight set points and their modification in response to interventions as varied as high fat diets and pharmacotherapy.

Evidence for regulation of body weight in humans is derived from Key's study of starved volunteers and from sims study of overfed volunteers. In each case, when the subjects were allowed free access to food their body weight rapidly returned to normal.

The idea that body weight is regulated helps to explain four traditional problems in the treatment of obesity: dropping out of treatment, symptoms during treatment, limited weight losses and the regaining of weight lost during treatment. In each case, the problem can be ascribed to the attempt to reduce body weight in the face of opposing physiological regulations. Another clinical problem - the transiency of the effects of appetite suppressant medication - can be similarly explained. Reasons for the relative success of behaviour therapy of obesity are provided by the regulation of body weight.

REFERENCES

1. Adolph, E.F. (1947): *Am. J. Physiol.*, 151: 110-125.

2. Cohn, C., and Cohn, J.D. (1962): *Yale J. Biol. Med.*, 34: 598-607.

3. Craighead, L.W., Stunkard, A.J., and O'Brien, R. (1981): *Arch. Gen. Psychiatry*, 38: 763-768.

4. Cruce, J.A.F., Greenwood, M.R.C., Johnson, P.R., and Quartermain, D. (1974): *J. Comp. Physiol. Psych.*, 87: 295-301.

5. Fantino, M., and Cabanac, M. (1980): *Physiol. Behav.* 24: 939-942.

6. Fantino, M., Faion, F., and Rolland, Y.: *Am. J. Physiol.*, (in press).

7. Faust, I.M., Johnson, P.R., and Hirsch, J. (1977): *Science*, 197: 393-396.

8. Faust, I.M., Johnson, P.R., Stern, J.S., and Hirsch, J. (1978): *Am. J. Physiol.* 235: E279-E286.

9. Hamilton, C.L. (1969): *Ann. N.Y. Acad. Sci.*, 157: 1004-1017.

10. Hervey, G.R. (1959): *J. Physiol.*, 154: 336-352.

11. Hoebel, B.G., and Teitelbaum, B. (1966): *J. Comp. Physiol. Psychol.*, 61: 189-193.

12. Keesey, R.E., Boyle, P.C., Kemnitz, J.W., and Mitchell, J.S. (1976): In: *Hunger: Basic Mechanisms and Clinical Implications*, edited by D. Novin, W. Wyrwicka, and G.A. Bray pp. 243-255. Raven Press, New York.

13. Keys, A., Brozek, J., Henschel, A., Mickelson, D., and Taylor, H.L. (1950): *The Biology of Human Starvation*, University of Minnesota Press, Minneapolis.

14. Levitsky, D.A., Strupp, B.J., and Lupoli, J. (1981): *Pharmacol. Biochem. Behav.*, 14: 661-667.

15. Liebelt, R.A., Ichinoe S., Nicholson, N. (1965): *Ann. N.Y. Acad. Sci.*, 131: 559-582.

16. Mandenoff, A.T., Lenoir, T., and Apfelbaum, M. (1982): *Am. J. Physiol.*, 242: 349-351.

17. Mrosovsky, N., Powley, T.L. (1977): *Behav. Biol.*, 20:205-223.

18. Odum, E.P. (1960): *Am. J. Clin. Nutr.*, 8:621-629.

19. Pengelley, E.T., and Fischer, K.C. (1963): *Canad. J. Zool.*, 41: 1103-1120.

20. Sims, E.A.H., and Horton, E.S. (1968): *Am. J. Clin. Nutr.*, 21: 1455-1470.

21. Stunkard, A.J. (1957): *Am. J. Med.*, 23: 77-86.

22. Stunkard, A.J. (1975): *Psychosom. Med.*, 37: 195-236.

23. Stunkard, A.J. (1982): *Life Sci.*, 30: 2043-2055.

Pharmacology of Eating Disorders: Theoretical and Clinical Developments, edited by M. O. Carruba and J. E. Blundell. Raven Press, New York © 1986.

Metabolic Action of Leptogenic (Anorexigenic) Agents on Feeding and Body Weight

Stylianos Nicolaidis and Patrick Even

Laboratoire de Neurobiologie des Régulations CNRS UA 637, Collège de France, 75231 Paris Cédex 05, France

Therapy for "overweight" now makes increasing use of medication as opposed to other forms of treatment. The drugs used to decrease food intake are designated "anorectics" (or better "anorexigenic" agents). This term reflects the underlying idea prevailing in the medical world that "overweight" is due to "overeating". Not only is the meaning of the prefix "over" in both words unjustified but it is surprising that half of the regulatory processes, i.e. those concerned with energy expenditure rather than intake, are neglected. Curiously enough, some of the early treatments of obesity used thyroid or dinitrophenol preparations, thereby emphasizing the increase of metabolic rate as a strategy to reduce body weight.

Today, on the base of the recently postulated ischymetric hypothesis (56, 57) it can be hypothesized how the physiological stimulus acts upon neural structures to enhance hunger and arousal (decreasing metabolic rate) or to induce satiety and sleep (increasing metabolic rate). Consequently, the distinction between a primary action of drugs on feeding or a primary action on metabolism is becoming inappropriate. Indeed, it seems that energy expenditure and intake are intimately inter-related in physiological normal as well as pathological situations.

To the extend that the goal of medication is the reduction of body weight, the most appropriate term for active compounds should be "leptogenic (from greek leptos = lean) agents" (instead of anorexigenic). This suggestion will appear more appropriate as the argument proceeds and will be reiterated in the concluding remarks.

LEPTOGENICS

On theoretical grounds, leptogenic agents may act exclusively or conjointly in a variety of ways:

a) They may interfere with the monoaminergic, or other neurochemical pathways which appear to transmit the signals of depletion thereby leading to ingestive behaviour and/or its complementary functions (i.e. gastric and intestinal clearance).

b) Leptogenics may proceed as above but their final effect may lead to metabolic corrective responses via neural and/or endocrine controls. For example, changes in secretion of insulin, growth hormone, glucagon or catecholamines can readily modify the way macronutrients are metabolized by cells. Various partially known mechanisms may bring about a real caloric wastage possibly inducing futile cycles. This concept will appear several times in this chapter dealing with basal of feeding-associated thermogenesis, or with the newly demonstrated phenomenon (25, 27) of increased energy expenditure during locomotion. In all of these cases, leptogenic agents would act on energy in a manner similar to the manner in which diuretics act against "overhydration".

c) Leptogenic agents may change the value of the body weight set-point and/or may act on the system which translates regulatory signals into feeding and metabolic response. If leptogenics bring about a lowering of the "set-point" the subject would naturally be expected to show reduced feeding in parallel to greater energy losses until the new set point has been reached. This would then reinstate pretreatment levels of intake and expenditure and establish a new body weight plateau.

d) Leptogenic agents may act simultaneously upon more than one of the above regulatory mechanisms by means of some common "key" or simply because regulatory processes are interactive. For example, primary anorexia and underabsorption of energy affect neuroendocrinological secretions and metabolism; changes of metabolic rate determine the onset of hunger (according to the ischymetric hypothesis) and both anorexia and energy wasting affect the set point as much as they are themselves affected by set point changes.

e) Central vs peripheral actions: In addition to the above functions, leptogenics may act selectively at the central nervous system (CNS) level or at both CNS and peripheral levels.

Since central anorexigenic mechanisms are being dealt with elsewhere (see Carruba et al., this volume), this chapter will be restricted to the properties of those anorexigenic agents which justify the description of leptogenics.

Peripheral effects of leptogenics are important to understand, not only for a better therapeutic practice, but also because they throw light upon the central integration of the multiciplicity of responses which achieve energy balance.

Before describing the overall metabolic effects of leptogenics, some consideration will be given to their specific action on glucide, lipids, and on some hormone and biochemical reactions.

LEPTOGENICS AND GLUCIDIC METABOLISM

The overall handling of glucose may be modified by leptogenics. Soon after fenfluramine was reported as an anorexigenic agent it was shown to improve glucose tolerance in maturity-onset diabets (6, 21, 23, 39, 47, 51, 62, 68, 69, 73). This phenomenon was not due to an augmented insulin secretion and could be found in patients with peripheral arterial desease (6). Unlike fenfluramine, amphetamine does not improve glucose tolerance. Mazindol however was also found to produce improvement in oral glucose tolerance together with the reduction of insulin secretion in obese human subjects. Norfenfluramine has hypoglycaemic effects in man, in addition to its hypolipidaemic effect. Fenfluramine was reported to produce an improvement in *obese* maturity-onset-diabetic patients (70). A number of findings may account for this antidiabetic effect of leptogenics.

An important observation was that fenfluramine, mazindol and ciclazindol produce significant increases in glucose uptake in human isolated skeletal muscle (29, 45). In addition, fenfluramine increases uptake into human forearm muscle *in vivo* (11, 43, 45). In *in vitro* studies fenfluramine, norfenfluramine and trifluorex also display an effect on glucose uptake in therapeutic concentrations and in the presence of insulin (3, 40, 41). However, fenfluramine does not increase tissue glycogen (29, 40) but does increase lactate (42). Fenfluramine and, in higher doses, mazindol exert a dose-related inhibitory effect on the specific binding of human insulin to human adipocytes (35). However, unlike mazindol, fenfluramine enhances conversion of ^{14}C-glucose to $^{14}CO_2$ by human adipose tissue. Fenfluramine may also contribute to the antidiabetic action through inhibition of hepatic neoglycogenesis from lactate, pyruvate and alanine but not from dihydroxyacetone (34). It is of importance that most of the metabolic effects of fenfluramine can be inhibited by methysergide, a selective 5-hydroxytryptamine (5-HT) receptor antagonist (44). This observation allowed Turner (65) to suspect the possible role of 5-HT in the peripheral action of fenfluramine. Indeed by its CNS action 5-HT was known to produce hypoglycaemia in mice pretreated with a MAO inhibitor, and this effect was blocked by methysergide and cyproheptadine (17, 30). A 5-HT agonist action, recognized first by Duhault and Verdavaine (20) is also believed to be responsible for the anorexigenic and glucose uptake effects of metachlorophenyl piperazine (32) anf benfluorex (64) or to contribute more generally to the process of satiety (33).

The interaction between glucidic metabolism and fenfluramine is important since it can explain a number of interesting observations including, for example, the action of fenfluramine on the utilization of glucose during locomotion (25, 27 and present article) in carbohydrate craving (75) and in the blockade of 2-Deoxy-glucose or insulin elicited feeding (12).

LEPTOGENICS AND LIPID METABOLISM

Before considering particular aspects of lipid metabolism there is one recent finding (25) which summarizes the action of fenfluramine. Fenfluramine administration in rats was shown to produce a massive and prolonged lipolysis and to increase cellular utilization of the liberated lipid substrates. This was clearly demonstrated by the time course of the respiratory quotient (RQ) which rapidly reaches a value close to 0.72. This level of the RQ is the pathognomonic signal of lipid utilization. The fact that the composition of the food of theses subjects was mainly carbohydrates rules out an exogenous origin of lipid substrates. Therefore the substrates must come from adipocyte stores, the only source able to provid metabolites during periods of one or more days.

This phenomenon is substantiated by a number of earlier observations. For example, in fenfluramine treated animals Duhault and Boulanger (18, 19) have shown a decrease of epidydimal fat tissue while free fatty acids (FFA) were released. This was confirmed by Chandler and al. (13) and shown to take place in isolated adipocytes when lipolysis was elicited by adrenaline, noradrenaline (NA), 3'5'-cyclic AMP and growth hormone (16). Broadly speaking fenfluramine increases plasma free glycerol, FFA and ketone bodies but decreases plasma triglycerides and total lipids (59, 67). The decrease of triglycerides induced by fenfluramine in human serum was confirmed (14, 52) and extended to other species such as rabbit (38) and rat (9, 53). Similar observations were made with amphetamine and norfenfluramine (9, 53). Moreover, fenfluramine inhibits lipogenesis both *in vitro* and *in vivo* (15, 74). Fenfluramine inhibits FFA synthesis and NA release in the rat (16) and, like mazindol, it prevents the lipogenic hormone, insulin, from binding to human adipose tissue and isolated fat cells (35, 36). In human adipose tissue fenfluramine and mazindol enhance conversion of glucose to CO_2 (35, 36). In addition to slowing gastro-intestinal emptying, fenfluramine reduces gastrointestinal lipid absorption as a result of inhibition of lipase/colipase/bile salt system (7) and of microsomal monooleinacyl transferase in the rat intestine (16). Therefore in man fenfluramine decreases triglyceride absorption and increases the faecal excretion of fat and bile acids (63). This is an additional phenomenon which may contribute to a reduction of lipid synthesis in the presence of fenfluramine as shown both in humans and in rats by ^{14}C-glucose incorporation studies (16, 74) and also in isolated liver or adipose tissue (5, 38, 54). The biochemical mechanism of this fenfluramine action is being explored. Interaction with insulin appears to be complex since both facilitating and inhibiting actions have been reported (35, 36, 58) and 5-HT was shown to release insulin (28, 31). Fenfluramine inhibits glycerolipid synthesis in the liver at the step of glycerophosphate incorporation into neutral lipids and other amphiphilic compounds which increase phospholipid synthesis (9). In hepatocytes, oxidative phosphorylation and fatty acid synthesis is not affected by fenfluramine although ketogenesis from long chain but not from short chain fatty acids is depressed (34). It is postulated that mitochondrial CoA concentration is decreased and the site of action might well be at the level of carnitine acyltransferase.

EFFECT OF DEXTROFENFLURAMINE ON BODY-WEIGHT OF PAIR-PATTERN-FED RATS

From the above data it would be expected that pair-fed fenfluramine treated animals should lose more weight than their control sham injected partners. Indeed data from the literature tend to confirm this hypothesis (13) although other data are apparently in opposition (71). To assess "pair feeding" it is necessary to do more than simply match the number of calories given to treated and to control yoked pairs since the control group necessarily receives a restricted ration which is immediately consumed within a limited time during the light period of the circadian light-dark cycle. To avoid such distorting factors when studying energy efficiency of nutrients a pair-pattern-feeding schedule was set up (Even and Nicolaidis unpublished data).

In the experimental procedure each of a pair of rats was given a cup into which could be delivered a semi-liquid complete diet (Renutryl 500, Shopharga Laboratories). The dextrofenfluramine-treated partners (12 mg/kg/day given i.p. in two portions) obtained food from a syringe by pressing a bar. This system controlled another syringe located in parallel, which delivered exactly the same amount of Renutryl to the partner at the same time.

Two experiments were carried out over five and fifteen consecutive days respectively. Body weight was measured daily. Body weight variations were observed to remain identical between control and pair-pattern fed subjects throughout the time course of the experiments.

These data favoured the idea that dextrofenfluramine under "perfect" pair-feeding conditions does not increase energy expenditure by affecting metabolism and/or thermogenesis. However, a careful observation of animals' behaviour led to a more cautious interpretation of our data. Intake was indeed perfectly matched but the energy producing events were not. In particular the dextrofenfluramine treated rats appeared to be very calm, owing to the sedative action of dextrofenfluramine at doses used in this experiment (48, 76). In contrast to the dextrofenfluramine treated subjects the control partners were observed to become increasingly agitated as the diet was restricted. Therefore, the equal body weight loss of the control group was observed despite increased energy expenditure through locomotor behaviour.

LEPTOGENICS AND ENERGY EXPENDITURE

The experiment reported above points out the need to monitor all possible parameters capable of influencing the experimental outcome. In other words, when mechanisms of action of leptogenics are studied both intake and expenditures must be closely controlled. On one hand quantitative and qualitative intake should be assessed only following faecal analysis. On the other hand, energy expenditure is not equivalent to thermogenesis but includes also locomotion. For example, it is easy to decrease total energy expenditure by preventing locomotor activity even if the subject otherwise shows intense thermogenesis. Similarly, hypo- and normo-thermogenic subjects would show increased energy expenditure if they were simply made hyperkinetic or if their locomotion used more fuel than in untreated subjects. Finally, if thermogenesis *per se* was increased it could be related either to basal metabolism or to the feeding associated heat production, and/or to extra losses triggered by muscular contraction.

It may be noted that the mechanisms responsible for extra losses, may be due to futile biochemical cycles of synthesis and degradation triggering a less efficient and otherwise useful chain of reactions (e.g. hexoses vs pentoses cycle) or to costly musculo-hepatic-type or to brown adipose tissue (BAT) hepatic cycles.

A possible thermogenic effect of leptogenics was proposed by several authors working with ephedrine (10, 24, 55). Although the initial hypothesis was inclined towards the muscular origin of increased glucose uptake (see above), later investigations revealed the possible importance of BAT. BAT is generally considered to be the effector of cold-induced thermogenesis (37). Increase and/or decrease of activity of BAT has subsequently been suspected to determine negative and/or positive energy balances leading respectively to leaness and/or obesity (60). It was therefore natural that the leptogenic-induced thermogenesis was suspected to originate within the BAT and to be feeding associated (1, 2, 49, 61). Extensive work indicated that leptogenic activated Na^{+} -K^{+} - ATPase activity in the BAT was presumably the cause of feeding associated thermogenesis for compounds as widely different as amphetamine, fenfluramine, mazindol and cyclazindol. This peripheral effect is however elicited by a central controller activating β-adrenergic receptors (10, 37, 61). This indicates how leptogenics could exert a peripheral effect though a central action might also include an effect on general activity.

The possible influence of drug-induced increase in motor activity was examined by recording metabolic rate of either free moving or anesthetized animals treated with amphetamine, diethylpropion, mazindol and cyclazindol (46). In those preparations it was observed that amphetamine, mazindol and also diethylpropion produced increases in metabolic rate of anesthetized animals. In contrast, cyclazindol was ineffective in increasing metabolic rate of anesthetized animals. These findings indicate that, at least for some leptogenics, motility-related rather than BAT metabolism may account for the overall increase of thermogenesis. Other mechanisms of action have been forseen. Mazindol has been shown to increase thyroxin levels, another way (additional or exclusive) of increasing thermogenesis in long term treatment. Temperature was also shown to increase in fenfluramine-treated subjects (4).

LEPTOGENICS AND ENERGY METABOLISM

Metabolic effects of dextrofenfluramine were studied by using a computerized device performing mutliparametric measurements. It allowed the investigation of the effect of dextrofenfluramine treatment simultaneously on a) meal pattern, b) total and resting energy expenditure, c) intensity and metabolic cost of locomotor activity and d) qualitative metabolism through RQ, to answer the question which of the main fuels (glucids, lipids), is being used in resting as well as during locomotion.

It was thus possible to answer some questions on the mechanisms of leptogenic action of dextrofenfluramine (for more details see 27).

We studied two groups of rats fed *ad libitum* throughout 22 hours recording: an untreated group of 7 rats, and a group of 5 rats treated by an initial single i.p. injection of dextrofenfluramine at the dose of 7 mg/kg. The results show that food intake was strongly reduced. The average body weight loss was 10.5 g.

The light/dark cyclicity of energy expenditure, also related to cyclicity of food intake, RQ and locomotor activity, was completely abolished. This absence of cyclicity of all the metabolic and behavioural parameters in the dextrofenfluramine treated group is probably related to the near total inhibition of food intake.

Despite the nearly complete anorexia, total energy expenditure throughout the 22 hours was almost identical for the two groups. It thus appeared that anorexia in the dextrofenfluramine treated group did not reduce energy expenses as would be expected from untreated starved rats. This phenomenon can be interpreted through the ischymetric hypothesis for the control of food intake which proposes that satiety is maintained by a high metabolic rate whereas hunger is generated by a decrease. The anorexia of the dextrofenfluramine treated rats could be the consequence of the high metabolic rate induced by the drug. Since this anorexia seems to be mainly a consequence of metabolic changes, it occurs without any adaptive reduction of energy expenditure.

The long and short term changes in RQ after dextrofenfluramine treatment point to possible mechanisms maintaining high metabolic rates and anorexia. In contrast to the control group, in which RQ fluctuated according to the well known light period of lipolytic vs dark period of lipogenic processes, RQ of the dextrofenfluramine treated animals appeared to be lower than that of untreated rats at the very beginning of the recording sessions, and to decrease progressively during the following hours, until it reached 0.80 (versus 0.93 in the control group).

These results show that dextrofenfluramine produced immediately a preferential lipid utilization which is progressively increased and maintained throughout the 22 hours of measurement. This increased utilization of endogenous lipid stores may be the way dextrofenfluramine treatment maintains high metabolic rate, and thus produces anorexia through an ischymetric and/or lipostatic control of food intake.

This possibility was further strengthened by the results observed in short term changes in RQ and Total Energy Expenditure (TEE) in relation to locomotor activity. At the dose used in this experiment, locomotor activity in the dextrofenfluramine treated group was reduced by 33%. This quantitative reduction occurred together with large qualitative changes. During the five hours following the treatment continuous movements of small amplitude were recorded. Then activity returned to a more normal pattern of resting/locomotor periods but locomotor episodes remained shorter and weaker than in control animals.

The study of TEE and RQ in relation to the locomotor events showed that the dextrofenfluramine treatment produced a great increase of the apparent energy cost of muscular contraction (2.528 Watts/Unit Act./Kg vs 0.589 Watts/Unit Act./Kg in untreated controls). In addition, the RQ was simultaneously increased in direct relation with the intensity of locomotor activity and metabolic changes 0.14 Unit/Unit Act. (Corr. Coef. = 0.981) vs 0.007 Unit/Unit Act. (Corr. Coef. = 0.514) in the control group .

The present data show that in addition to the initial increase of resting metabolism in the dextrofenfluramine treated animal, the muscular work produces further metabolic changes of (RQ and overall energy expenditure), and that this new phenomenon could play a role in the leptogenic action of dextrofenfluramine.

In dextrofenfluramine-treated subjects, the high degree of lipolysis and lipid utilization were apparent from the RQ which approximated 0.80. If this RQ were corrected by taking into account its abnormal increase during the scarce episodes of locomotor activity the figure would drop to a value of RQ close to 0.72 expressing an almost pure utilization of lipids except during locomotion.

In summary, from the present data it appears that

dextrofenfluramine strongly modifies peripheral metabolism by enhancing metabolic pathways associated with locomotor activity. This results in an increased thermogenesis despite the reduced locomotion. A through examination of the participation of energy expenditure in the leptogenic action of a substance should compare paired groups which eat equal amounts of food and show comparable locomotor activity. Since in this experiment neither feeding nor locomotor activity were comparable, it is difficult to draw firm conclusions on the effect of dextrofenfluramine on overall energy losses. However, the dramatic increase of the cost of locomotor activity prompts us to suggest that treated subjects which have recovered normophagia and close to normal locomotor activity lose a large proportion of nutrients through increased cost of muscular contraction.

GENERAL DISCUSSION

Currently most available data suggest that the so-called anorectic agents do more than decrease hunger and food intake. Even though anorectics belong to different neurotransmitters, they also affect several metabolic processes which lead to a negative energy balance and to body weight loss. This leads us to prefer to replace "anorexigenic" by the term "leptogenic".

The example of fenfluramine is significant. Fenfluramine clearly induces a sequence of events resulting in both anorexia and increased energy expenditure. Its initial action is to produce a massive lipolysis and to increase lipid utilization. This assertion is supported by almost all of the *in vivo* and *in vitro* measurements, and is demonstrated in the whole animal by the decrease in the RQ. As expected the fenfluramine-induced lipolysis is accompanied by an inhibition of lipogenesis and, to some extent by an inhibition of the intestinal absorption of triglycerides. Lipidic metabolites are made available from both white and brown adipose tissues. The role of brown adipose tissue has been recently emphasized; however the small amount of fat contained by this tissue cannot account for the long lasting lipid utilization after fenfluramine treatment. Besides metabolic reactions that synthesize ATP, lipids may possibly participate in futile cycles resulting in pure thermogenesis like those associated with thermoregulation. All these reactions may co-exists in order to bring about both extra-losses of energy and increased availability of cellular fuel, the latter being most important in bringing about the anorexigenic action of leptogenic agents. Indeed, according to the ischymetric hypothesis, the physiological stimulus for hunger is a diminution of metabolic rate at the cellular level, whereas satiety takes place when restoration of the metabolites and of their co-factors of cellular utilization restore the metabolic rate. Therefore, the increased availability and cellular utilization of lipidic substrates induced by fenfluramine treatment should be sufficient to induce satiety, together with or independently from the well established activation of the central serotoninergic system (20).

However, the central modifications of 5-HT and other neurotransmitters may not be the primary stimulus for hunger and satiety, but rather the way the CNS amplifies the triggering signal (which may be ischymetric) and/or mediates the neuroendocrine and behavioural responses to this initial signal of depletion/repletion. In this case, there is no contradiction between the above suggested sequence of events and the classical conception of the central indolaminergic mechanism of action of fenfluramine. To summarize, the fenfluramine-induced release and utilization of endogenous lipids could deplete fat stores and, as a result, increase satiety by alleviating the cellular metabolic turn-over.

In addition to lipolysis and utilization of lipidic substrates there is an augmentation of glucose uptake and utilization by muscles and possibly by other cells. This phenomenon was well described from specific preparations and has recently been further substantiated by comparing the extra-cost of energy expenditure durig locomotor activity between control and treated subjects (see above). As a result fenfluramine induces a supplementary loss of metabolites during locomotion which becomes a more costly process. Such an effect may further contribute to body weight decrease. In this case, carbohydrates also appear to be used as fuels for biochemical futile cycles.

The question remains whether peripheral effects are directly elicited by leptogenics. In particular, it is possible that the primary action of leptogenics triggers brain mechanisms which, in turn, controls metabolic processes and/or feeding. For example, fenfluramine could affect the activity of the central serotoninergic system which could induce neuroendocrine responses leading to both lipolysis and special glucose uptake and utilization. Alternatively, fenfluramine could affect both peripheral and neural responsiveness by means of some common metabolic properties. For example, serotonin elicits insulin secretion from the pancreas and, possibly, from brain tissue. Fenfluramine may induce activation of a more general lipolytic factor via β-sympathetic receptors and some complementary unknown neuroendocrine system. Presently, there is only a partial answer to these questions. Fenfluramine was shown to affect both lipolysis and glucose uptake *in vitro*. These observations favor the idea of either a peripheral or a combined action of fenfluramine which could affect a more universal membrane property which would favor catabolic reactions. Changes of broad biological reactions by fenfluramine, such as the increase of guanosine 5'-diphosphate binding, may be involved in the action of this compound and of leptogenics in general.

The last possible mechanism of leptogenic agents would be a direct action upon brain structures which tune the set-point of body weight. If a substance could decrease the set-point, it would be expected to bring about a decrease of feeding together with an increase of overall energy expenditure until the new set-point is reached. Precisely this has been observed in the case of fenfluramine treatment whose leptogenic efficiency is reduced if body weight is diminished prior to treatment.

ACKNOWLEDGEMENTS

This work was partially supported by ADIR Co. and INSERM No.857009. We thank Henri Coulaud and Jean-Luc Aucouturier for their precious assistance; John Blundell for improving the English version and Jeanine Asmanis for secreterial assistance.

REFERENCES

1. Acheson, K.J., Zahorska-Markiewicz, B., Pittet, P., Anantharaman, K., and Jequier, E. (1980): *Am. J. Clin. Nutr.*, 33: 989-997.

2. Arch, J.R.S. (1980): *Alim. Nutr. Metab.*, 1: 217.

3. Bajaj, J.S., and Vallence-Owen, J. (1974): *Horm. Metab. Res.*, 6: 85.

4. Balmagiya, T., and Rozovski, S.J. (1982): *Fed. Proc.*, 41: 942 (Abstr. n. 3932).

5. Bizzi, A., Bonaccorsi, A., Jespersen, S., Jori, A., and Garattini, S. (1970): In: *Amphetamine and related compounds.* Edited by E. Costa and S. Garattini, pp. 577-595. Raven Press, New York.

6. Bliss, B.P., Kirk, C.J.C. and Newall, R.G. (1972): *Postgrad. Med. J.*, 48, 409-413.

7. Borgstrom, B. and Wollesen, C. (1981): *FEBS Lett.*, 126: 25-28.

8. Bray, G.A. and Lupien, J.R. (1984): *Excerpta Med. Intern. Series* No 642, p. 797.

9. Brindley, D.N., and Bowley, M. (1975): *Postgrad. Med. J.*, 51 (Supp. 1): 91-95.

10. Bukowiecki, L., Jahjah, L.J., and Follea, N. (1982): *Int. J. Obes.*, 6: 343-350.

11. Butterfield, W.J.H., and Wichelow, J.J. (1968): *Lancet*, 2: 109.

12. Carruba, M.O., Ricciardi, S., Spano, P.F., and Mantegazza, P. (1985): *Life Sci.*, 36: 1739-1749.

13. Chandler, P.T., Dannenburg, W.N., Polan, C.E., and Thomson, N.R. (1970): *J. Dairy Sci.*, 53: 1747-1756.

14. Chremos, A.N., Dannenburg, W.N., and Noble, R.E. (1971): *Diabetes*, 20 (Suppl. 1): 351.

15. Comai, K., Triscari, J., and Sullivan, A.C. (1978): *Biochem. Pharmacol.*, 27: 1987-1994.

16. Dannenburg, W.N., and Kardian, B.C. (1970): In: *Amphetamines and related compounds*, edited by E. Costa and S. Garattini, pp. 597-610. Raven Press, New-York.

17. Darwish, S.A.E., and Furman, B.L. (1974): *Experientia*, 30: 1306-1307.

18. Duhault, J., and Boulanger, M. (1965): *Rev. Fr. Etud. Clin. Biol.*, 10: 215-216.

19. Duhault, J., and Boulanger, M. (1966): *Journées Annuelles de Diabétologie de l'Hôtel Dieu*, p. 67. Editions Médicales Flammarion, Paris.

20. Duhault, J., and Verdavainne, C. (1967): *Arch. Int. Pharmacodyn. Ther.*, 170: 276-286.

21. Durnin, J.V.G.A., and Womersley, J. (1973): *Br. J. Pharmacol.*, 49: 115-120.

22. Dykes, J.R.W. (1973): *Postrgrad Med J.*, 49: 318-324.

23. Dykes, J.R.W. (1973): *Postgrad. Med J.*, 49: 314-317.

24. Evans, E., and Miller, D.S. (1977): *Proc. Nutr. Soc.* 36: 136A.

25. Even, P., and Nicolaidis, S. (1985): *Proc. Intern. Symposium on the Metabolic Complications of Human Obesities.* Marseille, May 30, June 1.

26. Even, P., and Nicolaidis, S. (1982): *J. Physiol.* , 78: 4A.

27. Even, P., and Nicolaidis, S. (1985): Submitted to *Pharmacol. Biochem. Behav.*

28. Feldman, J.M., and Lebovitz H.E. (1972): *Trans. Assoc. Am. Physicians* 35: 279-294.

29. Frayn, K.N., Hedges, A., and Kirby, M.J. (1974): *Horm. and Metab. Res.*, 6 : 86.

30. Furman, B.L., and Wilson, G.A. (1978): *J. Pharm. Pharmac.* 30: 53P.

31. Gagliardino, J.J., Zieher, L.M., Iturriza, F.C., Hernandez, R.E., and Rodriguez, R.R. (1971): *Horm. Metab. Res.*, 3: 145-150.

32. Garattini, S., Caccia, S., Mennini, T., Samanin, R., Consolo, S., and Ladinsky, H. (1979): *Curr. Med. Res. Opin.*, 6 (Suppl. 1): 15-27.

33. Garattini, S., and Samanin, R. (1975): In: *Appetite and food intake*, edited by T. Sylverstone, pp. 83-108. Dahlen Konferenzen, Berlin.

34. Geelen, M.J. (1983): *Biochem. Pharmacol.*, 32: 3321-3324.

35. Harrison, L.C., King-Roach, A., Martin, F.I.R., and Melick, R.A. (1975): *Postgrad. Med. J.*, 51 (Suppl. 1): 110-114.

36. Harrison, L.C., and King-Roach, A. (1976): *Clin. Exp. Pharacol. Physiol.*, 3: 503-506.

37. Himms-Hagen, J. (1976): *Ann. Rev. Physiol.*, 38: 315-351.

38. Kaye, J.P., Tomlin, S., and Galton, D.J. (1975): *Postgrad. Med. J.*, 51 (Suppl. 1): 95-99.

39. Kesson, C.M., and Ireland, J.T. (1976): *The practitioner*, 216: 577-580.

40. Kirby, M.J., and Turner, P. (1975): *Postgrad. Med. J.*, 51 (Suppl. 1): 73-76.

41. Kirby, M.J., Carageorgiou-Msarkomihalakis, J., and Turner P. (1975): *Br. J. Clin. Pharmacol.*, 2: 541-542.

42. Kirby, M.J., and Turner, P. (1976): *Nature*, 262: 617.

43. Kirby, M.J., and Turner, P. (1976): *J. Pharm. Pharmacol.*, 28: 163-164.

44. Kirby, M.J., and Turner, P. (1977): *Arch. Int. Pharmacodyn. Ther.*, 225: 25-28.

45. Kirby, M.J., and Turner, P. (1977): *Br. J. Clin. Pharmacol.*, 4: 459-462.

46. Lang, S.S., Danforth, E. Jr., and Lien, E.L. (1983): *Life Sci.*, 33: 1269-1275.

47. Larsens, S., Vejtorp, L., Hornnes, P., Bechgaard, H., Sestoft, L., and Lyngsoe, J. (1977): *Br. J. Clin. Pharmac.*, 4: 529-533.

48. Le Douarec, J.C., and Schmitt, H. (1964): *Thérapie*, 19: 831-841.

49. Levitsky, D.A., and Schuster, J.A. (1985): Submitted to *Intern. J. Obes.*

50. Levitsky, D.A., Strupp, B.J., and Lupoli, J. (1981): *Pharm. Biochem. Behav.*, 14: 661-667.

51. Luntz, G.R.W.N., and Reuter, C.J. (1975): *Postgrad Med. J.*, 51 (Suppl. 1): 133-137.

52. Mace, P.B., Malcom, K.P. Outar, K.P., and Pawan, G.L.S. (1972): *Proc. Nut. Soc.*, 31: 14A.

53. Marsh, J.B., and Bizzi, A. (1972): *Biochem. Pharmacol.* 21: 1143-1150.

54. Marsh, J.B., Guaitani, A., Bartosek, I., and Bizzi, A. (1972): *Proc. Soc. Exptl. Biol. Med.* 139: 753-754.

55. Massoudi, M., and Miller, D.S. (1977): *Proc. Nutr. Soc.*, 36: 1235A.

56. Nicolaidis, S. (1974): Proc. of the *XXVI Inter. Congress of Physiol. Sci.*, Vol. 10, pp. 122-123, New Dehli.

57. Nicolaidis, S., and Even, P. (1984): *C. R. Acad. Sci. Paris* t. 298, Série III, No 10.

58. Pasquine, T.A., and Thenen, S.W. (1981): *Proc. Soc. Expt. Biol. Med.*, 166: 241-248.

59. Pawan, G.L.S. (1969): *Lancet* 1: 498-500.

60. Rothwell, N.J., and Stock, M.J. (1979): *Nature* 281: 31-35.

61. Rothwell, N.J., Stock, M.J., and Wyllie, M.J. (1981): *Br. J. Pharmacol.*, 74: 539-546.

62. Salmela, P.I., Sotaniemi, E.A., Vikari, J., Solkivi-Jaakola, T., and Jarvensivu, P. (1981): *Diabetes Care* 4: 535-540.

63. Sian, M.S., and Rains, A.J.H. (1979): *Postgrad. Med. J.* 55: 180-187.

64. Slusarczyk, H., and Turner, P. (1980): *Br. J. Pharmacol.*, 73: 272P.

65. Turner, P. (1978): *Inter. J. Obes.*, 2: 343-348.

66. Turner, P. (1979): *Curr. Med. Res. Opin.*, 6 (Suppl. 1): 101-106.

67. Turtle, J.R. (1973): *La vie Médicale au Canada Français*, Special issue for the International Symposium on Fenfluramine: 95-103

68. Turtle, J.R., and Burgess, J.A. (1973): *Diabetes*, 22: 858-867.

69. Verdy, M., Charbonneau, L., Verdy, I., Belanger, R., Bolte, E., and Chiasson, L.J. (1983): *Int. J. Obes.*, 7: 289-297.

70. Wales, J.K. (1979): *Acta Endocr.*, 90: 616-623.

71. Wales, J.K. (1981): In: *Anorectic Agents: Mechanisms of Action and Tolerance*, edited by S. Garattini and R. Samanin, pp. 239-240. Raven Press, New-York.

72. Wellman, P.J. (1983): *Res. Commun. Chem. Pathol. Pharmacol.* 41: 173-176.

73. Wells, H.M. (1975): *Postgrad Med J.*, 51 (suppl. 1): 137.

74. Wilson, J.P.D., and Galton, D.J. (1971): *Horm. Met. Res.*, 3: 262-266.

75. Wurtman, J., Wurtman, R.J., Mark, S., Tsay, R., Gilbert, W., and Growdon, J. (1985): *Int. J. Eating Disorders* 4: 89-99.

76. Yelnosky, J., and Lawlor, R.B. (1970): *Arch. Int. Pharmacodyn. Ther.*, 184: 374-388.

Pharmacology of Eating Disorders: Theoretical and Clinical Developments, edited by M. O. Carruba and J. E. Blundell. Raven Press, New York © 1986.

Abnormal Regulation of Carbohydrate Consumption

Judith J. Wurtman

Department of Nutrition and Food Science, Massachusetts Institute of Technology, Cambridge, Massachusetts 02139

The control of food intake has traditionally focused on mechanisms that regulate energy intake. Considerably less attention has been given to the regulation of macronutrient consumption. One consequence has been the belief that disorders in food intake resulting in obesity are synonymous with disorders in the regulation of calorie consumption. It is assumed that the obese individual or animal consumes more calories than needed because of an abnormality in the regulation of energy intake. The possibility that the animal or human may be ingesting too many calories because mechanisms regulating the intake of a specific macronutrient are abnormal is rarely considered. Therapeutic measures used to produce weight loss reflect this belief ; the dieter is told to reduce his intake of excess calories regardless of its nutritional source.

Recent developments in the study of food intake regulation suggest that animals and humans are able to regulate their consumption of protein and carbohydrate independent of calorie intake (4, 8, 9) and that the inability to regulate consumption of carbohydrate may be involved in the obesity of some people (11, 12). These people consume excessive calories, primarily as carbohydrate snacks. When their food intake is measured over 24h, their consumption of calories, carbohydrate and protein from meals appears to be moderate (12); only their intake of carbohydrate snack calories is excessive. This disorder of carbohydrate intake seems to involve the brain neurotransmitter serotonin. When individuals who eat excessive amounts of carbohydrate are treated with a drug that increases serotoninergic neurotransmission (dextrofenfluramine) they significantly decrease their consumption of carbohydrate snacks (11, 12).

ANIMAL STUDIES

Studies on whether macronutrient intake is regulated independent of calorie intake were made possible by the development of an experimental paradigm that allowed the investigator to distinguish between an animal's ingestion of a specific macronutrient for its nutritive value or for its caloric value (4). Animals are allowed to choose their foods from a pair of diets containing identical calories but dissimilar amounts of a test macronutrient. Using this technique, Musten et al. (4) showed that rats can regulate their consumption of protein independent of their consumption of calories and our laboratory demonstrated that rats regulate their carbohydrate intake independent of their calorie consumption (8, 9).

We became interested in whether this regulation of carbohydrate intake involved brain serotonin. Earlier studies showed that the synthesis and release of brain serotonin depends on the relative proportions of protein and carbohydrate eaten in the previous meal (1, 2). When a carbohydrate-rich meal is consumed, the pattern of plasma amino acids changes such that tryptophan uptake into the brain is increased. This results in an increase in the synthesis and release of tryptophan's neurotransmitter product, serotonin. The consumption of a protein-rich meal does not bring any changes in the synthesis and release of brain serotonin (1, 2). Thus it seemed possible that brain serotonin was involved in a feedback loop in which the consumption of a carbohydrate-rich food increased serotonin synthesis and release and this, in turn, caused a decrease in subsequent carbohydrate intake.

To see whether brain serotonin was indeed involved in the regulation of carbohydrate consumption, animals were treated with drugs known to enhance serotoninergic neurotransmission and their subsequent carbohydrate consumption measured. Such treatments caused the animals to decrease their consumption of a diet high in carbohydrate but not of a diet considerably lower in carbohydrate (3, 9, 11). We tested our hypothesis further by determining whether the consumption of carbohydrate itself would reduce subsequent carbohydrate ingestion. Animals consumed a small pre-meal (6 calories) containing only carbohydrate or a mixture of carbohydrate, protein and fat. Ninety minutes later, all animals were given a pair of isocaloric diets containing the same amount of protein, but either 25% or 75% carbohydrate. The group that had been given the carbohydrate pre-meal ate significantly less of the high-carbohydrate diet but the same total number of calories as those animals eating the mixed nutrient pre-meal (7). This study thus strengthened the evidence linking the regulation of carbohydrate intake to brain serotonin.

HUMAN STUDIES

These studies on the regulation of carbohydrate intake were extended to humans to see whether such regulation might be found among normal and overweight individuals. A pilot study with normal volunteers was done first. These subjects claimed to have an appetite for carbohydrate-rich foods particularly as snacks and these claims were evaluated by interviews and food intake records. In this and the subsequent human studies to be described, all volunteers signed consent forms that had been formally approved by the MIT

(Massachusetts Institute of Technology) committee on Use of Humans as Experimental Subjects and by the Clinical Research Center Committee, which oversees studies on human volunteers. The eleven subjects studied consumed 60% or more of their snacks as carbohydrate-rich foods and each tended to snack at very specific times of day or evening rather than randomly (10). Subjects were then treated with tryptophan (2g), fenfluramine (20g) or placebo (controls for these compounds) in a double-blind crossover schedule. Each treatment period lasted 5 days. The subjects were asked to restrict their snacking to pre-chosen high-carbohydrate foods (such as potato chips or cookies) and to take their designated pills one hour before the onset of their carbohydrate snack period. The group as a whole responded to fenfluramine by significantly reducing the number of carbohydrate snacks eaten; they did not as a group respond in a similar fashion to tryptophan but three of the subjets did significantly reduce snack intake with this treatment (10).

This pilot study revealed that some individuals have a definite need to snack on high-carbohydrate foods and that this need involves serotonin; it thus seemed possible that this appetite for carbohydrates might be exaggerated in obese people and explain their excess for calorie intake. The abundance of reports of excessive carbohydrate intake among 'failed dieters' made this possibility seem even more likely.

A second clinical study (10) was carried out to see whether obese adults who consider themselves carbohydrate cravers would indeed snack preferentially on high-carbohydrate foods if allowed 24-hour access to an assortment of both isocaloric carbohydrate-rich and protein-rich foods. The study was designed to distinguish between a general inability to control calorie intake; i.e. the consumption of too much food regardless of its nutrient content and a specific inability to control carbohydrate intake. The study lasted 4 weeks and was conducted on an in-patient basis. Subjects were encouraged to snack freely from ten isocaloric high protein and high carbohydrate foods dispensed in a computer-driven vending machine. The fat contents of the snacks were similar and subjects were told repeatedly that the calorie contents of the snacks were all the same. They were not allowed to diet during the study. The snacks were available at all times except during meals. The calorie and nutrient contents of the meals were fixed to prevent subjects from skipping meals in order to snack.

Twenty-three subjects completed the study. The first two weeks were used to obtain baseline food intake information and the second, to test the effect of fenfluramine (15 or 20 mg/dose), l-tryptophan (800 mg/dose) or placebo, administered three times a day.

The group consumed significantly more carbohydrate than protein snacks per day (4.1 ± 0.4 vs 0.8 ± 0.3). As with our normal weight subjects, these volunteers also consumed their snacks at very characteristic times of the day or evening.

Fenfluramine reduced their carbohydrate snack intake significantly while tryptophan decreased carbohydrate snack intake among three of the six subjects in its treatment group.

It was not possible to measure the voluntary choice of nutrients at meals among these carbohydrate cravers because meal choices were fixed in this study. Thus a third clinical study was carried out to determine whether obese carbohydrate snackers would choose a high proportion of carbohydrate to protein at meals as well as snacks (12). This in-patient study was shorter; subjects spent 2 days a week for 4 consecutive weeks at the MIT Clinical Research Center. Dextrofenfluramine (15 mg at 7 am and 4 pm) or its placebo was administered for 8 days in a double-blind crossover schedule. Food intake was measured in the Clinical Research Center on days 1, 7 and 8 of each treatment period. Subjects were allowed to live at home during days 2-6. They were not allowed to restrict their food intake during the study. To determine how much protein and carbohydrate the obese carbohydrate-craving subjects would choose to eat from both meals and snacks, a variety of isocaloric high-carbohydrate and high-protein foods was offered at meals. As in the previous study, five isocaloric protein and five isocaloric carbohydrate snacks were dispensed in a computer-driven vending machine. The choice of food remained the same throughout the study to minimize the possible effects of novelty. The foods represented those commonly eaten in this geographic area. All meal foods were weighed before serving and after subjects had left the dining room.

The results of this study pointed out significant differences between the nutrient choices made at mealtime and as snacks (Table 1). As in previous studies, the subjects ate primarily carbohydrate-rich foods as snacks. However, they did not show a similar preference for carbohydrates at mealtime. Contrary to our expectations, they ate similar amounts of protein and carbohydrate at meals (Table 1). Moreover, their caloric intake at meals was moderate and would not account for their obesity. The addition of carbohydrate snack calories increased their caloric intake to levels above their energy needs.

Dextrofenfluramine caused our subjects to decrease their calorie intake from snacks by 41 %. However it dit not cause the same reduction in mealtime calorie intake. Calorie intake at meals was reduced only by 16 % and this decrease was not caused by an equal reduction in protein and carbohydrate intake. Rather, dextrofenfluramine caused our subjects to eat less only of the carbohydrate-rich meal foods; they dit not change their intake of the protein-rich meal items. The subjects ate too few protein snacks to assess the effects of dextrofenfluramine on protein snack intake.

These results suggest that the need to snack specifically on

TABLE 1. Effect of dextrofenfluramine on meal and snack consumption

	MEALS			SNACKS		
	CALORIES	PROTEIN (g)	CHO (g)	CALORIES	PROTEIN (number/day)	CHO
PLACEBO	1940	104	121	707	0.7	5.8
DEXTROFENFLURAMINE	1630*	93	94*	414*	0.5	3.4*
% REDUCTION	16	10	23	41	28	41

Twenty obese carbohydrate-craving subjects received dextrofenfluramine (15 mg bid) or a placebo for consecutive 8-day periods. Food choice was measured on days 1, 7 and 8 of each. Subjects chose from among 6 isocaloric foods at meals and from among 10 foods for snacks; half of the foods available at any time were rich in protein and half were rich in carbohydrate.

* $P < 0.01$ differs from placebo group.

carbohydrates and the consumption of carbohydrates along with protein at meals may be motivated by different regulatory mechanisms. Perhaps the desire to consume a certain proportion of carbohydrate to protein at meals involves a regulatory mechanism concerned with maintaining adequate nutrient intake. The need of our subjects to consume carbohydrate snacks unaccompanied by any protein in the mid-afternoon or evening may reflect the brain's 'desire' to enhance serotoninergic neurotransmission and may be unrelated to the body's nutritional needs.

In addition, the hypothesized relationship between nutrients ingestion and brain chemistry could be further extended. We are beginning to accumulate evidence that some subjects may ingest a carbohydrate-rich meal in order to produce specific changes in mood state. Studies measuring changes in mood and performance after a morning or afternoon meal of protein or carbohydrate revealed that carbohydrate consumption in the afternoon increased feelings of calmness, relaxation, and drowsiness among 184 normal men and women (6). Protein consumption had no such effects. We are now questioning carbohydrate cravers participating in an on-going study to determine whether they experience mood changes after eating carbohydrate and also testing them directly with carbohydrate or protein-rich meals to measure changes in mood and sleepiness. The possibility that the consumption of carbohydrate-rich snack foods may be motivated, at least in part, by the psychopharmacologic effects of carbohydrate consumption is based on the similarity between the effects of carbohydrate intake and the action of many antidepressant drugs. Such drugs share with dietary carbohydrates the propensity to enhance serotonin-mediated neurotransmission (either by blocking serotonin's intracellular metabolism by monoamine oxidase or by suppressing its re-uptake into the presynaptic terminals that release it). The subgroup of obese people who demonstrate the need to eat carbohydrates at specific times may, in reality, be consuming these foods in order to produce a specific change in their mood. The increased consumption of sweet carbohydrates found among people suffering from a type of depression known as Seasonal Affective Disorder reinforces this possibility (5).

REFERENCES

1. Fernstrom, J.D., and Wurtman, R.J. (1972): *Science*, 178: 414-416.

2. Fernstrom, J.D., and Wurtman, R.J., Hammarstrom-Wiklund, B., Rand, W.M., Munro, H.N., and Davidson, C.S. (1979): *Am. J. Clin. Nutr.*, 32: 1912-1922.

3. Moses, P., and Wurtman, R.J. (1984): *Life Sci.*, 35: 1297-1300.

4. Musten, B., Peace, D., and Anderson, G.H. (1974): *J. Nutr.*, 104: 563-572.

5. Rosenthal, N., Sack, D., Gillin, C., Lewy, A., Goodwin, F., Davenport, Y., Muller, P., Newsome, D., and Wehr, T. (1984): *Arch. Gen. Psychiatry*, 41: 72-80.

6. Spring, B., Maller, O., Wurtman, J.J., Digman, L., and Cozolino, L. (1983): *J. Psychiatr. Res.*, 7: 155-167.

7. Wurtman, J.J., Moses, P., Wurtman, R.J. (1984): *J. Nutr.*, 113: 70-78.

8. Wurtman, J.J., and Wurtman, R.J. (1979): *Curr. Res. Opin.*, 6: 28-33.

9. Wurtman, J.J., and Wurtman, R.J. (1979): *Life Sci.*, 24: 895-904.

10. Wurtman, J.J. and Wurtman, R.J. (1981): In: *Anorectic Agents: Mechanisms of Actions and Tolerance*, edited by S. Garattini and R. Samanin, pp. 169-182. Raven Press, New York.

11. Wurtman, J.J., Wurtman R.J., Growdon, J.H., Henry, P., Lipscomb, A., and Zeisel, S. (1981): *Int. J. Eating Disorders*, 1: 2-11.

12. Wurtman, J.J., Wurtman, R.J., Mark, S., Tsay, R., Gilbert, W., and Growdon, J. (1985): *Int. J. Eating Disorders*, 4: 89-99.

Pharmacology of Eating Disorders: Theoretical and Clinical Developments, edited by M. O. Carruba and J. E. Blundell. Raven Press, New York © 1986.

A Pharmacological Analysis of Human Feeding: Its Contribution to the Understanding of Affective Disorders

Trevor Silverstone and Elizabeth Goodall

Academic Unit of Human Psychopharmacology, Medical Colleges of St. Bartholomews, and the London Hospitals, London, United Kingdom

The clinical pharmacological approach to the study of appetite has both theoretical and practical implications for the understanding and management of psychopathology especially in the field of major affective disorders.

It is accepted that disturbances in appetite and weight are important features of depressive states and have been used to assess both the nature and severity of the illness. Disturbance may be manifest as either an increase or a decrease in appetite or weight (40) although the direction of the change is probably associated with severity of the depression.

Weight loss is a diagnostic feature in endogenous depression (18) and is one of the symptoms which distinguishes depression with melancholia from major depression in DSM-III criteria.

Return to appetite is one of the earliest and most reliable signs of recovery (32) and improvement in appetite has been shown to be one of the 10 symptoms which can be used as a reliable measure of response to desipramine treatment (26).

In a recent survey of 193 moderately depressed out patients, 54 % gave a history of decreased appetite, while 27 % had noted an increase in their appetite associated with over-eating in times of stress (19). Changes in appetite in either direction were associated with more severe depression, a finding consistent with Paykel's findings (29). Thus alterations in appetite, particularly anorexia would appear to be inextricably bound up with depressive illness, and knowledge of the physiological and neurochemical mechanisms underlying these appetite changes might well lead to a greater understanding of the pathophysiology of the illness itself.

According to the monoamine hypothesis of affective disorder (33) central monoamine neurotransmitter systems are closely involved in the pathogenesis of affective disorders. This is still believed to be the case although the hypothesis, as originally stated, is now thought to be oversimplified (23).

Anorectic agents have been shown in animal studies to exert their influence by the release of the same monoamines (catecholamines and indolamines) which are implicated in the etiology of affective disorders.

Drugs which are administered primarily to alter abnormal psychological processes (as in the treatment of psychopathological states, such as depression) can at the same time affect appetite and thereby lead to alterations in body weight. An understanding of the ways these drugs act can throw light on the neurochemical mechanisms underlying those disease states for which the drugs are being administered and can also lead to a perhaps greater understanding of how these often unwanted effects on appetite and weight can be managed.

The clinical pharmacological approach involves the application in human subjects of pharmacological tools developed from animal research such that the action of drugs which alter the amount or effect of a specific neurotransmitter at the synapse can be studied. These include agonist drugs which increase the availability of the neurotransmitter by promoting release, blocking re-uptake or inhibiting breakdown; antagonists which act at the receptor (either pre or post-synaptic) to block the action of the neurotransmitter, and precursors of neurotransmitters which promote their synthesis.

AMPHETAMINE ANOREXIA AND AFFECTIVE DISORDER

Amphetamine is a drug with potent anorectic stimulant and euphoriant properties in human subjects (38). In laboratory animals amphetamine has been shown to act in the brain largely by releasing pre-formed dopamine (DA) and noradrenaline (NA) from pre-synaptic neurones (9). Given this dual pattern of neurochemical actions, could it be that the effect of one neurotransmitter might underlie the drug's anorectic effect, with its stimulant action being related to an action on the other neurotransmitter ?

We have attempted to answer this question by examining the interaction of amphetamine with a number of relatively specific receptor blocking compounds. In a series of studies involving normal human subjects, we have used both subjective and objective measures to evaluate the effects of such interactions. For rating of subjective changes we used visual analogue scales (VAS); for objective measure of arousal we used skin conductance (22) and for objective measurement of food intake we used an automated solid food dispenser (35). In order to determine the effect of DA receptor blockade on the stimulant and anorectic action of amphetamine we have used the selective DA receptor blocking drug pimozide (3).

In our first experiment with pimozide we administered a single oral dose of 2 mg of the drug or matching placebo, two hours before giving a single oral dose of 10 mg d-amphetamine or a second matching placebo to eight healthy female subjects. The subjects completed VAS ratings for arousal, mood and hunger before receiving the first tablet and at hourly intervals thereafter for the next six hours. Unfortunately we were unable to determine the effects of pimozide in d-amphetamine-induced euphoria as the dose of d-amphetamine used did not produce a significant elevation of mood. However, Jonsson (20), using a much higher dose of d-amphetamine, had reported that pimozide inhibits the euphoriant effect of the drug in previously addicted subjects. Thus, the available evidence supports the view that the euphoriant action of d-amphetamine is likely to be DA-mediated.

As far as subjective arousal is concerned we did observe a significant effect of d-amphetamine; and this effect was significantly attenuated by pretreatment with 2 mg pimozide. This finding suggests that d-amphetamine is also DA-mediated.

In contrast, hunger VAS ratings, which were markedly reduced by d-amphetamine remained unaffected by pimozide, indicating that d-amphetamine anorexia, unlike d-amphetamine arousal and euphoria, is not mediated primarily through DA pathways.

In a second study involving pimozide we measured the response to d-amphetamine objectively by recording skin conductance before and after a single oral dose of 20 mg of the drug, with and without pretreatment with 2 or 4 mg pimozide (Jacobs and Silverstone, in preparation). As before, matching placebos were used to maintain strict double-blind conditions. d-Amphetamine increased both the basal level of skin conductance and the number of spontaneous fluctuations in skin conductance. Pimozide reversed these changes in a dose-related manner, another result in keeping with d-amphetamine arousal being DA-mediated.

Thymoxamine is considered to have a relatively specific action on α -NA receptors (7), and has been shown to be active centrally. In order to assess the effects of NA blockade on d-amphetamine arousal and anorexia we administered 80 and 160 mg thymoxamine, or matching placebo one hour before giving a single oral dose of 20 mg d-amphetamine to 12 healthy male volunteers. As far as subjective mood ratings were concerning, thymoxamine, if anything, d-amphetamine-induced euphoria and irritability. A similar pattern was seen in the VAS arousal ratings, with thymoxamine enhancing the effect of d-amphetamine. Changes in skin conductance measurements were consistent with those observed in the subjective ratings.

In sharp contrast to what was observed with d-amphetamine-induced arousal d-amphetamine-induced anorexia was partially by the higher dose of thymoxamine. This finding suggests that d-amphetamine anorexia may well be NA-mediated, a view consistent with some of the animal data (1). However in a second study involving healthy female subjects in which we measured food intake directly in addition to assessing subjective hunger we failed to replicate our previous finding that thymoxamine attentuates d-amphetamine anorexia (Goodall, Silverstone and Trenchard, in preparation). But in this second study food intake was measured two hours after the drug had been given whereas the most marked effect of thymoxamine in the first study had not occurred until some three to four hours after it had been given. Thus the lack of agreement in the two studies may well be more of a reflection of the methodological differences between them than a true pharmacological inconsistency.

We found propranolol, a centrally active β-NA receptor blocking drug (28), to be completely without effect on either d-amphetamine-induced arousal or anorexia in normal female volunteers. Nor did it influence the reduction of food intake brought about by d-amphetamine. Such a complete lack of interaction between d-amphetamine and propranolol argues strongly against a primary involvement of β -NA receptors in d-amphetamine-induced arousal or anorexia.

From the results we have obtained in our series of experiments in human volunteers we can be reasonably confident that the stimulant activity of d-amphetamine, and probably its euphoriant activity as well, is mediated through central DA pathways.

As manic illness also appears to be, at least partly, DA-mediated (34), d-amphetamine-induced arousal in normal subjects might provide a useful model for mania. Further evaluation of this possibility has yielded some striking similarities in symptomatology, endocrine changes and pharmacological response between the model and the clinical correlation (Jacobs and Silverstone, in preparation).

The situation with regard to the mediation of d-amphetamine anorexia is less clear than that of arousal; certainly neither DA nor β-NA receptors appear to be primarily involved. Whether α -NA receptors are implicated, remains unresolved; in one study there did appear to be a definite inter-relationship between the α -NA receptor blocking drug thymoxamine and d-amphetamine anorexia. If it turns out to be confirmed that d-amphetamine anorexia is NA mediated then the possibility arises that other anorectic states, such as those which occur in depressive illness may be a consequence of an abnormality in central NA neurotransmission.

To this end we have examined the effect of a single intravenous injection of 15 mg methylamphetamine as compared to sterile water under strict double-blind conditions in 21 depressed subjects (Silverstone and Cookson, in preparation).

The questions we were asking were : a) if methylamphetamine improved the mood of any of our depressed patients was there an associated improvement in appetite, as occurs during recovery from a depressive illness, and b) was any such improvement in appetite suppressed by the direct anorectic action of the drug ? Two intriguing findings emerged. First, as was expected from uncontrolled studies (10), only a third of our twenty-one patients responded to methylamphetamine (but not to placebo) with an unequivocal improvement in mood. This suggests an impairment of the responsiveness of central DA pathways in some severely depressed patients, but not in all. While the essential differences between methylamphetamine responders and non-responders remains to be elucidated, there appears to be a distinct possibility of delineating different categories of depressive illness on pharmacological grounds.

The other intriguing finding which emerged from this study in depressed patients was that six of the seven who responded to methylamphetamine with a marked improvement in mood, also experienced a concomitant increase in hunger. If d-amphetamine anorexia is in fact NA-mediated then in these methylamphetamine responders the absence of methylamphetamine-induced anorexia may reflect a disorder of central NA neurotransmission in at least some depressed patients. This possibility has also been proposed by others on neuroendocrinological grounds (11).

These results raise the question of the extent to which loss of appetite and lack of interest in food are linked to the etiology of depression. It could be argued that when weight loss occurs in depression it is due to a functional deficit in central DA systems causing a general reduction in activity (including eating) rather than a primary lessening of appetite. Whereas in stress, a deficit in NA transmission might be causing a primary alteration in appetite and consequent weight change.

SEROTONINERGIC MECHANISMS, APPETITE AND DEPRESSION

A case has also been made for the involvement of 5-hydroxytryptamine (5-HT) in depression particularly in those patients who manifest suicidal behaviour. A bimodal distribution of the serotonin metabolite 5-hydroxyindoleacetic acid (5-HIAA) was found in the cerebrospinal fluid of depressed patients, with those patients who had committed suicide or made a violent suicide attempt having low levels of 5-HIAA (5, 6).

Goodwin and Post (16) reviewing the literature of 5-HT metabolism and depression suggested that low 5-HT may be a feature of all those with suicidal or impulsive/aggressive tendencies regardless of purely depressive psychopathology.

The anorectic drug fenfluramine is known to act via the release and prevention of re-uptake of serotonin in presynaptic neurones (14).

Our studies have shown that fenfluramine (both the racemic mixture and the dextro-isomer) have anorectic properties in normal volunteers (21, 36, Silverstone, Smith and Richards, in preparation). Fenfluramine has also been shown to be an effective weight reducing agent in obese people (25). In two studies, depression has been reported following abrupt withdrawal of the drug (27, 41). As fenfluramine (a 5-HT releaser) has been shown to cause anorexia in humans and sudden withdrawal to induce depression, it is possible that the low levels of 5-HT noted in some depressed patients might be associated with an increase in appetite and in weight gain. However it remains uncertain whether there is any correlation between increased appetite and weight gain and low 5-HT levels in such patients. Indeed, the interrelationships between transmitter levels, rate of turnover and the density of receptors make interpretations of clinical findings extremely problematical.

Further evidence for the involvement of 5-HT in feeding comes from the use of post-synaptic 5-HT receptor blocking drugs. Metergoline has been shown to antagonise fenfluramine-induced anorexia in rats (8) but not that induced by d-amphetamine. We have recently examined the role of metergoline in eating in normal volunteers. In our first study, we gave a single oral dose of 4 mg metergoline or matching placebo together with a single oral dose of 10 mg d-amphetamine or placebo to healthy female subjects two hours before access to the automated solid food dispenser. As expected, d-amphetamine had a significant effect on both subjective hunger rating and food intake. Metergoline alone was associated with increased food intake which was significant after 70 minutes when compared to placebo (15).

The mean consumption of food when metergoline was given with d-amphetamine was significantly higher than that following d-amphetamine alone. However, the difference between the effect of metergoline on placebo and its effect on d-amphetamine was not significant, suggesting that there was no direct interaction between metergoline and d-amphetamine. These results are consistent with the view that 5-HT is involved in human feeding, and indicate that d-amphetamine-induced anorexia is not 5-HT mediated.

Our findings with metergoline are in keeping with earlier reports that cyproheptadine, a 5-HT receptor antagonist, produces significant weight gain in thin healthy volunteers (37).

ANTIDEPRESSANT DRUGS, APPETITE AND CHANGES IN BODY WEIGHT

Another way of examining the relationship between appetite and mood is to examine the changes in appetite which occur during treatment of depressed patients with antidepressant drugs. As we have already seen, improvement in mood in depressed patients is frequently accompanied by an increase in appetite, thus it would be expected that effective treatment with an antidepressant drug might well be associated with a gain in weight. However, any gain in weight over and above that associated with general clinical improvement could lead to undesirable consequences. A potential for excess weight gain has been particularly remarked upon with the antidepressant drug amitriptyline.

Arenillas (4) was the first to draw attention to the frequency with which patients on amitriptyline gained weight, and he pointed out that this weight gain appeared to be the result of a craving for carbohydrate containing foods. The suggestion that this carbohydrate craving might be due to an effect of amitriptyline on insulin was postulated by Winston and McCann (42); they reported data on two patients receiving a combination of antidepressants who had gained weight and in whom circulating insulin levels appeared to be elevated. Paykel, Muller and de la Vergne (30) examined the relationship of amitriptyline to weight gain which was over the above that which might have been expected simply as a result of clinical improvement. They found that patients who were being maintained on prophylactic amitriptyline, having previously recovered from a depressive illness, gained significantly more weight than a matching control group who were being maintained on placebo. As before, the increase in weight appeared to be secondary to an increase in a desire for carbohydrate containing foods. In addition to an action upon an NA neurons, amitriptyline also appears to affect central serotonergic receptors mechanisms (24, 31) and it may be this property which is responsible for the increase in weight.

Several effective 5-HT re-uptake inhibitor antidepressants have been developed following the evidence that a defect in indolaminergic transmission may be involved in some depressive illnesses. Theoretically these drugs would be predicted to cause weight loss as their neurochemical function is to increase the availability of 5-HT at the synapse.

Fluoxetine has been reported to cause reduction in food intake in animals (13), and another 5-HT re-uptake blocking drug, zimelidine, was noted to cause significantly greater weight loss than placebo in a group of healthy obese volunteers (39). Coppen et al. (12), comparing amitriptyline and zimelidine in depressed patients found that while those on amitriptyline showed significant weight gain those on zimelidine showed no such change, and Gottfries (17) also reported weight loss in depressed patients treated with zimelidine.

Questions concerning anorexia and mood now arise, similar to those previously discussed in relation to amphetamine and depression. What is the relationship between improvement in mood and appetite in patients treated with an antidepressant which simultaneously improves mood but decreases appetite ? Does decrease in appetite adversely affect potential improvement in mood ? Or are those patients (with presumably low 5-HT) who are responsive to the drug a subgroup with *increased* appetite and weight gain when depressed ? If this were so, such patients should respond to antidepressant treatment, which decreased their appetite, without any detrimental effect on their mood. Unfortunately, since changes in weight and appetite are frequently not reported in studies on depressed patients, this issue presently remains unresolved.

It may be concluded from our studies and those of others that appetite and mood are often inextricably linked with changes in one causing changes in the other. While many questions remain unanswered detailed examination of the way drugs act in *human* subjects to simultaneously cause changes in mood and/or appetite have shed some light on the extremely complex neurochemical mechanisms involved. It is, we believe, from such investigation that progress in our knowledge of the pathogenesis of affective disorders will come, followed closely by corresponding advances in treatment.

REFERENCES

1. Ahlskog, J.E. (1974): *Brain Res.*, 82: 211-240.

2. Amin, M.M., Ananth, J.V., Coleman, B.S., Darcourt, G., Farkas, T., Goldstien, B., Lapierre, Y.D., Paykel, E., and Wakelin, J.S. (1984): *Clin. Neuropharmacol.*, 7 (Suppl. 1): 580-581.

3. Anden, N.E., Butcher, S.G., Corrodi, H., Fuxe, F., and Ungerstedt, U. (1970): *Europ. J. Pharmacol.*, 11: 303-314.

4. Arenillas, L. (1964): *Lancet* i:432-433.

5. Asberg, M., Thoren, P., Traskman, L., Bertilsson, L. and Ringberger, V. (1976): *Science*, 191: 478-480.

6. Asberg, M., Traskman, L. and Thoren, O. (1976): *Arch. Gen. Psychiatry* 33: 1193-1197.

7. Besser, G.M., Butler, P.W.P., Ratcliffe, J.G., Rees, L. and Young P. (1968): *Br. J. Pharmacol.*, 39: 196P-197P.

8. Blundell, J.E., and Latham, C.J. (1980): *Pharmacol. Biochem. Behav.*, 12: 717-722.

9. Carlsson, A. (1970): In: *Amphetamines and Related Compounds* edited by E. Costa and S. Garattini, pp 289-300. Raven Press, New York.

10. Checkley, S.A. (1978): *Br. J. Psychiatry* 133: 416-423.

11. Checkley, S.A. (1980): *Psychol. Med.* 10: 35-53.

12. Coppen, A., Rao, V.A.R., Swade, C., and Wood, K. (1979): *Psychopharmacologia* 63: 125-129.

13. Fuller, R.W., and Wong, D.T. (1984): *Clin. Neuropharmacol.*, 7 (Suppl. 1): 202-203.

14. Garattini, S., Buczko, W., Jori, A., and Samanin, R. (1975): *Postgrad. Med. J.*, 51: 27-35.

15. Goodall, E., and Silverstone, T. (1984): Presented at *14 th C.I.N.P. Congress*, Florence, June 1984, Abstract P. 850.

16. Goodwin, F.K., and Post, R.M. (1983): *Br. J. Clin. Pharmacol.* 15: 3935-4055.

17. Gottfries, C.G. (1981): *Acta Psychiatr. Scand.* 63 (Suppl. 290) : 353-356.

18. Hamilton, M. (1960): *J. Neurol. Neurosurg. Psychiatry* 23: 56-62.

19. Harris, B., Young, J., and Hughes, B. (1984): *J. Affective Disord.* 6: 219-239.

20. Jonsson, L.E. (1972): *Eur. J. Clin. Pharmacol.*, 4: 206-211.

21. Kyriakides, M., and Silverstone, T. (1979): *Neuropharmacology*, 18: 1007-1008.

22. Lader, M.H. (1975): *The Psychophysiology of Mental Illness.* Routledge and Kegan Paul, London.

23. Maas, J.W., Koslow, S.H., Davis, J.M., Katz, M.M., Mendels, J., Robins, E., Stokes, P.E., and Bowden, C.L. (1980): *Psychol. Med.*, 10: 759-776.

24. Maj, J., Lewandowska, A., and Rawtow, A. (1979): *Pharmakopsychiatria*, 12: 281-285.

25. Munro, J.F., and Ford, M.J. (1982): In: *Drugs and Appetite*, edited by T. Silverstone, pp. 125-158. Academic Press, London.

26. Nelson, J.C., Mazure, C., Quinlan, D.M., and Jatlow, P.I. (1984): *Arch. Gen. Psychiatry*, 41: 663-668.

27. Oswald, I., Lewis, S.A., Dunleavy, D.L.F., Brezinova, V., and Briggs, M. (1971): *Br. Med. J.*, 3: 70.

28. Patel, L., and Turner, P. (1981): *Med. Res. Rev.*, 1: 387-410.

29. Paykel, E.S. (1977): *J. Psychosom. Res.*, 21: 401-407.

30. Paykel, E.S., Mueller, P.S., and de la Vergne, P.M. (1973): *Br. J. Psychiatry,* 123: 501-507.

31. Peroutka, S.J., and Snyder, S.H. (1980): *Science,* 210: 88-90.

32. Russell, G. (1960): *Clin. Sci.,* 19: 327-336.

33. Schildkraut, J.J. (1965): *Am. J. Psychiatry,* 122: 509-522.

34. Silverstone, T. (1978): In: *Depressive Disorders,* edited by S. Garattini. pp. 419-430. Schattauer Verlag, Stuttgart.

35. Silverstone, T., Fincham, J., and Brydon, J. (1980): *Am. J. Clin. Nutr.,* 3: 1852-1855.

36. Silverstone, T., Fincham, J., and Campbell, D.B. (1975): *Postgrad. Med. J.,* 51: 171-174.

37. Silverstone, T., and Schuyler, D. (1975): *Psychopharmacologia,* 40: 335-340.

38. Silverstone, T., and Wells, B. (1980): In: *Amphetamines and related stimulants,* edited by J. Caldwell. CRC Press,Boca Raton.

39. Simpson, R.J., Lawton, D.J., Watt, M.H., and Tiplady, B. (1981): *Br. J. Clin. Pharmacol.,* 11: 96-98.

40. Spitzer, R.L., Endicott, J., and Robins, E. (1978): *Arch. Gen. Psychiatry,* 35: 773-782.

41. Steel, J.M., and Briggs, M. (1972): *Br. Med. J.,* 3: 26-27.

42. Winston, F., and McCann, M.L. (1972): *Br. J. Psychiatry,* 120: 693-694.

Pharmacology of Eating Disorders: Theoretical and Clinical Developments, edited by M. O. Carruba and J. E. Blundell. Raven Press, New York © 1986.

The Limited Role of Drugs in the Treatment of Anorexia and Bulimia Nervosa

Gerald F. M. Russell, Stuart A. Checkley, and Paul H. Robinson

The Institute of Psychiatry and the Maudsley Hospital, Denmark Hill, London SE5 8AF, United Kingdom

Different drugs have in recent years been administered to patients with anorexia nervosa and bulimic disorders. The choice of drug has usually been made according to theoretical principles. In the case of anorexia nervosa, for example, the aim has often been the simplistic one of stimulating hunger, in the hope of increasing food intake. On the whole, this approach to drug treatment has met with little success. This review will concentrate more on empirical observations, and will take as its point of departure the clinical features of these two disorders. The limitations of the theoretical models will be briefly considered. Finally, an appraisal will be made of the limited role of drug treatments in anorexia and bulimia nervosa, when compared with more general and psychological methods of treatment.

ANOREXIA NERVOSA

Clinical Features

Anorexia nervosa is much commoner in girls than in boys. The reason for this sex difference is not clear, but it is generally acknowledged that the main clinical features are remarkably similar in boys and in girls (6, 9). This article will therefore concentrate on the illness in girls. In them anorexia nervosa usually occurs within a few years of the menarche so that the age of onset is usually between 14 and 17. But the illness may also afflict more mature women or younger adolescents before their menarche.

The onset is insidious, over weeks or months. The young woman reduces her intake of those foods usually considered to be "fattening" by the layman (bread, potatoes, pastries, biscuits). She explains that she is merely following a diet with the aim of acquiring a slim figure and improving her appearance - a pursuit which nowadays is generally viewed as unexceptional. Yet, underlying this behaviour and partly concealed, is the patient's morbidly exaggerated dread of fatness, a state she wishes to avoid at almost any cost. Weight loss is slow at first. Menstruation ceases at an early stage of the illness and persists throughout its course. Within a few months body weight may become reduced to very low levels - 35 kg or even less - and the patient may show various features of severe malnutrition: irritability, restlessness and depression are among the commonest psychological sequelae. Insomnia, sensitivity to cold and loss of interest in the opposite sex also follow. More serious features and complications of malnutrition include severe wasting, hypotension and hypothermia. Especially during attempts at rapid refeeding, peripheral oedema, pancytopenia with purpura, and myopathy may supervene (1).

There are three sets of clinical disturbances which are characteristic of anorexia nervosa and virtually essential for the diagnosis:

1) A specific psychopathology consisting of the overvalued idea that fatness is a dreadful state which should be avoided at all costs.

2) A self-induced loss of weight, caused by the systematic avoidance of "fattening" foods, often combined with excessive exercise.

3) A specific endocrine disorder expresses itself in the female as amenorrhoea.

It is important to note that the characteristic weight loss of anorexia nervosa is not simply due to a diminution of hunger. Few of these patients have a true loss of appetite (29). The term "anorexia" nervosa is really a misnomer. The patient may comment on her attitude to food, providing explanations for the unwillingness to eat. She may express feelings of guilt after eating, or she may complain of feelings of abdominal fullness and discomfort after a small meal. The illness is best understood as an abnormal need to control body weight. The German term *Magersucht* (the pursuit of thinness) introduced by Kylin (31), is most descriptive. It has also been suggested that the anorexic patient experiences positive sensations from her self-starvation such as feelings of calm and being "in control". Thus her behaviour is said to resemble that seen in other syndromes of dependence (e.g. alcohol dependence) (55). For all these reasons a treatment aimed at merely increasing the patient's hunger and appetite is inappropriate: her reduced food intake is purposive and aimed at reducing body weight.

Theoretical Models governing the Choice of Drug Treatments

In spite of much research in recent years the fundamental causes of anorexia nervosa remain elusive. More is known about the disturbed mechanisms which affect mental and bodily function and contribute to the genesis and perpetuation of the illness. These disturbances constitute secondary causes, making it difficult to disentangle primary aetiology from pathogenesis and psychogenesis. That socio-cultural factors are important aetiologically may be surmised from the impressive evidence that anorexia nervosa has become more common during the past thirty or forty years (28, 54, 56). The most plausible explanation for this increased incidence is that culturally-determined attitudes contribute to the genesis of anorexia nervosa (30). For example, social pressures in Western cultures lead young girls and women to believe that a thin body shape is to be preferred, a message which is echoed repeatedly by the fashion industry, news media and women's magazines. In the present state of limited knowledge it is usually assumed that psychosocial and biological factors interact in causing the illness and producing its manifestations (18, 48). In attempts to unravel the possible causation of anorexia nervosa, several writers have formulated theoretical models. Some of these models have led to various drugs being chosen for the treatment of anorexia nervosa.

Anorexia nervosa viewed as secondary to other psychiatric disorders

Anorexia nervosa is usually regarded as a primary psychiatric illness in its own right (18, 47). Nevertheless it has been argued that anorexia nervosa may be the expression of an underlying depressive illness. For example, it has been pointed out that depressive symptoms are frequent in anorexic patients and a high proportion of first degree relatives have a history of affective disorder (10, 63).

For these reasons antidepressant drugs have been administered to patients with anorexia nervosa. Mills et al.(36) treated a large number of patients with tricyclic antidepressants and claimed beneficial results. The limitations of uncontrolled trials of antidepressants are illustrated in one study (40) where the main criterion of improvement after administering amitriptyline was one of weight gain which ranged from 2.8 to 16.9 kg. As will be mentioned later, however, more predictable weight gains can be observed merely by admitting the patient to a psychiatric unit where skilled nursing care is available. Moreover, an assessment of outcome in anorexia nervosa requires evidence of improvement in several aspects of the patient's life in addition to weight gain: her mental state, her attitudes to eating, her psychosexual and social adjustment, as well as a return of menstruation. These improvements should be sustained and the assessment of outcome usually requires that the follow-up covers at least 4 years (25,38). In this respect the use of antidepressant medication has proved disappointing as it did not influence the long-term outcome of the illness. It is perhaps surprising that a fully controlled clinical trial of an antidepressant in anorexia nervosa has not yet been carried out.

The search for a possible relationship between anorexia nervosa and affective disorders has been pursued further, and has led to the administration of lithium carbonate in the hope that this drug might improve the course of the illness. A pilot study was carried out by Barcai (4) and a controlled trial by Gross et al. (21). In the latter study, which was combined with a course of behaviour therapy, the lithium-treated group of patients on average gained more weight than the placebo-treated group (6.8 kg compared with 5.2 kg). There was thus some justification for the authors' conclusion that lithium carbonate augmented weight gain in patients who were simultaneously being treated with behaviour modification. But the study was limited to 4 weeks duration. A potentially toxic drug such as lithium carbonate should not be administered to anorexic patients until careful studies show that it does indeed shorten the course of the illness.

Anorexia nervosa viewed as a disorder in the hypothalamic control of food intake.

The first studies on the central nervous regulation of food intake were based on the effects of hypothalamic lesions in animals. Anand and Brobeck (3) found that bilateral lesions in the extreme lateral regions of the hypothalamus led to self-starvation in rats. Later work suggested that these lesions would interfere with the principal monoamine pathways ascending to forebrain structures. The monoamine pathways comprise those of noradrenaline, dopamine and 5-hydroxytryptamine (5-HT) (11, 57).

In view of the potent effects in experimental animals of drugs acting upon central neuroamines, trials have been conducted to investigate the therapeutic value of such drugs in the treatment of patients with anorexia nervosa. This extrapolation from findings in normal experimental animals to the complex clinical situation of anorexia nervosa is made mainly as an empirical search for improved treatment. Apart from the results of these treatment studies there is scant clinical evidence in favour of any biochemical hypothesis relating to the pathogenesis of anorexia nervosa.

Dopamine antagonists. Chlorpromazine was introduced in the 1960s as a treatment for anorexia nervosa but although clinicians reported a beneficial effect (13, 14), no controlled trial was conducted. More recently such studies have been reported for the more selectively acting dopamine antagonists pimozide (59) and sulpiride (58). Active treatment resulted in only a very small gain in body weight and little change in psychological attitude. Whether any of these effects were due to non-specific effects of sedation or to a specific action upon the regulation of eating behaviour remains to be clarified.

Dopamine agonists. In keeping with Mawson's views (34) that anorexia nervosa might be due to dopaminergic underactivity, two small uncontrolled studies of dopamine agonists have been reported. Johanson and Knorr (26) reported a small weight gain following treatment with l-DOPA as did Harrower et al. (24) in a similar study using bromocriptine. It is impossible to interpret such small drug effects in the absence of a placebo control.

5-HT Antagonists. In view of the potent inhibitory effect of 5-

HT upon eating behaviour in experimental animals the 5-HT antagonists cyproheptadine has been investigated in comparison with placebo (20, 60). The drug-treated group gained 1 kg more than the placebo-treated group but this difference was neither clinically nor statistically significant. However, cyproheptadine has other pharmacological actions including the blockade of dopamine, histamine and muscarinic receptors and these actions could modify the effect upon eating of 5-HT receptor blockade. Furthermore cyproheptadine only poorly crosses the blood brain barrier. When more satisfactory centrally acting 5-HT antagonists become available for clinical study these could be investigated in anorexia nervosa.

Other pharmacological approaches. On the basis of animal studies, both alpha agonists (33) and antagonists (44, 45) have been proposed for testing in anorexia nervosa. No such studies have as yet been reported.

Daily infusions of naloxone have been reported to result in weight gain of 1 kg per week in 12 patients with anorexia nervosa (37). Without a placebo control the discussion of the mechanisms underlying this possible effect (19) remains premature.

A hypersensitivity of the hypothalamus to oestrogens has been proposed (64) though not investigated in treatment studies.

Conclusions. No controlled study has reported a statistically and clinically significant drug effect upon body weight in anorexia nervosa. Consequently there is no established place for the use of drugs in the management of the eating disorder in these patients.

It is, however, of some theoretical interest that the blockade of dopamine and 5-HT receptors may result in small degrees of weight gain. It will be seen (below) that the stimulation of these same receptors reduces overeating in patients with bulimia nervosa under acute experimental conditions.

The amenorrhoea of anorexia nervosa viewed as a disorder of hypothalamic endocrine regulation.

There is overwhelming evidence that the amenorrhoea of anorexia nervosa is due to an endocrine disorder involving the hypothalamic anterior pituitary-gonadal axis (8, 35, 39, 48). The nature of the hypothalamic disorder has been explored by studying the sequence of endocrine recovery following weight gain and clinical recovery over time. Blood levels of gonadotrophins (LH and FSH) and oestrogens gradually rise. The action of gonadotrophin-releasing hormone returns to normal. There is a return of hypothalamic responsiveness to the negative- and positive-feedback effects of exogenous oestrogen on LH-release. The return of positive-feedback effects is delayed longest and mirrors the final recovery of the hypothalamic response (61).

There is a role for the treatment of persistent amenorrhoea in anorexic patients if the menses have not returned spontaneously in a young woman in spite of having achieved an optimun weight and having maintained it for several months. The patient may respond to one or two courses of clomiphene citrate (50-100 mg daily for 7 days) which induces gonadotrophin release through blocking the negative-feedback effect of endogenous oestrogen on the hypothalamus. If there is no response to clomiphene, this signifies that the positive-feedback hypothalamic response has not yet recovered. It can be mimicked by giving an infusion of LH-releasing hormone in physiological saline 14 days after commencing the clomiphene, when ovulation will usually be induced (62).

Results of the Empirical Treatment of Anorexia Nervosa

It is understandable that most studies of therapeutic outcome should concentrate on the weight gain which is achieved. The malnutrition as such impairs physical health and may even imperil life. It also contributes to the patient's psychological disturbances, so much so that it is seldom possible to implement psychotherapeutic methods without first restoring body weight to an optimum or at least a reasonable level.

The empirical methods of treatment will only be summarized briefly, and the interested reader should refer to fuller texts (12, 50). Because the patient often rejects in part the idea of submitting to a full treatment programme, it is usually necessary to elicit her confidence. This is best achieved over the course of two or three interviews devoted to an exploration of distressing antecedents and consequences of her illness, an approach which enables the clinician to obtain a greater measure of trust from his patient. Although out-patient interviews may succeed in initiating some weight gain, a more reliable and efficacious method is to admit the patient to a psychiatric unit with a team of well-trained nurses experienced in the treatment of anorexic patients. The nursing programme relies mainly on practical psychotherapeutic measures with the nurses establishing a relationship of trust with the patients. The programme is carefully structured and it is made clear to the patients that they are expected to gain weight steadily by consuming all the food presented to them by the nurses. The patients are thus asked to allow the nurses to decide for them how much food is consumed each day. Reassurance is provided to the patient that she will not become "fat" as a result of this agreement, but at the same time the weight aimed at is decided according to objective criteria and not by the patient herself, whose views are distorted. A great deal of nursing skill and sympathy is necessary for success, but with an experienced team a return to an optimum weight can always be achieved. As a rule weight is gained at a rate of 200 - 400 g daily, so that most patients can achieve an optimum weight (generally over 50 kg) within 6 to 10 weeks, even if on admission they only weighed 35 kg. This is the yardstick for weight gain against which other treatments should be gauged.

After discharge from hospital a proportion of patients, perhaps as many as 50 per cent, remain well or at least maintain a weight level sufficient for continued out-patient treatment. In other patients, however, the illness may run a more precarious course with recurrent weight loss which may require further admissions to hospital.

Currently therapeutic trials are being undertaken at the Maudsley Hospital and elsewhere, testing the efficacy of family therapy, individual psychotherapy and cognitive behavioural therapy. Criteria for success will include measures such as a diminution in the patients' distorted attitude to their body weight, fewer hospitalisations, a reduced duration in the course of the illness, and a more favourable outcome assessed at the end of 4 or 5 years.

Criteria of Success in the Use of Drug Treatments in Anorexia Nervosa

From the foregoing discussion it can be concluded that drugs should not be selected by their appetite-stimulant properties, as true loss of appetite need not occur in anorexia nervosa. On the other hand a drug which facilitates weight gain might be advantageous if its effectiveness compared favourably with established methods of nursing treatment. Although weight gain is a prerequisite of successful treatment in anorexia nervosa, it is not sufficient without a marked reduction in the patient's abnormal attitudes, especially those which prevent an acceptance of optimal weight levels. A drug which improves the patient's abnormal mental state and maintains this improvement should be a real asset, but unfortunately none has been discovered so far.

BULIMIA NERVOSA AND OTHER BULIMIC DISORDERS

Clinical Features of Bulimia Nervosa

Bulimia nervosa is the most destructive bulimic disorder and can be viewed as a late sequel of anorexia nervosa. Often the previous espisode of anorexia nervosa has been a minor one, with a phase of dieting leading to only a moderate degree of weight loss and amenorrhoea, the episode lasting only a few months. The patient appears to improve after the anorexic phase, in that she is no longer able to suppress her eating, and gives way to bouts of voracious eating. Consequently her weight rises and she ceases to cause great concern. On the other hand, weight gain is not matched by an improvement in her mental state, and her dread of fatness remains unaltered. She strives to maintain a harsh control over her weight. A carefully taken history of the changes in her weight over the previous few years, dating from the time of puberty, will usually reveal that she is rigidly maintaining her weight some 7 kg (or more) below her original "healthy" level. This is defined as the weight which prevailed before the onset of symptoms and the excessive dieting.

The efforts to maintain her weight below a self-imposed threshold level (e.g. 47 kg) give rise to persistent cravings for food. The patient succumbs intermittently to these cravings so that episodes of gorging food take place (referred to as "eating binges" by patients, and by authors who neglect the true meaning of the word "binge"). Because she remains desperately anxious to control her weight, the patient resorts to self-induced vomiting or abuse of laxatives in an attempt to mitigate the natural consequences of overeating. This behaviour becomes repetitive and habitual. Patients' hands may become scarred at the site of abrasions caused by harsh rubbing of the skin against the upper incisors, whenever vomiting is induced by rough pushing of the fingers down the throat. The abuse of laxatives may be excessive in the extreme with upwards of 20 purgative doses ingested daily, resulting in chronic diarrhoea. Self-induced vomiting and purging add their toll to the nutritional and metabolic complications which may occur. They include erosion of dental enamel (from regurgitated gastric acid), swollen salivary glands, injury of the myenteric plexuses of the large bowel, and the consequences of hypokalaemic alkalosis: cardiac arrhythmias, muscular paralysis, renal impairment, epileptic seizures and tetany.

The clinical disturbances characteristic of bulimia nervosa can be summed up as follows:

1) A specific psychopathology, similar to that of anorexia nervosa, with an excessive dread of gaining weight above a self-imposed weight threshold.

2) Persistent cravings for food to which the patient succumbs with frequent episodes of overeating.

3) Harmful habitual devices aimed at countering the "fattening" effects of food: self-induced vomiting, purgative abuse, alternating starvation, dependence on diuretics, appetite suppressants or other drugs.

4) A previous episode of frank anorexia nervosa, or a minor form with moderate weight loss and transient amenorrhoea.

This last feature links the bulimic disorder with anorexia nervosa and thus earns the title of bulimia nervosa for the syndrome. Less clearly defined bulimic disorders have been reported as unduly prevalent among young women, especially in the United States (23, 27, 43). These are bulimic subjects identified by surveys conducted in special populations at risk (e.g. high school or college students) using DSM III criteris (2) which are less precise and less stringent than those listed above. This group of bulimic disorders is heterogeneous and much less severe than the group with true bulimia nervosa, but the two groups represent overlapping populations. In any treatment trial on bulimic patients it is thus essential to specify the diagnostic criteria, and establish objective measures of severity of the disorder, such as the degree of associated physical and mental ill-health.

Theoretical Models Governing the Choice of Drug Treatments

Bulimia viewed as secondary to depressive illness

In view of the frequency of depressive symptoms in bulimia nervosa (49) it is not surprising that some authors have considered the syndrome of bulimia as representing a form of affective disorder. In one study indeed, the investigators reached this conclusion because they found that the tricyclic antidepressant imipramine brought about an amelioration of symptoms (42). They reported a reduction in the frequency and intensity of episodes of overeating, a diminution in the preoccupation with food and a relief of depressive symptoms.

The subjects tested in this placebo-controlled trial were likely to have had a milder form of bulimic disorder as they were recruited by advertising in a local newspaper. In contrast, another placebo controlled trial of an antidepressant, this time mianserin, failed to find any reduction of bulimic symptoms that could be attributed to this drug (51). These authors concluded that bulimia is not a manifestation of an underlying affective disorder. The patients they tested were all referred to a hospital clinic and were therefore likely to be suffering from more severe forms of bulimia. The difference in these findings makes it desirable to undertake further trials of antidepressant drugs.

Bulimia viewed as a disorder in the hypothalamic regulation of food intake

In contrast with anorexia nervosa, the symptoms of bulimic disorders can be more readily conceptualized as due to a disordered neuro-regulator of food intake. This is the case because the behaviour of bulimic patients can be equated with increased hunger or decreased satiety induced in experimental animals after hypothalamic lesions. Mammals, including man, overeat when the ventromedial hypothalamic areas are damaged. The overeating occurs only with palatable foods, an observation which has led to the conclusion that the brain mechanisms take into account hedonic as well as nutritional consideration (22). Bulimic patients admit to preoccupations with food and giving way to their cravings by overeating. Yet it should be noted that they frequently deny that they sense increased feelings of hunger (49). The craving for food may be viewed as excessive hunger (in spite of the patients' denial) or as a defect in satiety control once eating has commenced. Such cravings may constitute a response to a state of moderate but chronic undernutrition. It should also be borne in mind that the state of undernutrition is primarily maintained through psychopathological mechanisms, i.e. the patient's determination to control her weight at a sub-optimal level.

The effects of anorexic drugs on bulimic behaviour

The possibility that bulimic behaviour represents a disturbance in the normal regulation of food intake led us to investigate the response of bulimic patients to anorexic drugs under laboratory conditions. Two drugs were tested - fenfluramine and methylamphetamine. These drugs have in common the capacity to reduce the weight of food ingested. The actions of fenfluramine and amphetamine have been contrasted in animals and man by Blundell et al. (7). They act differently on brain neurotransmitters, fenfluramine acting mainly on 5-hydroxytryptamine, amphetamine mainly on dopamine and noradrenaline. They differ also in the way they influence eating: in general terms fenfluramine mainly slows the rate of eating whereas amphetamine delays its onset. It may be surmised from these observations that fenfluramine predominantly affects satiety whereas amphetamine affects hunger. Two separate experimental studies were undertaken, one with fenfluramine, the other with methylamphetamine. The experimental designs were similar except that fenfluramine was administred orally (60 mg) and methylamphetamine intravenously (15 mg/75 kg body weight). Each patient arrived in the experimental ward at 9 a.m. after an overnight fast, and completed visual analogue scales every half four. The patient was tested on two occasions, once with the active preparation and once with a placebo, under double-blind conditions and with a randomised order of administration. Two hours after the drug (or placebo) was given the patient was left alone for 30 minutes with a liberal amount of food of her own choice. She was asked to eat as much as she wished, and the caloric content of the ingested food was subsequently calculated. The patient was also asked whether she felt her eating was so out of control as to constitute an "eating binge".

Effects of fenfluramine: 15 patients were tested (46). No patient experienced a bulimic episode during the test meal when given fenfluramine, whereas 6 did so after placebo ($p < 0.05$). The drug also had an effect in reducing the calories consumed during the test meal (mean of 234 cals. compared to a mean of 492 cals. after placebo, $p < 0.01$).

Bulimic patients were found to differ from normal controls in their subjective response to the test meal, both before and after the meal. They had been asked to rate their feelings of "hunger" and their "urge to eat" using the visual analogue scales. Before the test meal the bulimic patients rated themselves lower than the controls. After the test meal the bulimics differed from the normal controls in another important manner: whereas normal subjects rated themselves as less "hungry" and with a diminished "urge to eat", bulimic patients on placebo showed no such reductions in their ratings. After fenfluramine there was a tendency to return towards the normal response to a test meal: the ratings for "hunger" and "urge to eat" fell after the meal, whereas they had failed to do so under placebo conditions.

These results can be summarised as showing that bulimic patients report sensations of hunger abnormally, and their bulimic symptoms are reduced in the short term by the action of fenfluramine.

Effects of methylamphetamine: 8 patients were tested. The results on the bulimic symptoms were in part similar to those of fenfluramine. When given methylamphetamine no patient succumbed to a bulimic episode, whereas four did on placebo. The mean caloric consumption after methylamphetamine was 224 cals., whereas after placebo it was 943 cals. ($p < 0.02$). The effects of methylamphetamine in reducing self-ratings for hunger tended to be more definite than those of fenfluramine (41). The two drugs differed most clearly in their side-effects, however: methylamphetamine enhanced alertness and caused euphoria, whereas fenfluramine mainly caused drowsiness, and sometimes headache and unsteadiness.

Although the actions of fenfluramine and methylamphetamine differ in some respects, the effect they have in common when given to bulimic patients is a specific reduction in their abnormal eating behaviour.

Appraisal of the actions of fenfluramine: Fenfluramine is potentially the more interesting drug as a potential treatment in bulimia nervosa: methylamphetamine is ruled out in view of its stimulant effects and the dangers of drug dependence and drug-induced psychosis. The suppression of bulimic symptoms by fenfluramine may operate through a number of mechanisms:

(i) Bulimia nervosa may be associated with a disorder in the neuro-regulation of eating behaviour, a disorder which can be modified by a drug like fenfluramine.

(ii) Bulimia nervosa may be viewed as a failure of normal satiety control, a failure which can be reversed by fenfluramine.

(iii) Bulimic symptoms tend to occur when the patient's consumption of high caloric foods exceeds a certain threshold. Fenfluramine may act by reducing the intake of food below this threshold.

It will be seen that these mechanisms may overlap with each other.

Assessment of the Current Treatments of Bulimic Disorders

The role of drug treatments

The finding that fenfluramine suppresses bulimic symptoms in the short-term and under experimental conditions holds out some hope that it may be a useful treatment. This can only be established by means of a controlled double-blind therapeutic trial. It may be anticipated that certain difficulties will arise in the clinical use of a drug like fenfluramine. Bulimia nervosa is a disorder characterised by the patient's excessive need to exact harsh control over her body weight so as to maintain it below a self-imposed threshold level. A drug which facilitates weight loss might therefore be harmful if this effect transcends any benefit in reducing the urge to overeat. It is likely therefore that a drug treatment should only be used as part of a general programme of management which includes appropriate psychological treatments.

Antidepressant drugs already have a limited role in the treatment of bulimic patients when they develop severe depressive symptoms. The evidence that they might also be effective in controlling the bulimic symptoms themselves is less clear (42, 51) and requires that further therapeutic trials be undertaken in patients selected according to clearly defined diagnostic criteria.

Psychological treatments

Bulimic patients tend to seek treatment on their own terms and it may be difficult at first to persuade them to accept good advice regarding their eating habits and their attitudes to weight. Thus a supportive psycotherapeutic approach is an essential component of any treatment programme. In recent years various forms of psychological treatment with more specific aims have been given on an out-patient basis. Cognitive behaviour therapy tries to tackle the abnormal behaviour and attitudes of the bulimic patient. The treatment is intensive and the patient is seen at least 2 - 3 times weekly during the first 4 to 6 weeks, the entire programme lasting 4 to 6 months. The following elements are included: self-monitoring of the food eaten, the prescription of a regular eating pattern, the avoidance of vomiting, purgatives and diuretics, advice about sensible weighing, gradual exposure to foods otherwise avoided and "cognitive restructuring" (i.e. the patient is taught to identify the irrational basis of those thoughts which govern her behaviour, and thus dismiss them) (15, 16). In another study the treatment programme incorporated elements of behaviour therapy and group therapy (32). For example, the patient agreed with her therapist the terms of a written "contract" in which were stipulated the frequency of her attendance, her weight and diet. She kept a diary in which she recorded her food intake, episodes of bulimia, vomiting and laxative abuse, as well as thoughts which occurred to her when eating or giving way to bulimic symptoms. The group therapy sessions included counselling techniques as well as "insight directed psychotherapy". The treatment occured during weekly sessions over a total of ten weeks, and was judged to be successful in reducing bulimic symptoms and behaviour. This study, and another one which also supported the value of both cognitive and behaviour therapy programmes (17), depended on a comparison with a control group of patients who were simply left on a waiting list without any treatment.

In-patient treatment

Admission to hospital to a unit with nursing facilities, such as those described for the treatment of anorexia nervosa, may prove extremely beneficial in restoring the patient's eating to a normal pattern (50). Unfortunately the benefits tend to be of limited duration. Nevertheless, hospitalization may be required when physical or metabolic complications set in such as persistent hypokalaemia or when the patient is severely depressed or suicidal. An important aim of hospital treatment is to help the patient gain weight to a level which corresponds to a "healthy" level (as defined above), rather than her own "desired" level. Thus the patient is "desensitized" to her dread of gaining the necessary few pounds. When successful this treatment may result in a diminished preoccupation with food and weight, and a loss of depressive symptoms which may be enduring.

Criteria of Success in the Use of Drug Treatments in Bulimic Disorders

For a drug to be useful in the management of bulimic patients it should be effective in suppressing the episodes of overeating. It can be predicted that such an improvement would remove the patient's urge to induce vomiting or abuse laxatives. To be of value the reduction of bulimic symptoms should be at least as great as that obtained with psychological treatments.

There should be no unwanted effects from the drugs. In particular there should be no increase in carbohydrate restriction or weight loss to which bulimic patients are prone.

The drug treatments should be shown to be useful in bulimic patients who are most in need of effective treatments, i.e. those who are referred to hospital clinics with the more severe forms of bulimic disorders including bulimia nervosa.

REFERENCES

1. Alloway, R., Reynolds, E.H., Spargo, E., and Russell, G.F.M. (1985): *J. Neurol. Neurosurg. Psychiatry*, (in press).

2. American Psychiatric Association (1980): *Diagnostic and statistical manual of mental disorders. DSM-III.* American Psychiatric Association, Washington, DC.

3. Anand, B.K., and Brobeck, J.R. (1951): *Proc. Soc. Exp. Biol. Med.*, 77: 323.

4. Barcai, A. (1977): *Acta Psychiatr. Scand.*, 55: 97-101.

5. Barry, V.C., and Klawans, H.L. (1976): *J. Neural Transm.*, 38: 107-122.

6. Beumont, P.J.V., Beardwood, C.J., and Russell, G.F.M. (1972): *Psychol. Med.*, 2: 216-231.

7. Blundell, J.E., Latham, C.J., Moniz, E., McArthur, R.A. and Rogers, P.J. (1979): *Curr. Med. Res. Opin.*, 6 (Suppl. 1): 34-54.

8. Boyar, R.M., Katz, J., Finkelstein, J.W., Kapen, S., Weiner, H., Weitzman, E.D., and Hellman, L. (1974): *New Engl. J. Med.*, 291: 861-865.

9. Burns, T., and Crisp, A.H. (1984): *Br. J. Psychiatry*, 145: 319-325.

10. Cantwell, D.P., Sturzenberger, S., Burroughs, J., Salkin, B., and Green, J.K. (1977): *Arch. Gen. Psychiatry*, 34: 1087-1093.

11. Coscina, D.V. (1977): In: *Anorexia Nervosa*, edited by R.A. Vigersky, pp 97-107. Raven Press, New York.

12. Crisp, A.H. (1985): In: *Anorexia Nervosa and Bulimic Disorders: Current Prespectives*, edited by G.I. Szmukler, P.D. Slade, P. Harris, D. Benton, and G.F.M. Russell, J. Psychiatr. Res. (in press).

13. Dally, P.J., and Sargant, W. (1960): *Br. Med. J.*, 1: 1770-1773.

14. Dally, P.J., and Sargant, W. (1966). *Br. Med. J.*, 2: 793-795.

15. Fairburn, C.G. (1981): *Psychol. Med.*, 11: 707-711.

16. Fairburn, C.G. (1984): In: *Eating and its Disorders*, edited by A.J. Stunkard, and E. Stellar, pp. 235-258, Raven Press, New York.

17. Freeman, C., Sinclair, F., Turnbull, J., and Annandale, A. (1985). In: *Anorexia Nervosa and Bulimic Disorders: Current Perspectives*, edited by G.I. Szmukler, P.D. Slade, P. Harris, D. Benton, and G.F.M. Russell, J. Psychiatr. Res. (in press).

18. Garfinkel, P.E., and Garner, D.M. (1982): *Anorexia Nervosa: a Multidimensional Perspective*, pp. 20-26. Brunner Mazel, New York.

19. Gillman, M.A., and Lichtigfeld, F.J. (1981): *J. R. Soc. Med.*, 74: 631.

20. Goldberg, S.C., Halmi, K.A., Eckert, E.D., Casper, R.C., and Davis, J.M. (1979): *Br. J. Psychiatry*, 134: 67-70.

21. Gross, H.A., Ebert, M.H., Faden, V.B., Goldberg, S.C., Nee, L.E. and Kaye, W.H. (1981): *J. Clin. Psychopharmacol.*, 1: 376-381.

22. Grossman, S.P. (1984): In: *Eating and its Disorders*, edited by A.J. Stunkard and E. Stellar, pp. 5-13. Raven Press, New York.

23. Halmi, K.A., Falk, J.R., and Schwatz, E. (1981): *Psychol. Med.*, 11: 697-706.

24. Harrower, A.D.B., Yap, P.L., Nairn, I.M., Walton, H.J., Strong, J.A., and Craig, A. (1977): *Br. Med. J.*, 2: 156-159.

25. Hsu, L.K.G., Crisp, A.H., and Harding, B. (1979): *Lancet*, 1: 61-65.

26. Johanson, A.J., and Knorr, N.J. (1977): In: *Anorexia Nervosa*, edited by R.A. Vigersky, pp. 363-372. Raven Press, New York.

27. Johnson, C., Lewis, C., Love, S., Lewis, L., and Stuckey, M. (1984): *J. Youth and Adol.*, 13: 15-26.

28. Jones, D.J., Fox, M.M., Babigian, H.M., and Hutton, H.E. (1980): *Psychosom. Med.*, 42: 551-558.

29. Kay, D.W.K., and Leigh, D. (1954): *J. Ment. Sci.*, 100: 411-431.

30. Kendell, R.E., Hailey, A., and Babigian, H.M. (1973): *Psychol. Med.*, 3: 200-203.

31. Kylin, E. (1937): *Dtsch. Arch. klin. Med.*, 180: 115-152.

32. Lacey, J.H. (1983): *Br. Med. J.*, 286: 1609-1613.

33. Leibowitz, S.F. (1983): In: *Anorexia Nervosa: Recent Developments in Research*, edited by P.L. Darby, P.E. Garfinkel, D.M. Garner, and D.V. Coscina, pp 221-229. Alan R. Liss, New York.

34. Mawson, A.R. (1974): *Psychol. Med.*, 4: 289-308.

35. Mecklenburg, R.S., Loriaux, D.L., Thompson, R.H., Andersen, A.E., and Lipsett, M.B. (1974): *Medicine*, 53: 147-159.

36. Mills, I.H. Wilson, R.J., Eden, M.A.M., and Lines, J.G. (1973): In: *Symposium - Anorexia Nervosa and Obesity*, edited by R.F. Robertson, pp. 31-43. Royal College of Physicians, Edinburgh.

37. Moore, R., Mills, I.H., and Forster, A. (1981): *J. R. Soc. Med.*, 74: 129-131.

38. Morgan, H.G., and Russell, G.F.M. (1975): *Psychol. Med.*, 5: 355-371.

39. Mortimer, C.H., Besser, G.M., McNeilly, A.S., Marshall, J.S., Harsoulis, P., Tunbridge, W.M.S., Gomez-Pan, A., and Hall, R. (1973): *Br. Med. J.*, 4: 73-77.

40. Needleman, H.L., and Waber, D. (1976): *Lancet*, 2: 580.

41. Ong, Y.L., Checkley, S.A., and Russell, G.F.M. (1983): *Br. J. Psychiatry*, 143: 288-293.

42. Pope, H.G., Hudson, J.I., Jonas, J.M., and Yurgelun-Todd, D. (1983): *Am. J. Psychiatry*, 140: 554-558.

43. Pyle, R.L., Mitchell, J.E., Eckert, E.D., Halvorson, P.A., Neuman, P.A., and Goff, G.M. (1983): *Int. J. Eating Disorders*, 2: 75-85.

44. Redmond, D.E., Swann, A., and Heninger, G.R. (1976): *Lancet*, 2: 307.

45. Redmond, D.E., Huang, Y.H., Baulu, J., Snyder, D.R., and Mass, J.W. (1977): In: *Anorexia Nervosa*, edited by R.A. Vigersky, pp. 81-96. Raven Press, New York.

46. Robinson, P.H., Chekley, S.A., and Russell, G.F.M. (1985): *Br. J. Psychiatry*, 146: 169-176.

47. Russell, G.F.M. (1970): In: *Modern Trends in Psychological Medicine*, edited by J. Harding Price, pp: 131-164. Butterworths, London.

48. Russell, G.F.M. (1977): *Psychol. Med.*, 7: 363-367.

49. Russell, G.F.M. (1979): *Psychol. Med.*, 9: 429-448.

50. Russell, G.F.M. (1983): In: *The Handbook of Psychiatry, Vol. 4: the Neuroses and Personality Disorders*, edited by G.F.M. Russell and L.A. Hersov, pp: 285-298. Cambridge University Press, Cambridge.

51. Sabine, E.J., Yonace, A., Farrington, A.J., Barratt, K.H., and Wakeling, A. (1983)): *Br. J. Clin. Pharmacol.*, 15: 195S-202S.

52. Silverstone, T., and Turner, P. (1974): *Drug Treatment in Psychiatry*, p. 185. Routledge and Kegan Paul, London.

53. Szmukler, G.I. (1982): In: *Drugs and Appetite*, edited by J.T. Silverstone, pp. 159-181. Academic Press, London.

54. Szmukler, G.I. (1985): In: *Anorexia Nervosa and Bulimic Disorders: Current Perspectives*, edited by G.I. Szmukler, P.D. Slade, P. Harris, D. Benton, and G.F.M. Russell, J. Psychiatr. Res., (in press).

55. Szmukler, G.I., and Tantam, D. (1984): *Br. J. Med. Psychol.*, 57: 303-310.

56. Theander, S. (1970): *Acta Psychiatr. Scand.*, Suppl. 214: 24-31.

57. Ungerstedt, U. (1971): *Acta Physiol. Scand.*, Suppl. 367: 1-48.

58. Vandereycken, W. (1984): *Br. J. Psychiatry*, 144: 288-292.

59. Vandereycken, W., and Pierloot, R. (1982): *Acta Psychiatr. Scand.*, 66: 445-450.

60. Vigersky, R.A., and Loriaux, D.L. (1977): In: *Anorexia Nervosa*, edited by R.A. Vigersky, pp. 109-121. Raven Press, New York.

61. Wakeling, A., De Souza, V.A., and Beardwood, C.J. (1977): *Psychol. Med.*, 7: 397-405.

62. Wakeling, A., and De Souza, V.A. (1982): quoted by Szmukler, G.I. In: *Drugs and Appetite*, edited by J.T. Silverstone, pp. 159-181, Academic Press, London.

63. Winokur, A., March, V., and Mendels, J. (1980): *Am. J. Psychiatry*, 137: 695-698.

64. Young, J.K. (1975): *Physiol. Psychol.*, 3: 322-330.

Subject Index